BY THE SAME AUTHOR

JAMES HAMILTON-PATERSON

WHAT WE HAVE LOST

THE DISMANTLING OF GREAT BRITAIN

HEAD
of ZEUS

An Apollo Book

This Apollo book first published in the UK in 2018
by Head of Zeus Ltd
This paperback edition published in 2019
by Head of Zeus Ltd

9 7 5 3 1 2 4 6 8

A catalogue record for this book is available from
the British Library.

ISBN (PB): 9781784972363
ISBN (E): 9781784972349

Typeset by Adrian McLaughlin

Printed and bound in Great Britain by
CPI Group (UK) Ltd, Croydon CR0 4YY

Head of Zeus Ltd
First Floor East
5–8 Hardwick Street
London ECIR 4RG

WWW.HEADOFZEUS.COM

Contents

The author in 1977 with the 1938 BSA motorbike and sidecar he had just ridden from Alexandria to Hurstpierpoint.

M. T. S.

ave atque vale

1.
Formerly

'The repeated assertion by middle-aged men of the patriotic duty that events twenty or thirty years before they were born impose on the whole nation would be amusing were it not also a grim reminder of how deeply ingrained a whitewashed and heroic construction of the imperial past remains.'

—David Andress, *Cultural Dementia*

The streamlined *Duchess of Gloucester* leaves Euston Station for Glasgow in 1937. These powerful LMS 'Coronation Scot' expresses were specifically built to challenge the 'Flying Scot' service to Edinburgh.

S ome years ago, when I was researching a book about Britain's Cold War, I was given the name of a retired RAF officer living in Sussex. I was told he might be prepared to talk about his V-bomber squadron's activities in the early 1960s. My informant warned me that he'd had no contact with him since a reunion dinner some ten years earlier but had heard rumours that this octogenarian wing commander might be 'pretty eccentric and quite likely gaga. Still, you never know.' He turned out not to be in the phone book but since I had a free day I decided to drive down to his last address just on the off-chance.

The morning had followed a night's sharp frost and winter's dust lay on a vitrified landscape. Behind the village pub where I asked the way the Downs heaved up, white-crested, like frozen breakers. 'Good, you can check if he's okay,' the landlord said. 'We've not seen his car for a bit and since his wife died he's been a bit… you know. But with this brass monkey weather the oldies tend to stay indoors, don't they, and wait for the health visitor. Or the bloke with the scythe. Anyway, you'll find it a challenge if he invites you in, big fellow like you.' He wouldn't elaborate but smiled as he polished a glass. 'See for yourself.'

The isolated cottage proved quite small but hardly of the doll's house dimensions I was half expecting. A battered Volks-wagen Beetle stood outside, its windows opaque with frost ferns. I had bought a supplicant's bottle of Scotch at the pub and since there was no knocker on the door I gave it a good buffet or two with the base of the bottle. After a stage wait it was opened by a small grave-marked man in carpet slippers wearing a Mao-style quilted jacket with kapok leaking from its seams. 'Glad you've come,' he said. 'Can't shift the nut. Must be frozen. Perhaps you'll have better luck. This way. And close that bloody door.'

The reason for the landlord's mysterious parting shot now became apparent. I had finally met a hoarder. The passage behind the quilted figure was squeezed between tottering cliffs of newsprint, some bundled with string but most roughly heaped or lying in a knee-deep moraine, as at the foot of the upward slanting crevasse that was the staircase. The air in the house smelled of mildew and paraffin. I could see my breath. He led the way to the kitchen and out through the back door with a missing pane, the gap covered with Sellotaped brown paper. Evidently he needed to change the fat red propane cylinder that presumably fed the cooker and possibly heaters as well. He handed me a well-oiled King Dick adjustable spanner. The nut was not especially stiff and as I replaced the old washer and did it all up again it occurred to me he might have forgotten that gas installations are reverse-threaded. 'Good lad,' he said when it was done. 'A Halton boy, I bet, though you look a bit old. Disciplinary problems, no doubt.'

I followed him back through more newsprint canyons until we came upon a clearing in which a fireplace and a heaped sofa were revealed. There was also a card table and chair, the table unexpectedly neat with writing paper, pen and ink laid out on its green baize together with a supply of stationery and a cheque book. There was also a pile of stamped addressed envelopes. The wing commander lowered himself stiffly to his knees like an old camel and waved a crested Zippo lighter in front of the fire. The gas from the new cylinder took a while to replace the air in the pipe but eventually lit with a sudden balloon of blue flame and a *whump!* that rattled the window panes. I put the bottle of whisky on the table, cleared a space on the sofa and sat.

Very soon it was obvious I was not going to learn anything useful about flying Victor jet bombers in the Cold War. Evidently convinced I was still one of the RAF's Technician apprentices of the early sixties, he seemed to have lost all grasp of chronology since then. I gathered he had been born in Leicester in 1925 but that was about the only personal detail he vouchsafed. Yet his memory of the Second World War – indeed, of the first two decades of his life – was prodigious, especially for the trade names and multifarious products of the period. For an hour he spoke enthusiastically about Hobson aircraft carburettors, Rudge motorbikes, Allenbury's cereal ('Far superior to Grape-Nuts. No comparison… is that Scotch on the table? How very kind'), while sipping whisky from the bottle. He offered me none and after glimpsing the tip of his mauve tongue sliming into the neck of the bottle like a sinister reproductive organ I decided it didn't matter. Any question I asked him in an effort to drag him back to the aircraft he had flown from East Anglia and that tense, exhausting life of Quick Reaction Alerts and bombing competitions was deftly deflected and he retreated into what was evidently for him a far more congenial earlier world. The gas fire popped and whined softly. I steadily froze.

As the whisky in the bottle ebbed and his voice droned on I noticed that the magazines scattered in drifts around me were remarkably old, a couple of them back numbers of *Boy's Own* showcasing the wartime Biggles stories that W. E. Johns had contributed. Yet they clearly were not kept as collector's items, being like everything else on the floor much torn and creased and scuffed underfoot. It was all very peculiar. Against my better judgement I did elicit some details about his correspondence with what – if my intuition was right – must surely be defunct companies. For a while he rambled on about them with an almost boyish enthusiasm like a local historian walking around a cemetery and reading off the headstones as he went, although instead of people these were brands and trade names of evidently fond memory. Then without warning, as if he had given away too much and I might after all be laughing at him, he turned belligerent and ratty. Possibly the whisky accounted for this sudden change. It was clear that some highly empathetic and tactful questioning would be needed to restore his former mood and prompt further confession, but this was not what I had come for and by now the inner voice of experience was becoming insistent: *Don't go there*. In fact, just go.

So I did, on the way out thanking the wing commander for his time and asking if there was anything I could ask somebody to get him. 'Certainly not,' he said almost angrily. 'She left me to fend for myself and I'm fending. Bloody well, as it happens. You could drop these into the post somewhere. Goodbye.' And the front door was firmly shut, leaving me staring at it with a clutch of envelopes in one hand.

I stopped off at the pub for a much-needed hot toddy and gradually thawed out in front of the log fire. 'Well?' said the publican, in between serving his few customers, 'I assume our wing commander's still alive? That house – blimey, talk about a fire hazard. Amazing he's survived this long. Did you ever see anything like it?'

'Never,' I said, thinking that maybe after all I ought not to have changed the old fellow's Calor gas cylinder for him. But then, he might just as easily freeze to death as burn. 'He does seem pretty destitute.'

'Ah, he's gone down a lot recently. But he's not poor, you know. Draws quite a decent pension, thank you very much. Gets through two, three bottles of Famous Grouse a week? He once told us that after years of loyal service officers like him weren't expected to see out their days on NAAFI Woodbines and gnat's piss like Watney's Red Barrel or Double Diamond.'

'No friends?'

'Not recently, not so far as we can tell. Once he'd buried Sheila that was it. Bang – a recluse. But he must have pen friends because he's always sending off letters. Since our post office closed he drops them off here because thank God he doesn't drive much any more. We take them into town for him or else he gives them to the postie – always stamped and neatly written. He does get a few back, even the odd parcel he has to sign for. All those companies he writes to. And the postie says a lot of his letters get returned with Not Known At This Address. Strange, if you ask me. A nice enough fellow he used to be and he and Sheila were often in here of an evening. Popular locals, you know? But over the last years… Oh well, who's to say we mightn't go the same way when it's our turn? Now, you look as though you could do with our Cumberland sausage and mash for lunch. Bring the roses back to your cheeks.'

Later, fed and warmed, I stopped at Midhurst to post the wing commander's envelopes and drove on, musing. A wasted trip in terms of hearing inside stories from those paranoid Cold War years, but that was a familiar hazard of pot-luck research. Yet once back home I failed to shake off the morning's peculiar melancholy. Drawing parallels between the once vastly competent Victor captain who had been entrusted to deliver Britain's nuclear bomb and the hairless pensioner who couldn't change a gas cylinder seemed too obvious. That slow metamorphosis might happen to anyone if they lived long enough. More haunting was the form his survival had taken, his retreat into a warren of archives that pre-dated his own flying career and now sheltered him with its paper fortifications.

I remembered the faint smell of paraffin in the house and visualised a Valor oil stove upstairs in his bedroom, one of the comforting old ones that at night would throw a glowing orange stencil onto the ceiling so he could drowsily let its pattern drift him off to other times like a mantra made visible. So common is the bullying admonition always to live in the present that it feels like a moral failure or deliberately perverse to prefer the past. Yet surely it was reasonable that anyone might choose to forsake an intolerably cold and cheerless modern world and live in a remembered time still vivid and familiar and warmly reassuring, even if much of it had been in wartime? Nobody condemns someone who knows perfectly well their lifelong partner or friend is dead but who is daily conscious of their presence, close enough to be talked to. So why not be nostalgic for a much-missed country that in those days still held on to its wartime patch of moral high ground and whose post-war reconstruction hoped to build a more egalitarian society, a welfare state based on industrial enterprise? Health for all, homes for all, education for all, jobs for all. Was it surprising, given his young man's world stocked with thousands of household-name companies in dozens of industries, that in a pensioner's mind those years should still echo with promise? The air force he had joined was redolent of recent glory and was the world's second largest. Busy with pioneering futuristic jet propulsion at home, it also spanned the globe with its fleet of thousands of aircraft designed and built in Britain. Might not any keen youngster have given such an institution his loyalty and entrusted it with his future? The country of our youth is immutable, even fossilised. It is the present that erodes and fleets.

On the day following my visit I tried to put on paper what he had allowed me to glimpse of his inner world before clamming up and returning to the Grouse's contemporary solace.

There is a man who sits in Sussex. Each day he writes to an address he finds at random in one of the slumping heaps of old newspapers and magazines that fill his house. Mostly the address is that of a commercial premises. Other letters go to a PO box or house number. These are advertisements to which he replies, very often enclosing a stamped addressed envelope as requested and sometimes with a cheque for a modest amount. The only difficulty is with converting the old currency into new, but he has drawn up his own table so he can quickly read off the modern equivalents of prices like 5/11d. None of the ads is less than sixty years old. Some date back to the 1920s. The majority are those he encountered in his own boyhood and teens. Sturmey-Archer hubs, breeding pairs of white mice, crystal sets. As he licks the envelope flap he visualises neat but busy workshops in Birmingham and the Black Country or – as in the case of Folliboost hair restorer – a quiet residential road in Anstey, a tortoiseshell cat dozing in the sun on a low brick wall in front of a semi-detached house in whose back garden is a large hut. He can see it clearly. Inside the hut are cartons of empty bottles, a batch of which is being filled with various coloured liquids contained in a rack of carboys along one wall. There is a smell of camphor. The middle-aged man with the funnel has a fine head of hair. At the end of the hut his wife sits, writing addresses on gummed labels. Their daughter corks and wires each filled bottle with practised efficiency.

It is a home industry designed to assuage the hidden anxieties of men (and a good few women) up and down the country.

They are very real, these enterprises. They have street numbers and phone numbers and often cable addresses as well. Many have a nineteenth-century foundation date. They are going concerns and describe their own products enthusiastically, promising they will give years of service and offering immediate refunds in the unlikely event of dissatisfaction. There are their claims in black and white; there are the testimonials from satisfied customers that can be viewed at any time. The advertisements have no expiry dates so it stands to reason they must still be valid. If he took the trouble to visit Ellisdon's factory in Kempston Road, Bedford, he would undoubtedly find forty-odd employees in brown coats carefully assembling E & S's famous magic tricks and novelties like the Seebackroscope ('Just put it to your eye and you will see everything behind you! Amaze your friends!') Or he could go to Rotherham and watch J. J. Habershon & Sons Ltd making their equally famous high-tensile steel strip, just as they had for the aircraft industry in the war a year or two ago.

The more ads he responds to, the realer the past becomes. School leavers of fifteen are now offered training with excellent qualifications by the three Services, including the merchant navy, to replace the mass demobbing of the war's mostly unwilling conscripts. Or they can go to work with any of the thirty-five British car companies busily turning out models for a world where petrol will be unrationed and decent wages will turn every family man into a motorist. Britain's great industries are shaking off the wartime command economy and rebuilding for the future: coal, steel, shipbuilding, aircraft, the railways, electricity generation (there are even veiled hints of nuclear power).

Such is the delusory world these advertisements of yesteryear distil. The old widower in Sussex half-dead with cold behind his ramparts of newsprint elects to live in it, running on the potent twin fuels of whisky and nostalgia. It is conceivable that a part of him knows it is deluded. After all, he retired at a time when the world-spanning air force he had once joined was steadily becoming a ghost of its former self and was even then reduced to a comparative handful of aircraft – virtually none of which was any longer wholly British, the rest being products of international consortia or else entirely foreign. But at over eighty and with his wife dead he is surely free to live in whichever era he chooses and in an inner landscape of his own designing. For most surviving Britons of his generation the remembered actuality of those far-off days might be one of hard-bitten times with lingering rationing and short commons, when blackout material re-lined threadbare coats, wire mesh soap savers still hung above the sink in every scullery and young fathers went to the office wearing their demob suits. But by then the future wing commander was a recruit safe in the arms of the RAF, clothed and fed if not overpaid, with a myriad home-grown aircraft to pilot and a huge pink-coloured globe to fly around.

Predictably enough, that melancholy and haunting short visit to a complete stranger worked like yeast and brought a good many of my own childhood memories bubbling back to the surface. I was born in the depths of the Second World War and in my first twenty years I and my fellow Britons took for granted that nearly everything we bought or used or saw, whether in the street, in the sky or on the sea, was British made by a British-owned company. In 1950 practically every car or lorry on our roads had been designed and built in Britain. Only Fords and Vauxhalls were ultimately American-owned but built in Britain for the British market (Vauxhall had been bought by General Motors back in 1925). There were very few foreign cars about. The occasional Fiat or Delahaye, the odd Maigret-style Citroën – that was about it. A trip down to the London docks or any British port guaranteed that most of the ships there would be British registered, every one of which would have been built in a British shipyard. Even a good percentage of foreign-registered vessels would have come from a British yard since in those days we still built half the world's merchant fleets.

In those days Second World War-vintage propeller-driven aircraft were swiftly yielding to the early generation of jet aircraft, almost all of which were British designed and built. Practically all the screeching and roaring that went on overhead was of British military origin. The exception was around London Airport where the slow, droning, long-haul transatlantic propeller-driven American passenger aircraft such as Douglas DC4s, DC6s, Lockheed Constellations and Boeing's 'double bubble' Stratocruisers were still plentiful. But we schoolboys knew they were already dinosaurs. In the spring of 1952 the world's first jet airliner, de Havilland's Comet 1, went into passenger service followed a year later by the world's first turboprop airliner, the Vickers Viscount. On Christmas Eve 1952 the prototype Handley Page Victor bomber that my wing commander would one day fly as part of our nuclear deterrent made its maiden flight from Boscombe Down. Weird shrieks and whines and bangs from the sky brought us rushing outside to stare excitedly upward, hoping for a fleeting glimpse of some futuristic product of the country's lead in jet propulsion. Gloster Meteors and Supermarine Swifts held world speed records, English Electric Canberras held altitude and distance records. Come to that, John Cobb's Railton Special had held the world's land speed record since 1947 with a first-ever run of over 400 mph and in 1952 Cobb would also break the world's speed record on water at 200 mph.

British-built steam locomotives still pounded the country's extensive rail network, including the A4 class *Mallard* that had broken the world speed record for steam engines in 1938 (which still stands). Southern Rail's equally British electric trains served the London suburbs, leaving in their wake a faint smell of antiseptic as their hot condensers gave off phenolic wafts. London's brilliant double-decker trolleybuses that today would satisfy all kinds of environmental strictures swooshed silently about beneath their network of power lines. They, too, were British; as were the antique trams that still groaned and sparked uphill from Eltham station along Well Hall Road.

We took for granted that the very clothes we wore had been made in Britain. When I was sent away to school the name of the boy in the bed next to me in the dormitory was Bannerman. He naturally wore Banner brand pyjamas, made by his family's firm that had been founded in the early nineteenth century by Henry Bannerman, who owned cotton mills in Manchester. The rest of us mostly wore pyjamas of Viyella, a British cotton/wool blend invented in the late nineteenth century. In summer we naturally wore Aertex shirts, another nineteenth-century British fabric still made today, as well as Clarks sandals from Somerset with a sunburst of holes cut over the toes. In winter we ran about the playing field in Bukta shorts – yet another nineteenth-century Mancunian company.

The penknives or sheath knives we schoolboys carried, like the cutlery everybody ate with, were made in Sheffield of proudly marked Sheffield steel. The fountain pens with which many of us wrote our homework were made by Conway Stewart, a British brand dating to 1905. The bicycles we pedalled madly around on were Hercules or Raleigh or Humber or any one of a dozen brands, all of them British. The air rifle I potted pigeons with was made by BSA, the Birmingham Small Arms company that was also merely one of a dozen British firms making brands of motorbikes that were famous the world over and ubiquitous in those days of petrol rationing. And, of course, there were the toys and models advertised in the very magazines that sixty years later were heaped and trodden underfoot in an octogenarian's freezing house in Sussex. Microscopes; little Dinky and Matchbox models; Hornby trains; Keil Kraft balsa-wood glider kits; Mamod steam engines mounted on what looked like a Meccano steel base plate that when running gave off the familiar incense of burning methylated spirit and hot metal. My control-line aircraft was powered by an ED 'Bee' 1 cc engine that reeked agreeably of diesel and ether and was made by Electronic Developments in Surrey. Plus – appropriately enough for the new post-war Jet Age – Jetex jet motors that came in a variety of sizes and could power model cars, boats and aircraft. They had little cylindrical fuel pellets of a light ochre colour ignited by an inch or two of fuse that came in little round tins. British again. All British.

The shops in the high street were virtually all British, too; and with the exception of the ubiquitous Woolworths so also were the chain stores: Boots, W. H. Smiths, Timothy Whites, Dewhursts the butchers, Fifty Shilling Tailors. The scant luxury and labour-saving goods at home such as radios and electric irons were equally British. The radios were by any number of firms, including Bush and Pye and Cossor and Murphy and HMV; the iron might be by Morphy Richards. No-one in 1950 had a washing machine (my grandmother still had a washtub and mangle) but we certainly had a Goblin vacuum cleaner made in Leatherhead. British to the core.

And so it went on. That most of the raw materials from which everything was made were imported somehow didn't alter the goods' fundamental Britishness because so much was shipped from the Empire and the Dominions. Children tend to be anchored firmly in the present, so for many years I had no real perception that behind the scenes there had long been ominous signs that this happy state of affairs might not last indefinitely. Even when I was eleven a schoolfriend had a sophisticated clockwork car in glossy red whose roof had several slits in it. Invisible beneath them was a sensitive diaphragm that reacted to puffs of air. The idea was that the car could be voice controlled, and that by blowing or even just speaking into its roof one could make it start, stop, and even reverse. In those pre-electronic days this seemed magical; and had we not been so young we might have seen hovering in the room that Biblical cloud no bigger than a man's hand: the first sign of the deluge that was to come. For the car was made by Schuco, a well-established German toy company (still in existence today). Likewise, the best landscapes and buildings to go with our model railway layouts, if not by Bassett-Lowke of High Holborn, were also German. Within a few years I would be an exchange student visiting a town near Frankfurt am Main and, staring through the train window, would have the uncanny impression that I had been here before, so familiar was the look of the stations and their ancillary buildings.

At eleven, though, I was unwitting of decline and of any significance in India's now being an independent country, with the rest of the Empire slated to go the same way. I had no inkling that Britain had foolishly squandered the Americans' generous gift of Marshall Aid after the war by failing to divert it to renew the country's worn-out infrastructure, nor that Britain was about to become perpetually broke for the rest of my lifetime. Neither could I have guessed that within a decade or two most of those familiar brands whose eternal existence I took for granted would gradually become extinct or foreign owned. Over much the same period virtually all Britain's industries that had built the country and its infrastructure and had made it what it was would shrivel or collapse in acrimony and dust. The steel and coal; the ships and motorbikes and cars; the cotton mills and Witney blankets; even *aircraft*. And what didn't collapse my country's politicians would sell off to the highest bidder, no questions asked, like auctioneers clearing a ruined mansion of its last valuables. Everything that wasn't nailed down or green with mould would one day be sold: Great Britain as flea market, steadily disposing of itself for cash. Everything Must Go! Some famous brand names did survive even though now foreign owned, giving a false impression of unchanging familiarity until the shock of discovery suddenly hit. The very idea that one day well within my lifetime Bentley and Rolls-Royce cars might be German owned would have struck anyone of my or my parents' generation as about as thinkable as seeing the sun rise in the west.

As I reflected on that numbing winter's day in Sussex I found myself wondering if our national collapse had after all been inevitable, whether in industrial or less tangible form. Was it simply the inevitable outcome of world events or a succession of bad political decisions at home? Was it because rising living standards and hence increased labour costs in Britain obliged manufacturers to look for cheaper factories overseas? Had we British, as the founders of the Industrial Revolution, finally wearied of our dark satanic mills with their associated and corrosive class divisions, no longer caring very much where or by whom their consumer durables were made? And might it even be that the very idea of Britishness had been steadily diluted – not so much by immigration or EU membership and its free movement of peoples as by a weakening of the importance of national identity in an increasingly multinational world?

I suppose this book is an attempt to answer these questions well enough to satisfy my own curiosity, while knowing that like everyone else I am unable to escape my own past, in my case in a country long ago. The changes to Britain since I was born have been so vast and manifold as to give the whole concept of *back then* a vague imprecision. From the ever-sliding vantage point of the present it is like watching a conveyor belt passing relentlessly by, carrying today's succession of ever-smarter smart phones away to where in the shadowy distance long-defunct products drop off into the void as a shower of Flit guns and Brownie box cameras.

Recent political events – and especially the 2016 Referendum – have made the concept of nostalgia topical and unavoidable, to the point where assigning explanations for Britain's perceived industrial collapse becomes muddied with emotional ideas about contingency versus national destiny. Nostalgia can appear in many guises, but one variety in particular needs to be ruthlessly shorn of its imaginary components: that which celebrates fond memories of the home one never had. Until this is examined it will be hard to guess the basis for the series of political decisions taken both before and after 1979 by self-styled patriots presumably acting for the good of the country, but which have left that country increasingly unlike the 'Britain' that, constantly invoked, still quivers in the public imagination like a mirage.

The hastily taken, ill-informed and unthought-through decision to leave the European Union after forty-four years begged the question of exactly what kind of newly independent Britain the 'Leavers' were envisaging. There was no real consensus; but even those who believed in a shiny new twenty-first-century UK that would at last be free to forge its own trading links around the world and once again be the home-ruled master of a newly global destiny often seemed to paint a picture as much nostalgic as visionary. This was odd because no Briton under the age of fifty-five could possibly retain any detailed memory of what the country had actually been like politically and socially in 1973 when, together with Denmark and Ireland, it first signed up to join the 'European Communities'. In 2016 there was much talk of getting back to things as they had been before that watershed, but the imagery seemed based largely on old newsreels and the 'good old days' myth-making of tabloid newspapers.

The following year, on the day after Prime Minister Theresa May sent a letter to Brussels formally confirming Britain's intention to leave the EU, the internet-based market research company YouGov published a survey of the things Britons wanted to see brought back once the country had regained its independence. On 1 April the *Guardian* columnist John Crace noted some of them:

> Top of the list was the death penalty, with 52 per cent of those who voted leave wishing for its return. Just as well we didn't have a referendum for that, otherwise we might be up there with China, Saudi Arabia and the US for killing offenders. Other things that Leave voters were significantly more keen on than Remainers were the return of dark blue passports, pre-decimal currency, imperial measures, incandescent light bulbs, smoking in pubs and restaurants, and corporal punishment in schools. The idea that voting to leave the EU was a vote for an exciting new world of 21st-century British sovereignty, rather than a desire to head back to a nostalgic, rose-tinted vision of 1950s' and 1960s' Britain, is becoming harder to sustain. The mystery is why anyone who lived through '50s austerity Britain – I write as someone born in 1956 – would want to go back there.[1]

As someone born in 1941 with even better memories of post-war austerity than John Crace I find it beyond mysterious. There are not many advantages in being this old; but one of them is a perspective that confers the right to maintain an attitude of utter scepticism when hearing the solemn pronouncements of politicians half one's age. The banal fact of having lived so long is enough to make almost anything that hits the headlines seem familiar. Milan Kundera's dew of novelty no longer sparkles on the morning's news stories. They mostly seem like half-remembered but recognisable objects disinterred, encrusted with the dull crumbly aura of exhausted soil. 'Been there, seen that,' an inner voice says wearily as public excitement is whipped up over something that strikes younger reporters and two-thirds of the population as novel and alarming. Why (the voice continues), that's pretty much what happened in the fifties when we sent ill-supplied troops into an overseas conflict without the matter first being properly thought through. The same old lesson still unlearned...

Over this time span certain traits of a nation's character inevitably become clear. Although 'nostalgia', via its Greek roots, means homesickness, the Britain seemingly missed today by so many Britons never was their home since they were not even born then. Bafflingly, the Second World War, its pageantry and hardware, are still constantly evoked and trotted out like a fetish by grown adults who missed the entire thing by decades. I can remember the skies of my earliest childhood noisy with Spitfires, Hurricanes and Lancasters still flying live combat sorties; gigantic pre-cast sections of Mulberry Harbour scarcely able to negotiate the crossroads of Oxford's Carfax; and American troops massing for the D-Day invasion. At the time I must have inherited my mother's and other adults' war associations which, behind the resentment at having our lives turned upside down and our very existence daily threatened, were far more of blood and anguish and a deep anxiety for absent fathers and husbands than ever they were of victory. Maybe this is why my heart fails to leap up when cherished remnants of our former aerial armadas rumble overhead in yet another flypast to celebrate our having emerged on the winning side in a war so long ago that no-one younger than their mid-seventies can possibly have the least memory of it.

What is today's ten-year-old Briton supposed to think of this version of national glory? The equivalent for me at age ten would have been to witness a pageant celebrating the gallant but futile efforts of the British Army to relieve the besieged General Gordon in Khartoum in 1885, complete with howling Mahdists and camel-mounted troops with swords and pipe-clayed topees. That is the same distance from 1951 as is 2016. Would the grunting of camels have quickened my heart like the growl of Merlin engines? Absurd. So what magic could these old aerial lawn mowers now hold for children brought up on Airbus travel and virtual reality except maybe as curios? Apparently, half today's Millennials feel embarrassed at being seen by their friends wearing an Armistice Day poppy, and who can blame them? Again, the exact equivalent for me in the late 1950s would have been having to pretend in public that I was made thoughtful and moved by the Crimean War. Such things are not what interest and move teenagers. For the rest of us these comparisons can only provoke generalised and ironic reflection on the enormous gulf that separates Britain's erstwhile military might from its present threadbare defences.

If any nostalgia for the immediate post-war period is excusable in citizens my age it is surely because it was a time of reconstruction imbued with a feeling that, after nearly six years of a devastating war that no-one had wanted, things could only get better. The new Labour government whose election in 1945 so shocked the Tory *ancien régime* embarked on a programme of social improvements that had been overdue well before the war. Today we conveniently forget that although Britain in the 1930s was the motherland of the world's largest and wealthiest empire it also had Europe's worst slums, as the German Wehrmacht painstakingly noted in humiliating detail in its very accurate pre-invasion overview of Britain in 1940. After 1945 living standards for most Britons were obviously going to remain a bit basic for a few years; but there was comfort in the promise of a nationwide housing and slum-clearance programme, a free health service, free schooling for everyone up to the age of fifteen and a general feeling of progress towards a better future. The air raid sirens had at last fallen silent and in their place came the daily clatter of one-third-pint bottles of free milk arriving in heavy metal crates at schools throughout the land.

Anyone who can remember that time and plays down the rationing and fuel shortages (especially during the crippling winter of 1946-7 when we went to bed with wartime stone hot water bottles and wearing jerseys, socks and gloves) might be excused fond and even nostalgic memories of the promise of national recovery. Among themselves they might still reminisce about long-vanished household products and brand names, of popular radio programmes like *Workers' Playtime* or *Much Binding in the Marsh*, or of occasional outings to the flicks at the Gaumont, Odeon or Regal. But to imagine that thrifty and still rationed period as being worthy of returning to does seem strikingly perverse. The exterior shots of post-Blitz London in films such as *Passport to Pimlico* (1949) should be reminder enough of how Britons lived at the time – and that was in the capital city. Things were even worse in the industrial cities of the Midlands and the North.

Nearly seventy years later the Brexit Referendum revealed how far nostalgia is from being a unitary concept. Conservative types harrumphed wistfully about Britain's alleged former grandeur and international clout while Socialists evinced a left-wing nostalgia for the days of the Attlee government and Britain's social regeneration. There was clearly a conflict between these two radically different nostalgias, as between that and those many Brexiteers who weren't obviously nostalgic at all. They, with an entirely contemporary anger adroitly egged on by the right-wing press, just wanted to 'take their country back from the freeloaders of Brussels', and so on. And in addition there was the widespread nostalgia people everywhere and throughout history have always felt, telling them that things were better when they were young, back in those blissful days when their bodies were new and unused and they had no idea what was really going on.

When writing *The Ministry of Nostalgia* (2016) Owen Hatherley probably did not know that in 2017 British cinema-goers would be able to watch a film starring an actor pretending to be Churchill and another with thousands of uniformed extras re-enacting events on the beach at Dunkirk seventy-seven years ago. What he certainly did, and to good effect, was quote with revulsion the Second World War propaganda slogan 'Keep Calm and Carry On' and examine the implications of its success. Although it was never actually used during the war, the phrase has been widely appropriated for mugs and tea towels and T-shirts as presumably signifying some essential quality of the British character. Understandably, Hatherley finds it deeply embarrassing. I can match it with my own least favourite public address slogan, 'You Know It Makes Sense'. This accompanied ads in the late sixties and seventies to promote the wearing of seat belts in cars before they became compulsory. It survived into the Thatcher era as an increasingly nannyish nudge that for a while seemed to apply to everything and appeared everywhere, typically among the advertisements that Londoners glumly stared at in Tube carriages, guaranteeing one left the train in more mulish mood.

These are both examples of official exhortation invoking a supposed national character in a way that is more patronising than artless. They are perfect expressions of a ruling-class *de haut en bas* attitude towards the public it rules. This was already familiar from First World War recruiting posters with their mixture of exhortation and admonishment. 'It is far better to face the bullets than to be killed at home by a bomb', ran one. The implication of cowardice by failing to join up adroitly covered the government's and military authorities' complete inability to protect British citizens from the German Zeppelins' air raids that at the time were spreading increasing panic.

Even more laughably misjudged is a slogan that surely exceeds all others in ineptitude. It is one that practically every prime minister of the last sixty years has sooner or later announced, declaring with desperate emphasis that 'Britain is open for business'. To be sure, this was the basic message of the Festival of Britain in 1951 which was intended to reassure the world that despite the destruction and financial straits occasioned by the recent war, Britain and its industries had bounced back with renewed vigour and with all their world-leading inventiveness unimpaired. Since then the fateful reminder that Britain is open for business has been trotted out at regular intervals.

In sixty years it seems that nobody in government, not even one of its professional PR and marketing advisers in the erstwhile Central Office of Information, can ever have noticed the naff, self-defeating nature of this phrase. It epitomises the amateurish, like a seafront stall on whose closed door handwritten signs are pinned at the height of the season with messages: 'Sorry no whelks till Thursday' or 'Regret closed for month of August'. The clear implication of announcing that Britain is open for business is that you would be excused for thinking it wasn't until recently and might not be again at some point in the future; but meanwhile, as it is still feeling its way in this unaccustomed activity, it thanks the world for its indulgence.

Evidently we have never asked ourselves why we need to do this. When it comes to commerce other countries like Germany or Japan take for granted that they are businesslike, as do their customers. Only Britain seems to feel the need to reassure people that, despite appearances, it can still be traded with. And therein lies an awful truth: that at bottom Britain knows it is *not* businesslike in the contemporary sense, and arguably never has been except possibly back in the days when Napoleon Bonaparte famously disparaged us as a nation of shopkeepers. Even in the mid-nineteenth century, when Britain was at its apogee as the world's leading industrial nation, it barely needed to be competitive since most of its exports went to the Empire's vast and captive market. Still, at least being nature's shopkeepers argued the possession of housekeeping skills: buying and selling groceries and tallying up the weekly accounts to make sure incomings exceeded outgoings. This ethos of living within our means may have worked well enough for the nation's Mr Pooters and for little high street shops; but *pace* the shade of Mrs Thatcher it doesn't scale up to deal adequately with nationalised industries, or to plan an economy that must contain open-ended expenditure on such things as schools and prisons and a national health service while also making allowances for unforeseeable military commitments.

That takes much more complex and longer-term accounting, which in turn requires careful planning. What is more, no British government faces the same financial constraints as does a household since (as with quantitative easing) it can create as much money as it likes in sterling in order to buy assets such as bonds without having to borrow a single penny, which incidentally reveals the recent policy of austerity as essentially fraudulent.

Open for business. But business above all requires careful planning, and it is precisely in its inability to plan that Britain has consistently been found wanting. To someone of my age brought up with the full force of wartime and immediate post-war propaganda about our priceless heritage of rational administration, this seems all the odder. According to received opinion it was lesser, more hysterical nations that dithered and panicked and fell prey to Latin-style corruption and mafias; or else they simply overreached themselves with grandiose Teutonic or Soviet ideologies and plans of world domination. We Britons, on the other hand, were calm and measured and canny. As cricketers, we understood how to play a waiting game. I am not proud of the decades it took me to fully appreciate how hoodwinked I was by this fiction, which actually translates as a nation of fence-sitters, our apparent unflappability rather a mixture of indolence and indecision, shot through with the disguised anxiety of that archetypal figure Humpty Dumpty, forever debating on which side it would be the better to fall if indeed push came to shove.

One case I hope to make is that via a national tradition of laissez-faire indolence, Humpty Dumpty's stance has carried over into British attitudes towards industry, business and finance such that the ingrained short-termism of our governmental system is mirrored by a fatal national reluctance to commit itself to risk. This aversion has long been apparent in a disinclination on Monday to invest in anything that can't be guaranteed to produce a decent return for shareholders by closing time on Friday: a syndrome that reaches from the Treasury to the high street banks. Time and again a refusal to invest in a project or a new technology and give it serious governmental backing at a critical moment has seen it fail in Britain to only be snapped up and developed elsewhere. An example taken at random might be Eric Laithwaite's work on linear induction motors between the late 1940s and the early 1970s that led to the world's first magnetic levitation or maglev railway, a passenger shuttle at Birmingham Airport that, because it was never upgraded, closed in 1995 after eleven years' popular service. Today there is not a single maglev railway in Britain; but the technology has been steadily developed in South Korea, China and Japan, with high-speed versions either in service or proposed, especially for city-to-airport connections and with several other countries currently planning such lines.

Such stories are all too familiar in the general narrative of Britain's industrial decline. The question of whether or not the timorous Stock Exchange mentality (shared in spades by the Treasury) has constantly stymied the initial establishment or the proper development and support of an industry is not easily settled. Before that there is a central and rather knottier issue to decide: whose account of British industrial history ought one to believe?

2.
The Problem

(i)

'In the climate and activities of twentieth-century British government and business, we can see the picture of a nation, and an elite, at war with itself.'

—Martin J. Wiener

A Classics lesson circa 1951. Winchester College boys working their way through a Horace Ode with varying degrees of zeal and daydreaming.

(p. 49) The Duke of Edinburgh visits J. Lyons & Co.'s computer 'Leo' in March 1960. A pioneering British development, Leo was the world's first computer in daily use at a commercial enterprise.

From 1979 the focus of Britain's economic output shifted southwards from the industrial heartlands to London and the south-east. Manufacturing was increasingly replaced by service industries – principally banking, which as a purely parasitical activity has no right to dignify itself with the name of an industry since it manufactures absolutely nothing. Today these 'industries' account for up to 80 per cent of the British economy. If the real manufacturing industries largely collapsed within a mere couple of decades or so between the 1960s and the 1980s, what could have turned us so quickly and so consentingly from a nation of active producers to one of passive consumers?

As noted in the previous chapter, generations of government ministers have needed to keep reminding the world that Britain is open for business because the matter always seems in doubt. Buried in the British character, it is said, is an underlying cultural distaste for science and industry such that we are secretly relieved not to have to think about anything technical. The counter-allegation is that from the first Britain showed unusual technical genius and today remains a leading industrial nation whose industries have merely changed with the times rather than vanished.

Establishing where the truth lies between these two entrenched positions, each supported by impeccably researched references, has long been a historian's battlefield. The side we might call the 'cultural' thinks that from the very beginning of the Industrial Revolution Britons at all levels were equivocal about business generally and industry in particular. The other side, the 'scientific', maintains that the 'cultural' historians have wilfully misinterpreted much of the data and have ignored the rest; and that what decline there has been is purely relative: the outcome of the rise of other nations as economic powers, of changing economies and the shifting of world trade balances. These twin positions need closer examination before the fate of specific industries can be examined.

First, then, the 'cultural' explanation. Among those historians who favour it many (for example Eric Hobsbawm, Correlli Barnett and Martin Wiener) have blamed certain peculiarities of British education and social tradition for this perceived reluctance ever to have embraced industry or even commerce wholeheartedly. According to this thesis it was significant that the rapid growth of industry and manufacturing in the early nineteenth century happened to coincide with the beginnings of the English Romantic movement in literature and painting. This had itself grown out of the German *Sturm und Drang* movement as a reaction against the extreme rationalism of the Enlightenment. It soon embraced writers and artists like Walter Scott, William Wordsworth and John Constable. This prevailing spirit fostered an upsurge in the celebration of rural values, nationalism and even pantheism in Europe, and especially in Britain many embraced it as the antithesis of everything the new industrialism seemed to represent. Many viewed the rapidly expanding manufacturing cities as dirty, corrupt, money-grubbing, heartless citadels of Mammon. The countryside, by contrast, with its immemorial farms and close-knit rustic communities formed the true 'deep' England full of innate spiritual values where traditional cottage industries flourished and produced only what the craftsmen themselves needed for their daily lives.

This 'Merrie England' vision, accompanied by a growing interest in medievalism and the spiritual qualities of landscape, was instinctively promoted by the middle and upper classes and by artists and writers such as Samuel Palmer and William Blake. Admittedly this was well nourished by the often brutal way in which the first industrial towns grew, for the most part haphazardly and unplanned, while the workers they drew in from the surrounding countryside in search of a living wage were often peasants dispossessed by the various Enclosure acts who of necessity became urban slum-dwellers. There was scant acknowledgement that a life of toil on someone else's land had been no idyll. What was emphasised was the industrial hell into whose pitiless maw the sturdy English yeomanry was swallowed, a hell whose vile living conditions inevitably nurtured drunkenness and every kind of vice. This dichotomy was neatly encapsulated in Blake's phrases that every Last Night of the Proms audience knows today: dark satanic mills vs green and pleasant land.

This view was steadily endorsed by artists and thinkers such as William Morris and the Pre-Raphaelites and led to the revival of traditions that many had secretly hoped were decently buried, such as Morris dancing and folk song. In one form or another this obsession with the pastoral has flourished ever since, manured by a constant stream of books and films extolling country living and country values. Over the last 160-odd years innumerable memoirs and poems and novels have conspired to produce a mythical England of rose-girt cottage and cathedral close, of hospitable inns and Dickensian characters that eternally lies somewhere beneath the hideous ephemera of motorways and suburban sprawl and must surely one day resurface. Even books like Ronald Blythe's *Akenfield* (1969) that documented just how grim a life on the land often was managed also to convey a sense of lost virtues. Today a probable majority of white-collar workers dreams of retirement to the country as the reward for years of trudging an urban treadmill. Far fewer would elect to make the reverse journey and retire to the city. Until the dwindling of regular churchgoing in the later twentieth century this vision also consorted well with a national, Anglican vision of middle-class spirituality that somehow managed to commend the eternal values of 'simple folk' living in harmony with the natural cycles of soil and season; of ancient country churches, the King James Bible, the 1662 Prayer Book, Hymns A & M and an intense nostalgia. It was a version of rural Englishness much promoted by writers like Hilaire Belloc and G. K. Chesterton. P. G. Wodehouse captured one aspect of this, perhaps a shade too fondly for it to be out-and-out parody:

> There's something about evening service in a country church that makes a fellow feel drowsy and peaceful. Sort of end-of-a-perfect-

day feeling. ... They had left the door open, and the air was full of a mixed scent of trees and honeysuckle and mildew and villagers' Sunday clothes. As far as the eye could reach you could see farmers propped up in restful attitudes, breathing heavily; and the children in the congregation who had fidgeted during the earlier part of the proceedings were now lying back in a surfeited sort of coma. The last rays of the setting sun shone through the stained-glass windows, birds were twittering in the trees, the women's dresses crackled gently in the stillness.[2]

Nor was this cheerfully benign vision complete without the myth of a landowning gentry as genial squires whose values and sympathies were far better attuned to those of their cottagers, to field sports and rural concerns, than ever they were to things of the city such as government and commerce. This was a strain of Toryism that, while ruefully acknowledging the gentry's need for money to run their estates, was often bashful about mentioning it, instinctively feeling that an interest in money was vulgar. It was beneath a proper English gentleman precisely because it was something a *nouveau riche* mill owner might evince, and this despite many mill owners actually having a deep Puritan or Quaker opposition to any kind of ostentation. Proper gentlemen or not, the Brunels and Stephensons and the Quaker families like Cadbury and C. & J. Clark evidently tapped into a lively entrepreneurial spirit of the times that must have coexisted with the wider disdain.

There is a further important strand to this 'cultural' theory, one that allegedly would crucially affect Britain's future as an industrial nation and contribute to its post-1945 decline. This is the public school movement that coincided with the post-Wesleyan religious revivalism responsible for the rash of neo-Gothic churches spreading throughout the land from the early nineteenth century onwards. Until Thomas Arnold took over as headmaster of Rugby in 1828, the few ancient public (as opposed to grammar) schools were mostly degenerate relics whose wretched pupils were often so starved they survived only by scrounging and poaching in the neighbouring countryside. The inhuman floggings (so brutal that in one instance shreds of a boy's shirt had to be probed for and removed with forceps from the deep lacerations on his back), the equally brutal bullying and rampant homosexuality, drunkenness and local whoring, were a peculiar definition of any sort of education. If today people are misled into thinking schools like Eton have always been places of privilege for toffs, they might consider that in 1834 a report found that 'the inmates of a workhouse or a gaol are better fed and lodged than the scholars of Eton'. Jonathan Gathorne-Hardy has given a vivid picture of conditions at that time in the Long Chamber, a barn-like dormitory at Eton for fifty-two boys:

> It was filthy, stinking of corrupting rats' corpses, ordure and urine. … [At night] rats poured out of the walls and floors to feed on the filth, at which the fags would give chase, stuff them into socks and smash them against the beds. Their numbers can be gauged by

the fact that in 1858 two cartloads of rats' bones were taken from beneath the floorboards. Scenes of the coarsest and most flagrant indulgence took place, of a sort that participants (or victims) could later barely bring themselves to describe. ... And no-one came to see what went on. No-one else ever lived in the building. They were locked in at eight and left alone till morning. Their shrieks of pain and terror, their moans of pleasure, went alike unheard.[3]

Although this was taking place while Victoria was on the throne, the violence and anarchy to which the sons of the well-born were subjected was a survival of Regency England. The regime Dr Arnold set in motion at Rugby from his accession as headmaster in 1828 gradually changed things. Propaganda such as Thomas Hughes' novel *Tom Brown's Schooldays* (1857), set in the reforming Rugby the author had known in the 1830s, together with resonant stuff about the playing fields of a later Eton, produced the archetype of the 'muscular Christian': the clean-limbed Victorian boy who might have been (and often was) a barely educated academic dunce but whose instilled qualities of pluck, fair-mindedness and consciousness of duty made him an agent who with complete confidence could be sent overseas to administer the Empire, to play the game and keep a straight bat no matter what threats or temptation he faced.

The education the public schools offered in the latter half of the nineteenth century was heavily slanted towards the Classics. With the aid of regular canings the pupils learned to parrot reams of Latin and Greek authors while also attending Chapel services at least twice a day. The rest of the syllabus was sketchy. An ability to write a legible essay, some Shakespeare, some necessary geography so that the future administrators had a vague idea of where on the globe they might be sent, a smattering of arithmetic, geometry, algebra and trigonometry. But virtually no science, still less the physics that underpinned engineering. Victorian grammar schools did indeed teach science but the public schools did not believe the shaping of a gentleman required such knowledge. At Rugby Dr Arnold made his priorities clear: '[R]ather than have [physical science] the principal thing in my son's mind, I would gladly have him think that the sun went round the earth, and that the stars were so many spangles set in the bright blue firmament. Surely the one thing needful for a Christian and an Englishman to study is Christian and moral and political philosophy.'[4] Ironically, his son Matthew became a poet whose magnificent short poem 'Dover Beach' was to describe the sea's 'melancholy, long, withdrawing roar' as that of the outgoing tide of his father's generation's religious faith.

In 1859 Rugby did employ a science master who was grudgingly allowed to teach 'natural philosophy' for four hours a week provided that 'the experiments were performed out of sight, in the cloakroom of the Town Hall a hundred yards away down the road from the school, with the apparatus locked up in two cases so that the townspeople could use the space for other purposes at night'.[5] Even at the century's end many other public schools had little or no provision for science teaching.

According to the 'cultural' historians this mixture of Romantic ruralism and classical education resulted in widespread middle- and upper-class attitudes that were at best disdainful towards technologies they neither wished nor were able to understand. To them science and technology were associated with factories, industry, commerce and all the other things that ran counter to a gentleman's proper interests. Above all, the public school and Oxbridge classical education led in the next hundred years to Whitehall and Westminster being filled with people who knew a lot of Greek and Latin tags and, like *Yes, Minister*'s Sir Humphrey Appleby, could at a glance tell porcelain from china. Such people understood very little, if anything, about science and technology, while industry and commerce had a grubby air they instinctively shunned. This was to have a profound effect on British industry, business and politics throughout the nineteenth and twentieth centuries and its echoes are presumably still with us, as evidenced by the constant lament (now one and a half centuries old) that Britain is still not producing anything like enough engineers and science-literate graduates. This, the theory goes, is considerably responsible for the post-war collapse of Britain's former industrial might.

I can certainly testify that at my own public school in the 1950s in the heartland (one might say the Ground Zero) of Anglicanism there was still a faint but definite bias in attitude against science although allowances were made for either the very brilliant, who might go on to become famous boffins and look good in the school prospectus, or for those who were going to need science for an almost excusable profession such as medicine. There may have been boys in the school who were hoping for careers in industry, but if so they must have kept their intentions to themselves since I never met any. Later, in my final year at university, I bumped into the gowned and portly figure of Dacre Balsdon in the quad one morning. Dacre was a distinguished Classics don, a Greek scholar and friend of the poet Constantine Cavafy. 'Ah, James-dear-boy,' he said. 'Have you, I wonder, the remotest notion of what you might do when you go down?' I replied that I had none, adding facetiously that maybe I ought to get some careers advice. Dacre shied like Dracula on getting a whiff of garlic. 'Career?' he said faintly in Lady Bracknell tones. '*Career?* Nobody at Oxford – or even The Other Place – has a career. We have *lives*.' There spoke the voice of the humanities. Had I really wished to shock him I might have said I was toying with going into industry, but it would have been a lie.

That was only five years after this matter of viewing science and industry as though they were social leprosy was thrown into sharp relief. In 1959 C. P. Snow gave the Rede Lecture at Cambridge that expounded what almost immediately became known as the 'Two Cultures' thesis. Snow himself famously straddled the great divide, being a chemist and a physicist as well as a novelist. In his talk he made clear the abyss in Britain between the humanities and science:

A good many times I have been present at gatherings of people who, by the standards of the traditional culture, are thought highly educated and who have with considerable gusto expressed their incredulity at the illiteracy of scientists. Once or twice I have been provoked and have asked the company how many of them could describe the Second Law of Thermodynamics. The response was cold. It was also negative. Yet I was asking something which is the scientific equivalent of: *Have you read a work of Shakespeare's?* I now believe that if I had asked an even simpler question such as, What do you mean by mass, or acceleration, which is the scientific equivalent of saying, *Can you read?* not more than one in ten of the highly educated would have felt that I was speaking the same language. So the great edifice of modern physics goes up, and the majority of the cleverest people in the western world have about as much insight into it as their neolithic ancestors would have had.[6]

A few years later Snow's thesis was put to the test when the first vice-chancellors of Britain's new universities were appointed. Seven of the candidates were asked if they had any idea what the Second Law of Thermodynamics was about, and its significance. Only one of the seven passed. The bias seemed invincible. The historian Neil McKendrick, in comparing the two William Morrises, could write: 'Despite leaving one of the most popular cars in the world to bear his name, William Morris is completely overshadowed by his Victorian namesake in the mental reference map of most educated men and women.'[7] I should add here that my own experience of scientists is that they usually know far more about the arts than my British literary friends do about science although this may be sheer chance; it is not a scientific finding.

There is no doubt that attitudes in Britain have changed a good deal over the last thirty years. General science (if not technological) education has improved and there is a lively market in popular science books and magazines as well as TV programmes ranging from *The Sky at Night* to David Attenborough's remarkable documentaries. The representation on television of science-based subjects such as global warming and space exploration is both popular and serious. Perhaps more importantly, these days there is a limitless amount of scientific information and explanation instantly available on the internet. However, the apparent unfashionableness of industry still seems to make the humanities and social sciences the first choice of a majority of university students. This may be partly because engineering subjects, other than in their information technology and computing aspects, are thought to offer a more limited and more closely specified choice of jobs. As for commerce, and particularly banking, many of the old snobberies – and since the banking crisis of 2008 several new ones – still linger, if popular culture is anything to go by. Audiences clearly enjoyed films such as *Wall Street* (1987) and *The Wolf of Wall Street* (2013): the first because it portrayed a thrusting and amoral world that celebrated the American neoliberal ideal of free enterprise. Nearly a quarter-century later the second film – based on the true rags-to-riches-to-jail story of a Wall Street broker – showed the American dream traduced by corporate greed and personal ruthlessness while offering audiences the pleasure of seeing their own moral superiority vindicated.

The 'Big Bang' of 1986 when Margaret Thatcher deregulated the financial markets also offered a clash of cultures between the ex-public school, Varsity types who had drifted into 'something in the City' without making too much effort and the new currency brokers from state schools making quick fortunes. As a senior civil servant at the time observed later, '[T]his was the era of "yuppies" and the "wealth creators" – a bigger bunch of spivs not seen since the heyday of the nabobs.'[8] It was brilliantly depicted from the late 1980s by Charles Peattie and Russell Taylor's 'Alex' strip cartoons that appeared in the *Independent* and then the *Daily Telegraph*. The old public school snobbery is securely in evidence: Alex and his friend Clive have their weekend cottages and Range Rovers and go shooting and fishing. Else they are to be seen with their bank's clients in hospitality boxes at Ascot or Twickenham, making private asides about people who don't know the etiquette of passing the after-dinner port to the left and eating asparagus with the fingers. Likewise they decry the ghastliness of their northern industrial client's polyester ties. One of Alex's butts is the Cockney currency broker Vince, a wide boy always depicted wearing (horrors!) white socks. On one occasion Vince finds himself in a black tie at Glyndebourne and remarks to Alex that this is a new experience for him. Alex can well believe it and tells him he's in for a marvellous musical feast: *Die Zauberflöte*. When Vince looks blank Alex says 'Magic Flute,

47

Vince,' whereupon Vince looks down at his evening dress and says, 'Thanks, Alex. I bought it specially.'[9]

Such, then, is the 'cultural' historians' case: that the British executive and political class has always remained snobbishly ignorant of science and technology while favouring a deeper English tradition that, like Ruskin's loathing of the railways, sees industry as the inevitable despoiler of the countryside and its values. Once the Second World War was over such attitudes, together with other shortcomings, proved fatally damaging to Britain as an industrial nation. Whether or not they were the cause of Britain's alleged industrial decline, it is worth indicating that the decline itself was unequivocally noted by the American management guru Peter Drucker. His view was that it was a failure of business know-how rather than of native inventiveness:

According to its production of scientific and technical knowledge, Britain should have been the world's economic leader in the post-World War II era. Antibiotics, the jet engine, the body scanner, even the computer, were British developments. But Britain did not succeed in turning these knowledge-achievements into successful products and services, into jobs, into exports, into market standing. The non-productivity of its knowledge, more than anything else, is at the root of the slow and steady erosion of the British economy.[10]

(ii)

'The British economy has been one of the most efficient in the world: of the seven great powers of the interwar years ... only the US had higher levels of income per head than Britain. ... Britain has been one of the few great technological nations of the nineteenth and the twentieth centuries.'

—David Edgerton

On the other side of the debate, 'scientific' historians such as David Edgerton, Sidney Pollard, William Rubinstein and Donald McCloskey have poured a good deal of scorn on the 'cultural' historians' 'revisionist and declinist' explanations for the post-1945 collapse of large-scale British industries. For instance, Edgerton dismisses Correlli Barnett's theory that, as a result of Britain's elites having been classically educated and scornful of technology in the nineteenth century, our industrial lead was eclipsed by both Germany and the United States from around 1880. He points out that Germany, France and the United States also had their elites: there was nothing unique about Britain's increasingly formulaic and selective public (i.e. private) school education. This is surely true. Any nineteenth-century European society with overseas possessions to administer and defend probably required some administrative elite of this kind.

Then there is the accusation that British aristocratic values were anti-industrial. According to Peter Payne,

[A] veritable library of monographs reveals that the British aristocracy and gentry during the industrial revolution were the most economically-progressive and profit-oriented ruling class in Europe. They invested eagerly in agricultural improvement and enclosure, in trading ventures, mining, roads, river navigation and canals, docks, early railways, urban development and even, where circumstances permitted, in manufacturing such as brick-making, iron-founding and textiles.[11]

David Edgerton goes on to assert that it was not a lessening of Britain's industrial effort that led to its being overtaken by Germany and America towards the end of the nineteenth century. It was the inevitable consequence of those countries having had their industrial revolutions later than Britain's and being able to learn by refining and further developing the inventions and processes the British had so laboriously pioneered. This is simply the downside of pioneering: after-comers can usually manage to reap the rewards of mass production without the lengthy early period of trial and error.

A related popular British belief is that we are brilliant at ideas and inventions but much less good at marketing so it is always somebody else who makes a handsome profit out of them. This is one of the more enduring of the popular press's consoling myths, and not just in Britain since the media everywhere tend to be preferential in serving up stories about their own country's breakthroughs. Hence the myth's currency owes much to ignorance about how ubiquitous, as well as random, innovation has always been. Even in the nineteenth century Britain introduced many foreign techniques that became central to some of its most potent industries:

Classic examples are machinery for making small arms, imported from the USA in the 1850s; the [ammonia-soda] Solvay process for alkali first developed in Belgium; and from Germany the contact process for sulphuric acid, the Haber-Bosch process for producing ammonia, and the internal combustion engine. Similarly, foreign industries acquired British-innovated techniques: examples are the Bessemer converter [for producing steel from pig-iron], the spinning mule, and viscose rayon. A still more notorious case was the British innovation of synthetic dyestuffs, which was taken up by the German chemical industry. The failure of British firms to develop and produce synthetic dyestuffs for the giant British textile industry has long been condemned, despite the fact that the total value of such dyestuffs was small.[12]

The development of the internal combustion engine is a case in point. From the 1850s a variety of Belgian, French, Austrian, American, British and above all German engineers had invented various types of engine that could be called 'internal combustion' (as opposed to steam). Only in 1885 did Gottlieb Daimler produce an engine with a vertical cylinder and carburettor that was the clear antecedent of today's car engines. The following year he mounted it in the world's first four-wheeled motor vehicle. Only a full fifteen years later did the first indigenous British car appear: Herbert Austin's of 1900. That the originators of the Industrial Revolution lagged behind in this new technology was even more apparent only eighteen months later when an American broke the existing land speed record at 76 mph: a speed that was then far beyond Britain's capabilities. As late as the First World War British aircraft were still greatly dependent on foreign motors, particularly French-designed (and often built) rotary engines.

In short, the main problem the 'scientific' historians have with the 'cultural' argument is that it is far too imprecise. It is couched in such all-embracing terms that it cannot get to grips with specifics such as the effects of new products and processes at home and abroad – not to mention the pressures and special requirements of two world wars. To invoke 'cultural' causes for Britain's poor economic performance also lets ordinary human inadequacy off the hook: foolish politicians, dim-witted academics, inept businessmen, short-sighted trade unions and the rest.

Nor does the 'cultural' argument acknowledge how long it can take for people everywhere to change their ways of working – especially in industries employing thousands of workers. For example, in the 1880s the technology for the large-scale generation of electricity was developed, particularly in America. This was quickly spotted as offering great advantages over steam, which at the time was powering factories everywhere. The way steam was used in industry might typically involve a massive engine housed in a separate building driving a shaft that ran overhead the length of a shed containing rows of individual machines, for instance cotton looms. Each loom would be powered by a belt driven from the overhead shaft. This lay-out could be repeated in a series of parallel sheds all supplied with power from the same steam engine. It was pretty much immutable since the position of the looms as work stations was determined by their need to be connected directly to the constantly turning shaft overhead. It was not hard to see the great advantage in flexibility that electricity could offer. All that was needed in each shed was an external mains supply. Separate cables could then power any number of individual machines in any convenient position performing different tasks at different speeds, all of which could be stopped or started at will. The main steam engine would still be needed to drive a generator if the town was not yet centrally supplied with electricity; but the whole nature of production could be changed and made more efficient if different processes were no longer dependent on being beneath a common drive shaft turning at a uniform speed.

That it took well over half a century for general electrification to catch on even in industrialised countries might be singled out by 'cultural' historians as a peculiarly British phenomenon, presumably caused by a deep-seated lack of enthusiasm for new technology. Yet a rather better reason was that Britain had become the first urbanised country well before the electric light bulb was invented (severally by Joseph Swan in England and Thomas Edison in America). Its towns and cities had already invested hugely in a new infrastructure that piped coal gas to street lamps, homes, factories and offices. A dedicated industry employed thousands of people across the country making pipes and mantles and gasometers. City councils thus had little incentive to convert to electricity, especially since it was initially more expensive than gas.

'Scientific' historians point out that this slowness to adopt a new technology is common everywhere, partly because of

the expense of having to install an entirely new infrastructure
and retrain a vast corps of people to run it. This was just as
apparent in Germany or America, where electrification only
became universal after 1945. (Since then it has likewise taken
several decades for computers to slowly change traditional ways
of working.) It is a still-popular myth in Britain that in the
Second World War many of the country's industrial processes
were less advanced than those of Germany, at least initially.
The usual reason given is that after the First World War we
allowed things to stagnate, and after the Great Slump in the
1930s we were only goosed into belated and frantic activity
by Hitler's rearmament. This is broadly true; but it still has to
be explained how in the Second World War the German war
machine was dependent on 2.75 million horses and mules for
moving its supplies about, whereas the fully motorised British
military had none. German Romanticism, maybe?

Furthermore, one need not be a 'scientific' historian to point
out some key events of 1960s Britain. Those of us who can
clearly remember Harold Wilson's refreshing bid to end 'thir-
teen years of fuddy-duddy, old-school-tie Tory rule' (in *Private
Eye*'s phrase at the time) will also recall the speech he gave at
the Labour Party conference in 1963 as part of a more general debate on science that owed much to C. P. Snow's 'Two
Cultures' thesis four years earlier. Wilson stressed the vital
importance of higher education, an economy whose growth
would be driven by a Socialist scientific revolution, and a
proper balance between civil and defence R & D (this was, of

course, in the depths of the Cold War when defence spending was an urgent issue). Towards the end of the speech he famously said that if the country were to prosper, a new Britain would need to be forged in the 'white heat' of this scientific revolution. There was, he said, 'no place for restrictive practices or for outdated methods on either side of industry', and added that there was also no room for Luddites in the Labour Party, implying the Conservatives were a party of old-fashioned elitists, technophobes and backwoodsmen (which indeed many in both parties were). Later he would write that his ambition was to 'replace the cloth cap [with] the white laboratory coat as a symbol of British labour'.

One of the first things Wilson did on coming to power in 1964 was to set up a Ministry of Technology, immediately known as MinTech, that had close links with existing state-owned institutions such as the National Physical Laboratory at Teddington (founded in 1900) and the National Gas Turbine Establishment at Farnborough. The NGTE had grown out of a wartime merger of Frank Whittle's Power Jets Ltd and the Royal Aircraft Establishment's Turbine Division and was central to Britain's leadership in post-war jet propulsion. By 1969 MinTech had become one of Britain's biggest and most powerful ministries, having absorbed large parts of both the Ministry of Aviation and the Ministry of Power. Not unjustly, Wilson has often been accused of inconsistency and gross expediency – hardly rare charges against any politician – and for having thrown vast amounts of taxpayers' good money after bad on inherited prestige projects such as Concorde, TSR.2 and civil nuclear power (the Advanced Gas-cooled Reactor programme). Nevertheless his declared commitment to science and technology at a time when the future of several major British industries such as shipbuilding, cars and motorbikes looked bleak was surely proof of sensible intentions as well as representing the wisdom of the times. After all, most engineers and scientists of the day genuinely believed that civil nuclear power and civil aerospace were the way to go and represented the technologies of the future. Wilson's MinTech was equally convinced that if Britain wanted to survive as an industrial nation such projects needed heavy government support and investment: an extremely rare position for any British government to take, as we shall see.

It is obviously very difficult to second-guess the future, and David Edgerton's conclusion perhaps sounded more harsh than regretful when he wrote: 'Britain would have been *richer* had its government not subsidised civil aerospace and its nuclear programme. Grave as these losses were, they were almost certainly small by comparison to the losses incurred in defence R & D and procurement programmes.'[13] Whatever else, though, the enormous sums that successive post-1945 governments spent on R & D both civil and military, and the state backing for research institutes that were the equal of any in the world, might finally have banished the idea that in some mysterious but fundamental way the British are culturally and constitutionally opposed to science and technology.

That is, until one looks at education. Historians can claim the British have not been opposed to science education, but only if they are referring to the upper echelons of academe. At the level of ordinary state schooling the situation has in general been scandalously bad, for the most part demonstrably inferior to that of our most significant continental rivals. This subject will be taken up at greater length in the later chapter on engineering. For now it is enough to say that Harold Wilson's 'white heat' has at best been confined to quite limited foci and mostly has long since cooled to dull red where it is not already stone cold.

Such, then, are the outlines of the main arguments in the debate about the reasons for Britain's diminished status as an industrial nation. Yet it still needs to be explained why we seem to be so hopeless at translating our native inventiveness into cash. Indeed, we have always overvalued our inventions (radar, jet engines and all the rest of it) as though their discovery alone guaranteed a bumper crop on the money tree. But they never do. Crucially, such breakthroughs need to be translated into hard cash via production and marketing before they can benefit the national economy. Correlli Barnett quoted Masaru Ibuka, then president of the Sony Corporation, summarising this process succinctly in 1983: 'If the weight of invention or discovery is one, the weight to bring it to actual development should be ten, and the weight to produce and market it should be one hundred.'[14] In order to achieve this, not only do an industry's attitudes need to be right; it also needs to be flexibly capable of adapting quickly to market changes. This has seldom character-ised British industry, as will become apparent throughout this book: not because it lacked people who recognised the problem but usually because they could not make their arguments accel-erate their managements' inertial mass. In 1961 the economic journalist Michael Shanks observed, 'The backwardness of much of British industry is becoming almost a music-hall joke.'[15] At the time he apportioned some of the blame to badly organised and ill-disciplined trade unions. Yet in many areas this backwardness still exists today, and now has little to do with the unions. To explain why will require touching on the fugitive topic of national character: a phenomenon whose broad outlines both we and foreigners can recognise even if we may be hard pushed to define it.

We are unquestionably conservative with a small 'c', disliking change for change's sake. Most human beings share this dislike, but some societies seem better at overcoming it than we are. We are also deeply apprehensive of commitment, preferring to see ourselves as autonomous individuals with a horror of being tied down. Again, such individualism is vastly less appar-ent in Far Eastern societies where the idea of the common good takes precedence. Both these characteristics of resistance to change and reluctance to commit are precisely those that tend to hinder commerce, which usually entails a degree of risk-taking. One accusation commonly made by British company directors is of the prevailing 'Stock Exchange' mentality that in their view characterises the Treasury. Hence another national predisposition: that of hedging any agreement with 'opting out' or 'wait and see' clauses (our membership of the EU being the *locus classicus*). Similarly, our overpraised system of government with its precipitate elections and reversals of policy can seldom provide the long-term continuity that any industry's business strategy badly needs.

None of these characteristics, businesspeople reasonably claim, is promising when it comes to investing in the future and have continually stymied new industries. If it were not so, there would never be any need constantly to remind the rest of the world that Britain is open for business: it would surely be obvious. Business demands brisk decisions, firm commitment and now and then timely government backing, none of which has ever described the British system except in wartime. This is often compared with the way German governments, for instance, are prepared to make guaranteed long-term investments. It is a difference that has frequently been apparent when British companies have tried bidding in competition for major projects abroad, such as for dams or power stations. Outside the field of defence (for instance supplying aircraft or military equipment to foreign – notably Middle Eastern – buyers) there is no real tradition of solid long-term UK government backing even when foreign competitors are already known to have the generous support of their own governments.

Behind so much of this strangely lackadaisical approach to the way we British run our affairs there looms a ghost far more cultural than scientific. This is the Victorian fetish of the amateur as opposed to the professional: idolised in sporting (and especially cricketing) terms as 'gentlemen *vs* players'. This ethos is intimately bound up with the notion of being a good loser, with the implication that anyone who tries too hard may actually be a bit of a cad – or even worse, someone who needs the money. This has been reflected in politics as well as business. It is not so long since prime ministers expected to do very little office work in between hunting, shooting, fishing and other pursuits. The PM as micromanager is quite a recent invention. Nevertheless, the 'top table' attitude is still there even as the pretence of effortless superiority has worn threadbare; and the remains of a dandyish disdain for being professional about politics is surely reflected in a casual approach to thinking things through, most recently exemplified by David Cameron.

Britain's innate reluctance to commit itself, to make and stick to long-term plans and take firm decisions – on the contrary, apparently to *prefer* protracted fence-sitting – leads naturally to the next chapter.

3.
Trains and Planes

'No-one was ever decisive in a swivel chair.'

—George Patton

London Airport's departure lounge, 1946. Chintz-covered armchairs, a Western Union cables desk and artless vases of flowers fail to disguise a draughty army tent with celluloid windows, ad hoc lighting and coconut matting underfoot.

Britain's difficulty in drawing up and implementing long-term plans has been increasingly conspicuous, and in no sector more so than in transport. Clement Attlee's Town and Country Planning Act of 1947 seemed in theory to make certain public projects easier and more equitable to achieve since at last it made plain that private ownership of land did not confer the automatic right to develop it at whim. Planning permission was now a legal requirement and overrode personal property rights. However, in practice this public-spirited measure had the effect of guaranteeing planning disputes with hearings, inquiries and court cases that inevitably slowed things down and added layers of bureaucracy to the task of rebuilding Britain after the war.

It is hard to think of a single area of Britain's industrial and social effort that has not been still further frustrated by the lack of a clear programme as well as by chronic indecision. For instance: given the amount of damage that bombing raids in the Second World War inflicted on Britain's already ageing rail network – not to mention inadequate intercity road links – it is strange enough that there was no successful attempt to draw up and implement a properly integrated transport system for the country despite the 1951 Festival of Britain's message of a bright, new, efficient and technologically based economy. Even more extraordinary is that none has ever emerged in the ensuing seventy years. A small, highly industrialised nation without any blueprint for a rationalised network of joined-up travel and communications? But yes: even as the country's first motorway, the M1, was belatedly taking shape in the early 1960s Dr Richard Beeching was preparing his 1963 report *The Reshaping of British Railways* that resulted in the grubbing-up or closure of six thousand miles of railway lines and their stations by the end of the decade. The reason given was that the network was losing money and was challenged by road freight and increasing car ownership. The idea that *both* modes of travel might be organised over the long term for the benefit of all Britons and to be complementary rather than competing never took serious hold of the official mind. Since 1945 private cars have become Britain's sacred cows, unrestrainedly allowed to proliferate and clutter the landscape at will. Public transport, with its suspiciously socialistic overtones, has always come off second best, for all its obvious economic advantages.

The result has been a rail lobby and a road lobby each constantly striving for political preferment and funds. Far from integration, the system has tended towards still further disintegration. This was made inevitable by the dogma of 'sharing risk' that forced through the privatisation of British Rail and the London Underground between 1994 and 1997 in the teeth of widespread public opposition that included plenty of alarmed Tory voters. The policy duly made its investors rich while for the rest of the travelling public it resulted in a spectacular shambles: a balkanisation that makes a unified rail network impossible. Byzantine complexities of ticketing and pricing have added to chronic overcrowding to cause daily frustration and despair to millions of passengers. Most franchises last between seven and fifteen years, so trying to plan ahead by contracting for new rolling stock with a working life of thirty-plus years becomes practically unachievable. A further consequence has been that long-distance freight trains which have to travel across franchise boundaries are increasingly penalised by the Department for Transport, forcing more and more freight onto Britain's already overloaded road system.[16] Once again, the consequences to the nation of this brainless obedience to a rigid economic doctrine were never properly thought through. The final irony is that Britain's privatised rail network today is more heavily subsidised by the taxpayer than nationalised British Rail ever was.

Even worse in its way has been the sheer incompetence of Network Rail. After the spectacular bankruptcy of Railtrack in 1992 the government had to step in and effectively renationalise the remains as Network Rail, who have stoutly maintained their core incompetence ever since. A single example of this might be their project for the electrification of the Great Western line. On 1 March 2017 the Committee of Public Accounts described this as 'a stark example of how not to run a project'. This damning verdict was prompted by Network Rail's admission that the cost of this job had risen in a mere two years from £874 million to £2.8 billion. That's privatisation for you: layers upon layers of managers and accountants who know nothing about railways. The old British Rail alternative was layers upon layers of experienced railwaymen who knew nothing about accountancy but who did know exactly what electrifying a line entailed and simply got on and did it. The Public Accounts Committee's previous report in November 2015 had already referred to the project's cost increase since 2013 as 'staggering and unacceptable' when it became clear that Network Rail had not even devised a plan for obtaining all the necessary permissions from those along the line who would be affected by the works – local councils and the rest. Nor had they taken into account the tunnels and bridges that would all need modification. The truth was that the straightforward, well-established task of electrification 'is prohibitively costly and complex in a fragmented rail system that is riddled with conflicting interests and undermined by incompetence at the Department for Transport and Network Rail (which is part of DfT) while lacking overall leadership'.[17] In this dithering way whole years of drafting engineering plans and budgeting had gone by in which the project languished as the cost estimates steadily soared.

The problem of short-termism is built into the British political process. As will be seen over and over again in the course of this book, as a nation we are lousy at long-term forecasting and planning, especially in technological matters. Apart from anything else, one government's project may simply be cancelled by the next government either for ideological reasons or because the budgeted money is suddenly needed to plug a politically embarrassing gap elsewhere. Projects and even foreign alliances are suddenly abandoned because the government gets cold feet about mounting costs. A case in point was the 1974 attempt to build a Channel Tunnel. A mile of this was expensively bored through Kentish chalk before the government panicked over a new estimate of the total cost and the work was abandoned.

Sometimes, for reasons of vainglory and a refusal to do the market research, grandiose projects acquire a life of their own and can't be stopped when they should be. An egregious example was Concorde, which from the first was a political rather than a commercial project. Britain had hoped that an Anglo-French partnership might overcome General de Gaulle's resistance to Britain's application to join the Common Market. The agreed deal was that both governments would share the development costs while the manufacturers would then bear the production costs. Having drawn a glowing picture of the vast market awaiting the aircraft and falling for their own projections, the respective French and British aero companies were confident of being able to afford this. When the treaty (rather than a commercial contract) to build the aircraft was finally drawn up in 1962, Britain insisted on including a stiff penalty clause in the event of either party defaulting. True to form, some way into the project Cabinet members became alarmed over the rapidly increasing expense and seriously debated cutting and running. They were only dissuaded when Whitehall's legal advisers made it clear that the punitive damages France could demand would probably cost Britain as much as going ahead and finishing the two Concorde prototypes.

It had never been a secret at Cabinet level that the aircraft could never conceivably make a profit. Yet it was not until 1974 that Tony Benn, then the Secretary of State for Industry, admitted as much to parliament. He pointed out that the £600 million (£12.6 billion in today's values of economic cost) the government had already spent on the project was irrecoverably lost and that the contracted sixteen production aircraft would cost the British Aircraft Corporation and Aérospatiale a further £200 million to build. The Chairman of BAC, Sir George Edwards, then announced with consummate arrogance that BAC would not after all be paying for production and the government would have to do so. By then it was clear to everyone that Concordes could only ever be sold for a fifth of what they cost to build because the airlines had worked out how enormously expensive they would be to fly and maintain. Unfortunately, the media's triumphalist propaganda on both sides of the Channel had for years been steadily cranking up the volume; and so it was that the handful of Air France and British Airways Concordes finally flew with their little complements of fat cats and rock stars. They did it beautifully, glamorously, and noisily. Since a mere 6 per cent of the aircraft's weight was payload – human beings and their baggage – they also did it hugely uneconomically, if to widespread popular acclaim.

In 1977 David Henderson, an Oxford economic historian, described Concorde with endearing hyperbole as one of the three worst civil investment decisions in human history.[18] He calculated that by 1976 the Anglo-French aircraft had cost Britain alone £1.32 billion: some £22 billion at today's values. What was particularly sad was that from the British side, at least, the project when first proposed seemed to fulfil the economic shibboleth of 'picking a winner' and came at a time when Britain's once-illustrious aircraft industry was deeply dispirited after brutally enforced mergers. The thinking was that a prestige undertaking like Concorde would capitalise on the very real skills we still had and might reinvigorate the industry and halt its downward trend. Unfortunately, what the industry needed for its most promising projects was solid government backing, and once the true extent of the Concorde débâcle became clear, that was not about to happen.

A similar instance of havering and wavering was over the notion of a European 'air bus' to challenge America's hegemony in civil aircraft. Britain, still full of design ideas, signed the original Memorandum of Understanding in September 1967. Through Hawker Siddeley's participation BAC's projected 3-11 airliner was in a favoured position to be the first Airbus when in 1969 the UK got cold feet about the whole project and withdrew. It cited soaring costs as the reason, although in fact it was chiefly miffed that Rolls-Royce was no longer the consortium's engine maker of choice since by then the company was deeply mired in the well-publicised developmental problems of its RB-211 engine, which led to its bankruptcy two years later. BAC's highly promising 3-11 airliner was promptly abandoned. This was to be followed by yet another change of heart and in 1978 Britain rejoined Airbus, which hardly enhanced the UK's reputation as a reliable partner through thick and thin.

The granddaddy of all such examples of Britain's chronic indecision is, of course, its membership of the EU, with its initial delay compounded by de Gaulle's repeated '*Non!*' This was followed by years of uneasy membership marked by successive governments negotiating special concessions and opt-out clauses and general half-heartedness, culminating in the less-than-overwhelming mandate of June 2016 to unjoin again. The full consequences of this are likely to remain opaque for many a year. Britain continues to claim that it is open for business without (as of writing) the remotest certainty of who its future customers might be. With dogged optimism it continues to cite the fabled Anglosphere, which so far appears mostly tepid about a Britain newly open to the four winds of trade.

This chopping and changing according to the barometric conditions of Britain's governmental feet has become as familiar as jocular excuses are for the trains not running on time (the wrong kinds of snow, leaves, sunlight etc.). These days any Briton might be forgiven for finding much to be said for the old Soviet system of ten-year plans that had to be completed on time and within budget or else heads rolled. Under the British system failed ministers, chairpersons and managing directors clinking with lucre and knighthoods lamentably retain their heads. Instead of boarding a train to an Outer Hebridean gulag under an armed guard and clutching a little fibre suitcase, they tend to be elevated to the peerage and/or given a huge sum of money. Any little suitcase they might leave in the House of Lords cloakroom probably contains Masonic fancy dress. Yet short-termism is not alone responsible for failures of planning in Britain's infrastructure. There is also its close ally: chronic indecision. A single notorious example of vacillation in the transport sector that has now been sustained for well over half a century will suffice for the remainder of this chapter: that of London's main airport.

In 1945 an advisory panel was set up to choose a site for a new civil airport to serve the nation's capital and be 'capable of meeting the greatest foreseeable air traffic'. In 1946 the panel gave its verdict: the wartime RAF Transport airfield on what had once been Hounslow Heath between Staines and Hayes should be developed. It lay beside what in the days of stagecoaches was known as the Bath Road and had since become the Great West Road, so there was a direct road link into London right on its doorstep. Not only that, but the mainline railway from Paddington to Bristol lay a bare couple of miles from the airfield's northern boundary, promising a good rail connection to the west country as well. The row of houses overlooking the heath, the hamlet known as Heath Row, had already been demolished during the war.

In the 1920s and 1930s London had been increasingly served by Croydon Airport, with international scheduled flights to such capitals as Berlin and Paris. During the war Croydon was an RAF fighter base, but by the time the post-war advisory panel began its deliberations the airfield had become so embedded in suburbia that expansion was no longer possible and Croydon was dropped as a candidate for London's new airport. A second potential site for development was Northolt, an RAF station some six miles from what would become Heathrow, but for various reasons it was the latter that was finally chosen. It would be unfair to castigate this choice as stupid because no-one in 1946 could reasonably have predicted the rapid expansion of post-war aviation. Guesses as to 'the greatest foreseeable air traffic' were based on memories of civil aviation up to 1939. In those days flying the world's few air routes slowly and none too comfortably had been the affair of a comparative minority of suitably important or moneyed people that included politicians, company directors, absconding financiers and civil servants on Empire business. Middle-class folk rich enough to travel to places like the South of France for their holidays mainly preferred to do it far more luxuriously by rail or else by road, stopping off at agreeable hostelries on the way. In 1946 most people still associated aircraft with war rather than peace and it now seems excusable that the advisory panel got its predictions wrong. On the other hand, once having made the choice it was foolish not to have included some provision for a future need to expand.

And so the new London Airport was built over the rubble of Heath Row. Since the prevailing winds in southern England blow from the west, one problem with having an airport sited to the immediate west of the increasingly sprawling capital was that since aircraft prefer to land and take off into the wind (and anyway the majority approached from the Continent), inbound traffic had to overfly London at no great height, as it still does. Residents stoically accustomed to the noise of low-level wartime flying were probably philosophical about this at first; but with the early generation of jet aircraft from the 1950s onwards, when engines became both thunderous and screechy, London Airport's din became hard to bear for increasing numbers of citizens.

A second drawback was that building a hub airport on the edge of suburbia encourages suburbia to grow around it unless there is strict planning of land usage. A major airport is itself a massive business in whose shadow a host of secondary businesses flourish. Thousands of employees need to be housed locally; engineering workshops and hangars have to be built; so do warehouses, as well as offices for freight and ancillary services such as catering. Hotels need to be thrown up for transit passengers. By the early sixties it was becoming clear that Heathrow would have to expand, and above all that this would require at least one new runway to supplement the existing two. However, the developmental sprawl that had been allowed to surround the airport meant it would be better simply to find a completely new site for London's main aviation gateway. The old 1920s airfield at Gatwick, some thirty miles to the south-east in Sussex, had already engulfed a former racecourse and in October 1954 was officially cleared to be developed as London's second airport. With the expansion of popular air travel heralded by Freddie Laker's founding of Laker Airways in 1966 and the subsequent proliferation of charter airlines it was clear that passenger numbers everywhere were only ever going to increase steadily and by now Gatwick was providing useful overspill. All the same, it was clearly not enough.

Consequently, in 1968 the Roskill Commission began examining the possibilities offered by four alternative sites for a new airport. These were at Cublington in Buckinghamshire, Nuthampstead in Hertfordshire, Thurleigh in Bedfordshire and Foulness (aka Maplin Sands) on the Essex coast. It took the Commission nearly three years to think about this and in 1971 it finally recommended expanding the disused RAF Wing airfield at Cublington, seven miles north of Aylesbury. This news provoked immediate and widespread opposition that had CPRE nimbys (not in my back yarders) lighting hilltop beacons in protest. Not wishing to add to its already considerable woes by tangling with these fervent campaigners for the preservation of rural England, Edward Heath's Conservative government rejected Cublington on environmental grounds. Instead, it chose Foulness and in October 1973 the Maplin Development Act was passed. For several weeks the project to build the Thames Estuary Airport at Maplin Sands looked like a going concern until the largely Arab Organization of the Petroleum Exporting Countries (OPEC) announced an embargo on oil exports that hit the industrial nations hard. After five months of global oil crisis the price of oil had quadrupled and looked like increasing indefinitely. Horrified by the rising cost of the Thames Estuary scheme, Harold Wilson's incoming Labour government killed it off as being no longer economically viable. Instead, the wartime military airfields to the north of London at Stansted in Essex and Luton in Bedfordshire were further developed, having already become charter flight airports. It seems strange now that the Roskill Commission never examined Stansted as a likely site for expansion as London's new main airport, given that the countryside there is flat and was not over-populated. In any case the problem of finding a new site for a London hub airport remained unsolved.

In 1979 Margaret Thatcher's first government acknowledged that capacity at Heathrow was 'virtually exhausted' but all the same decided against the need for a new international airport. Instead, it backed the development of regional airports gener-ally and in 1981 a new City Airport was proposed as part of the London's Docklands development scheme and was in operation by 1987. This was, and still is, very small, however, and its reclaimed urban site meant it is only suitable for short-haul aircraft that can approach and take off at angles steep enough to avoid noise restrictions. After that an entire further decade dragged by until in 1990 the Conservative government commissioned yet another study: 'Runway Capacity in South East England', informally known to Heathrow campaigners as 'RUCATSE'. Yet another three years elapsed while the panel deliberated this now-venerable topic before it was ready to advise John Major's government that 'the greatest benefits' would be afforded by expanding Heathrow and that another runway would be urgently needed by 2005. Despite this, in a startling volte-face in 1994 the new Conservative transport minister, Brian Mawhinney, rejected the idea of new runways for both Heathrow and Gatwick because he believed that further capacity could still be wrung from both airports' existing runways.

One of the options the panel had listed was that of building a new east–west runway to the north of Heathrow's existing boundary. Environmentalists, local councillors and the scheme's other opponents were swift to point out that this would entail the bulldozing of 4,000 houses, a church and one of the country's finest tithe barns. Meanwhile the British Airports Authority (or BAA plc), which had been a member of the RUCATSE panel, dissented from the report's verdict by announcing, 'We must stress that this company is not planning or proposing to build a third runway at Heathrow. The airport requires extra terminal capacity rather than runway capacity.'[19] This apparent reversal of the conclusions of some thirty years' worth of studies was soon seized on by environmental groups such as Friends of the Earth, who viewed the proposed Terminal 5 as nothing but a Baldrickian cunning plan, a Trojan horse bound sooner or later to excrete a third runway.

In May 1995 an inquiry into the scheme to build Terminal 5 began. It was headed by Roy Vandermeer QC and after a further six years and six months had gone slowly by the Transport minister, Labour's Stephen Byers, could in November 2001 describe it with pride in the House of Commons as 'the longest [inquiry] in British Transport History'.[20] In fact it was the longest public planning inquiry in *all* British history and presumably not the least expensive seeing it was held in Heathrow's Renaissance Hotel. The upshot was that Terminal 5 was finally given the go-ahead more than eight years after the initial planning application had been made. Throughout the Vandermeer inquiry's six and a half year life BAA went on repeating its claim that the problem at Heathrow was a lack of *terminal*, and not runway, capacity. In May 1997 they had responded to the environmentalists' Trojan horse accusation by saying that 'some legitimate fears have been put to rest. We now know for example that there will be no third runway at Heathrow – a widespread concern before the inquiry started.'[21] The following year Tony Blair's New Labour government announced that the M25 would be widened between Junctions 12 and 15 to accommodate a new intersection for the spur road needed to connect with BAA's new Terminal 5. It was thus clear even before the outcome of the Vandermeer inquiry that the new terminal would be built. Still, the inquiry did conclude that a third runway could have 'unacceptable environmental consequences' and recommended limiting Heathrow's air traffic to 480,000 movements a year so that a third runway would not be needed.

Yet another six years drifted by until in 2003 New Labour's White Paper 'The Future of Air Transport' was published. This recommended the building of a third runway at Heathrow, the squeezing of still more flights onto the existing two runways (quite how was not plausibly explained) and the addition of another three runways at Stansted. In line with this BAA suddenly changed its tune by announcing that on second thoughts it *did* now want a third runway at Heathrow, claiming this was entirely compatible with the company's policy of 'responsible growth'. This predictably caused uproar among environmentalist groups, who variously called it 'the mother of all U turns' (HACAN – the Heathrow Association for the Control of Aircraft Noise); 'a sick joke' (Friends of the Earth); and 'lower than a rattle-snake's stomach' (*Planning* magazine). Just then, some two hundred miles away to the east as the airliner flies, Amsterdam Airport opened its fifth runway. Each year its manager sends a cake to his counterpart at Heathrow in gratitude for the delay in expansion and for enabling Schiphol to promote itself as a plausible alternative European hub. (It now has six runways.)

Four years later, in November 2007, the BBC reported that Heathrow was planning a third runway and also a sixth terminal (Terminal 5 having been tipped to open in 2008, which it did amid scenes of chaos involving the cancellation of five hundred flights and passengers' luggage going seriously astray). In 2009 Gordon Brown's Labour government threw its weight behind the idea of a third runway at Heathrow but by now the Tories had changed their tune once again and were opposing the idea. The following year the new Tory/Lib. Dem. Coalition ruled out any new runways at all, whether at Heathrow, Stansted or Gatwick. BAA reported that Heathrow was now operating at 99.2 per cent of its capacity. In the meantime, Frankfurt Airport had opened its fourth runway.

By 2012 it was obviously high time for another inquiry so the Airports Commission was convened to thrash out the whole matter yet once more. The following year plans for a third runway at Heathrow were made public. This new scheme was nothing if not original. It proposed the westward extension of the existing northern runway so that in effect it would become a double-length single runway, long enough for two aircraft to use simultaneously. The new section would require a slight gradient so as to form a westward ramp over the M25, thereby avoiding the daunting expense and disruption of putting fourteen lanes of motorway into a 600-metre-long tunnel. This work-around was greeted with a certain amount of public derision although the notion of a gently inclined runway was perfectly feasible. Many runways around the world are far from dead level.

All the same, this proposed solution to Heathrow's perpetual crisis was clumsy. It was all too obviously one imposed by decades of indecision and fence-sitting, not to mention a lack of planning that had painted Heathrow into the corner formed by the east–west M4 meeting the south–north stretch of the M25. Had that section of the M25 been sited a mere mile or so further west towards Windsor, expansion at Heathrow would have been comparatively straightforward, although of course the Queen, as Britain's nimby-in-chief, might have set up a howl. In any case by 2016, despite what the Tories had said in 2010, it looked as though David Cameron's government had finally plumped for further expansion of the Heathrow site with Terminal 6 and a new single runway.

The Airports Commission and several commercial pressure groups had meanwhile concluded that so much in the way of services essential to a hub had grown up around Heathrow it was impossible at this late stage to transplant them to a new site. In any case, where else to go? By now the population of south-east England had greatly increased. In view of its empti-ness a Thames Estuary site had always seemed a logical choice even though the area's marshland is favoured by nesting and over-wintering seabirds (in its derivation the name 'Foulness' means a promontory of fowls) and the danger of bird strikes would somehow have to be dealt with. Also needing pacification would be the environmental lobbyists who would rush to the birds' defence. Ministers would point out the enormous expense of building lengthy high-speed rail and road connections. Well, yes; that's what any modern hub airport needs if it wants to compete with Schiphol and Frankfurt. They're not an optional extra unless it is envisaged that passengers be left stranded in the Essex marshes at dusk, waiting for a shuttle bus service and listening to the honking of Brent geese. Britain being open for business surely includes getting its customers from the airport into the capital with maximum despatch. If the Japanese and Chinese can do it with bullet trains and maglev shuttles, why not the British? One can't hope to do major business on a shoe-string, not in the twenty-first century.

During his two terms of office as London's Mayor (2008–16) Boris Johnson drew up a grandiose if plausible plan for build-ing the airport on an artificial island in the Thames Estuary at Shivering Sands off Whitstable rather than on the extreme Essex coast. Again, if Hong Kong could build a completely new airport on an artificial island, why not the British? But 'Boris Island' was duly axed. Apparently it, too, would cost too much, although it is hard to believe it would in the long run have proved so much more expensive than an apparently endless future of inquiries, not to mention the destruction and blight caused by shoehorning another runway into Heathrow, especially as that could only ever be a stopgap measure. By the time the new extended runway is built – if it ever is – yet another runway will be needed in order for Heathrow to stay competitive with its continental rivals as a hub airport. A Dutch engineer has meanwhile floated the novel idea of a circular runway, which would take up less space while allowing more than one aircraft to use it at any one time. However, a great deal of research will be necessary to find out if it could ever be a practical solution. At the very least a new instrument landing system would have to be devised since the present system depends on a radio beam along which an approaching aircraft lines up and descends. Turning that beam into a spiral would clearly require considerable ingenuity, as would adapting the usual high-intensity lighting arrays leading to the runway touchdown. Furthermore, a strong headwind that during take-off or landing turned into a powerful crosswind would considerably test a pilot's skill.

In any case, after half a century's indecision the choice has apparently returned by default to Heathrow, no matter that there is more room for expansion at Gatwick or Stansted and far fewer people there to be incommoded by noise. Heathrow's position is more problematic than ever since the question of pollution has now become an added and major factor in the argument. The prevailing winds already carry the airport's voluminous exhaust fumes and particulate matter faithfully across an already overpolluted London. However, at the moment of writing this unsatisfactory extended runway solution has almost certainly fallen foul of unforeseen circumstances: not OPEC this time but the limbo imposed by Britain's Brexit negotiations with Brussels. This seems set to paralyse practically all economic life in the UK until the terms of Britain's departure have finally been made clear. Almost all decision-making has been put on hold if only because the negotiations are employing every last civil servant who can be recruited. There are none to spare for planning, budgeting and seeing through major infrastructure works that are not already well under way, like London's Cross-rail. For the foreseeable future uncertainty and indecision are therefore likely to prevail – which after all is Britain's familiar default position in almost everything.

One irony of the Heathrow saga is that the vast fortune in taxpayers' money spent over the previous fifty years on commissions, studies, white papers, inquiries and surveys could probably by now have financed an entirely new airport. In April 2017 Councillor Raymond Puddifoot, leader of Hillingdon Council, was quoted as saying it was time the government stopped 'wasting time and money' and turned its attention to finding a 'workable alternative' to Heathrow. 'The government spent more than £3.8 million of taxpayers' money on the expansion of Heathrow Airport in the 18 months between July 2015 and December 2016, and this figure has risen dramatically over the last few months and will continue to do so,' he said. 'We will continue to provide both the funding and the integrity necessary to both defend and represent our residents for however long it takes to win this battle.'[22]

To be fair, the worldwide expansion of air travel, especially in the last thirty years, has faced many other capitals in continental Europe with the same problem; but most were lucky enough to have more space and to have grasped the nettle earlier, earmarked a new site a suitable distance away, evicted and properly compensated any unfortunate residents, built proper rail and motorway connections and simply *got the job done*. Heathrow remains an anomaly in that at every point when it seemed a decision had been reached, something always happened to put matters on hold (such as an oil embargo or a new government taking office) or else indecision and a change of policy further delayed things and it all reverted to scratch once more.

In 2017 Lord Adonis, Chairman of the National Infrastructure Commission, conceded that 'Britain's historic weakness has been to underinvest in infrastructure, and to adopt a stop/go approach even where decisions are taken in principle. Nothing exemplifies this better than the long-running saga of Heathrow airport. A third runway was agreed in principle 14 years ago but there has still not been an unequivocal order to proceed. There's no point in saying Britain is open to the world if you can't get to and from the rest of the world because Heathrow is full.'[23]

Simply put, we have left it too late. While the sundry inquiries were coming to their slow and majestic conclusions, southeast England has been filling up with still more people. In the last thirty years many of them have become environmentally conscious, often militantly so. For excellent reasons that affect the quality of their lives and health they don't want the already noxious fallout of noise and pollution from a hub airport to worsen and are now well organised into pressure groups to oppose them. As HACAN's chair, John Stewart, said of a proposal in 2017 for a congestion charge of £15 to be levied on anyone driving to Heathrow, 'The very fact that it's being talked about shows that people realise how difficult it will be to control air pollution at a bigger Heathrow.'[24] This is a familiar British impasse in which lobby ritually clashes with lobby – in this case HACAN with the BAA, Hillingdon Council with the transport minister of the day and residents with their luckless MPs who are torn as ever between loyalty to their party and to those who elected them. It has become a sort of stylised adagio dance whose function seems designed more to exemplify the various poses of British democracy in action than ever to lead to any clear-cut conclusion. Nobody can possibly claim they are not getting a hearing. Objections are raised, overridden, raised once again. The intractability of planning in today's Britain is well portrayed by John Grindrod in his 2017 book *Outskirts*, which examines the history of the Green Belt and its politics:

Back in 1963, Michael Frayn described the difference between the two philosophies attempting to control Britain after the [Second World] war: the herbivores – guilt-bound liberal intelligentsia behind the BBC and the Festival of Britain – and the carnivores – 'if God had not wished them to prey upon all smaller and weaker creatures without scruple he would not have made them as they are'. The green belt was certainly created by herbivores, those Fabians and ramblers, town planners and grandees chomping on the green grass, protecting it and, in the process, the leafy places where they lived too. The policy was a way of neutralising the carnivores, preventing them from buying and selling the scenery around towns for swift profits, as had happened in the interwar years. These days it's all rather more confusing. Both carnivores and herbivores form coalitions on either side of the argument: the housing campaigners and town planners alongside the big developers; the environmentalists alongside the nimbys and vested interests. It's hard to tell if those are sheep grazing in the paddock or wolves creeping around in expensive woollen jackets.[25]

At Heathrow farmed fields run right up to the airport's southern boundary. Are their owners fighting a rearguard action to protect what is left of their immemorial green acres, or beadily waiting until the price is right to sell out? After all, their sheep may just as safely graze the flanks of Wraysbury Reservoir to the west, a bare mile away on the other side of the M25.

In the meantime, the fifty-year paralysis over the resiting or expansion of south-east England's hub airport continues. In late June 2018 a large majority of MPs voted in favour of a third runway. Nevertheless, it will not be completed 'until at least 2025'. The prevaricating phrase 'at least' had already been expanded by the Transport Secretary, Patrick McLoughlin, to mean 'by 2030'. He added: 'Business needs to be reassured that we are sticking by that date.'[26] Back in May 2017 the Institute of Directors called for a 'fast-track' commission to be set up to recommend locations for two additional runways – 'fast-track' then being defined as 'within a year'. Or possibly more.

At least one of these runways will surely have to be at Gatwick. In recent years it has been the strangest thing for visitors just landed at Heathrow or Gatwick to see hoardings extolling the competitive virtues of one or other airport, their rival messages taken up in full-page advertisements in the print media. To the citizens of most countries that take for granted the central planning of their nation's infrastructure it must seem most peculiar that a matter as important as the capital's new runways should be treated as though the two existing airports were competing brands, the choice made as much via a PR campaign as by rational planning. But at least this oddity must have provided a good introduction to a Britain open for business, to the experience of leaving the airport and thereafter trying to make sense of the country's wilfully discordant and overcrowded rail and road transport systems.

Of course, problems with large-scale projects like Heathrow are by no means confined to Britain. Contrary to myths about Germany's national efficiency, at least two projects there have been greatly delayed. Berlin's enormous new Brandenburg Airport, for which two entire villages were razed, was first planned in 1991. It was not until 2006 that construction began, with a projected opening date of October 2011. Thanks to bad planning, indifferent management and even corruption, the airport is still not ready and may not open until 2021 at the earliest. And a few years ago I found myself caught up during a visit to Stuttgart in a great public demonstration around the main station there. This was protesting Stuttgart 21: an immense railway redevelopment project affecting the station and considerable areas of the town. That plan had been announced in 1994; work started in 2010 and the new station is now not expected to open until 2021. However, it must be said that on both these projects work is well under way, and unlike at Heathrow neither required half a century's dithering indecision. Once the Heathrow question has finally and irrevocably been decided, botched or delayed construction and prodigious cost overruns will merely be the next step.

It is worth remarking that merely adding capacity to Heathrow and other British airports will not necessarily make things better for tomorrow's hard-pressed air traveller. It only takes the lemming-like surge of passengers that now ritually accompanies Bank Holidays and half-terms, plus the great summer and winter exeats, to show how whisker-thin are the operating margins. In July 2017 an Air Canada airliner blew a tyre on landing. This minor incident resulted in the temporary closure of the runway while it was cleared of debris. This in turn had a knock-on effect of cancelled slots, delayed flights and missed connections that stretched across Europe and even around the world. As an ex-BA executive later remarked, Britain's aviation system is 'operating at or near 100 per cent capacity' and has 'no resilience. There is no contingency capacity built in, be it runway, terminal, airspace, or road and rail access, so any delay or disruption anywhere in the system compounds very quickly. It may be good for airport bottom lines to squeeze the last gram of capacity out of their assets, but wholly unacceptable for passengers and the airlines who suffer the financial consequences of over-scheduling.'[27]

In sour mood one could read this as a symptom of the British disease in microcosm: laissez-faire government that, in its ideological obsession with shareholder profitability, puts off planning the nation's infrastructure in the hope that private enterprise will take care of the future: something that has yet to happen anywhere on earth. Nor is the problem of dangerously congested skies peculiar to the UK. They extend over nearly all southern Britain and on across Western Europe, especially over France. On any day, but above all at peak periods, air traffic control is stretched up to, and often beyond, the safety limit. However, as with accident black spots on roads, nothing will be done until the head count of fatalities and emotive pictures of piled-up teddy bears reaches a critical point. In Britain, ever since the death of Princess Diana such wayside shrines of rain-sodden floral tributes and sad messages have marked the newly expressed catharsis of public emotion. Road accidents also seem an appropriate subject by which to address the collapse of the country's erstwhile car industry, as we shall see in the next chapter.

Meanwhile, the chronic indecision, that national syndrome of Humptyish fence-sitting, continues. Further examples are legion but one in particular has real recursive charm since it involves Humpty's home fence. This is the constant failure to start urgent repairs to the Palace of Westminster. These are endlessly postponed and havered over, with each new estimate causing a fresh delay allowing the costs to multiply still further. Presumably the repressed hope is for the entire edifice to collapse in the small hours one morning forcing a relocation to, for instance, Buckingham Palace: the obvious choice since none of the royals has ever really seemed to like it since they so readily leave for Sandringham or Balmoral or Windsor at the earliest opportunity.

4.
Cars

*'This morning Chrysler
revealed their new Avenger.
And if all goes well, next month
they'll make another one.'*

—ROWAN ATKINSON:
unaired pilot episode for
Not the Nine O'Clock News (1979)

A 1928 4½ litre Bentley that accords with my memory of my uncle's 'Bomb'. As an ex-Brooklands racer his was in British Racing Green.

W hen I was a boy in 1950 the following were the thirty-five British-owned car makers registered with the Society of Motor Manufacturers and Traders: Allard, AC, Alta, Alvis, Armstrong Siddeley, Aston Martin, Austin, Bentley, Bristol, Daimler, Frazer Nash, Healey, Hillman, HRG, Humber, Invicta, Jaguar, Jensen, Jowett, Lagonda, Lanchester, Lea Francis, Lloyd, MG, Morgan, Morris, Riley, Rolls-Royce, Rover, Singer, Standard, Sunbeam Talbot, Triumph, Wolseley.

By 1994 virtually all were defunct or foreign owned. Today a mere seven of those listed still exist, of which Morgan alone remains entirely in British hands. Some, like Bristol and AC, are in semi-dormant form, while the names of others like Jensen and Lagonda are revived from time to time. Of Aston Martin (which also owns the Lagonda name), Germany's Daimler/Mercedes owns 5 per cent while the rest of the company is in the hands of multinational investment groups.

Including the thirty-five car companies listed above, a century's history stretches back that can be viewed as the automotive version of Canada's famous Burgess Shale, studded with the fossils of well over five hundred extinct British car marques, many of exotic and weird aspect that were evolutionary dead ends. No doubt the United States and most industrialised European countries that built early cars can point to a similar roll call of start-ups by young hopeful mechanics and engineers around the turn of the twentieth century whose endeavours survived a few years, occasionally even decades, by means of shoestring efforts to produce a model that would catch the attention of a limited marketplace. Today's motor world is the complete reverse, with a comparative handful of international corporations mass-producing cars and lorries for the global market while those few small independent companies that have survived slumps, two world wars, oil crises, increasing competition and brutal takeovers build expensive specialist cars for niche markets. In the UK hand-built Morgans and TVRs are the longest-surviving examples other than Aston Martin, and even TVR went into Russian ownership before returning to British hands. Yet strangely enough, there is today almost the same number of British car companies as there was in 1950, most having been started within the past twenty-five years. The majority of these are dedicated to building performance cars of often outlandish specification, such as Bowler Offroad's racing SUVs or the Keating Bolt, with its projected top speed of 340 mph (547 kph). Leaving aside trifling matters of legality, there is surely no existing road in Europe where such a speed could be attempted, let alone attained, so it is hard for those of us unsmitten by the lure of speed for speed's sake to grasp the point of such an enterprise.

British engineering skills in the automotive field remain world class even if mainly limited to such 'high end' sports cars and racing. Much of Formula 1's design and manufacturing takes place in Britain, as does even that of America's Indy cars. A good deal of this activity occurs in the region around the Silverstone motor racing circuit, and attracts many of the world's best engineers as well as specialised bespoke car makers. By contrast, today's mass-market production of ordinary domestic vehicles, together with that of most commercial trucks and buses, has long since passed from British hands into foreign ownership.

On the face of it this is odd for an industrial country that, having made a relatively slow start at building its own cars in the early twentieth century, thereafter made giant strides between the wars until by 1939 Morris and Austin between them commanded a considerable slice of the global output. At that point the top three vehicle manufacturers in the UK domestic market were Morris with 27 per cent, Austin with 24 per cent and US-owned Ford with 15 per cent. Immediately after the Second World War, with the United States concentrating on its own domestic market, Britain became the world's biggest vehicle exporter. By 1947 Austin was offering Europe's largest range of cars (even if most were pre-war technology given a slight face-lift in design) and by 1950 the UK was supplying over half the world's exported vehicles. That year it made 523,000 cars and exported 399,000 of them – most of those, admittedly, to the easy 'Empire' market. Yet over the next four decades the UK's indigenous car manufacturers dwindled one by one to the present-day rump of small firms catering for the wealthy few who like driving high-performance cars while wearing gloves with holes cut in them. On the way, and for the best part of two decades, Britain's failing motor industry became an international byword for industrial strife such that factory names like Dagenham, Halewood, Longbridge and Cowley became the media's shorthand for trouble, while the late Longbridge convener Derek Robinson achieved national notoriety as 'Red Robbo'. It was not that continental motor manufacturers were themselves immune to strikes, economic downturns, takeovers, badly made cars and misjudged models – far from it. It was just that in Britain's case the mixture was allowed to prove fatal. How this came about warrants examination.

From 1945, and despite a desperate post-war push for exports, Britain's domestic automotive scene was at first largely one of cautious convalescence. This matched the slowness in improving the country's infrastructure. There was not much money about and petrol was rationed. The main A roads were generally unrepaired after years of wartime military use and many of the B roads were barely passable. The initial stretch of the first motorway (the M1) – a mere sixty-two miles between Watford and Rugby – still lay a dozen years in the future, being just about open by 1960, albeit without crash barriers, lighting or speed limit. These days it is almost impossible to give anyone much under the age of sixty a credible impression of the still predominantly green and pleasant England I was lucky enough to grow up in. Most of the change for the worse has been wrought by the surging tide of motor vehicles that began swamping town and countryside alike: a hellish flood that today's citizens perforce accept as the norm in what the latest figures show is now Western Europe's worst country for traffic and one of the world's ten most gridlocked nations.[28]

In the post-war 1940s when a quarter of all British homes had no electricity, people would still refer with only slight irony to 'darkest Sussex' to describe where their eccentric relatives were living, where a few of the really small roads had yet to acquire tarmac and many of the signposts that had been removed on the outbreak of war had still to be replaced. In those days it was possible to get seriously lost and even stranded overnight with a broken fan belt in the middle of nowhere and not a light, let alone a garage, to be seen. With the exception of the wind and the occasional night creature it could also be quite soundless: a lovely silence practically never heard nowadays.

In 1948 there were just over one million cars on Britain's roads; and since petrol rationing was to last until 1954 sales of new vehicles remained comparatively low and largely limited to the professional middle class. My Uncle John, soon to be appointed head of BP's Hamburg office, seemed magically unaffected by a lack of petrol. He lived at the end of a cart track in Essex where he kept the cherished, massively thirsty 4½ litre Bentley he had raced at Brooklands before the war. On fine days he occasionally paid us a visit in it and would take me out for a spin down the old A20 London to Maidstone road, past those places whose names were familiar from the destination window on the Greenline buses that went through Footscray on their way to Swanley, Horton Kirby and Wrotham. On the left of the A20 just before West Kingsdown was the Brands Hatch racing circuit, a name full of dread to me as a child because of my mother's carefully toned-down accounts of the smashed-up young men she sometimes dealt with on race days as an anaesthetist at Queen Mary's Hospital, Sidcup. These were by no means all casualties of the racing. They were more often 'ton-up' bike boys who left Brands Hatch afterwards on their BSAs and Nortons and Vincents and, inspired by the excitement, played chicken with each other down the A20. At that time crash helmets were optional and hideous injuries would result.

I was a timorous child and frankly scared of Uncle John's Bentley, which he fondly called 'The Bomb'. It was open and horribly noisy. Sitting in what in his racing days had been his mechanic's seat I was hardly big enough to see over the cockpit coaming past the vast bonnet held down by leather straps. The gale of our clamorous passage was barely impeded by a little fold-up windshield in front of me. The wind buffeted my face and made my eyes water. I hated the whole thing but would have died rather than admit it. Worse: I admired my uncle but deep down I thought his car silly and rather ugly with its antique leather straps, gigantic headlamps and a tall handbrake that stuck up outside like an afterthought. There was also a large radiator cap with a lever that reminded me of a soda-water siphon. With the aerodynamics of a tank, it was plainly old-fashioned and I couldn't help comparing it with the sleek and beautiful car owned by the wealthy father of one of my schoolfriends, a new split-screen Jaguar XK120. That was fabulously streamlined and looked and sounded like a proper sports car. Every schoolboy knew it was called '120' because it could do 120 miles per hour: twice as fast as our family's Wolseley could ever have managed even downhill with the wind behind it and certainly very much faster than Uncle John's Bomb in which we howled along the A20, shouldering aside the occasional plodding little Standard or Hillman and Foden lorry. Hunched behind its immense steering wheel like Toad of Toad Hall, Uncle John would throw me a triumphant sideways grin and bawl 'She's touching *eighty*!' into the wind before he began slowing down well before Wrotham: well before because The Bomb's brakes seemed barely equal to the task of bringing that snarling, cantering tonnage of steel to a halt. On the return journey I only relaxed when we had reached Crittalls Corner and were at last obliged to chug along at a sensible speed. As a family I think we were all secretly relieved when Uncle John's wife Dorothy insisted he get rid of The Bomb: a wrench that nearly cost him his marriage. Years later, not long before he died and by which time I had grown very fond of him, Uncle John told me his beloved car was still alive and well and now in Australia and that he was in regular contact with its current and equally besotted owner. As I write this I discover that a Bentley like his is now worth a million pounds or so, even though I personally wouldn't accept the thing as a gift. But then, it's merely a car and not an aircraft. To me all cars, no matter how beautifully engineered, lack the crucial mystique of performing in three dimensions. Boringly, all they can do is go forward or backward in straight or curved lines and involve nothing like enough complex skills or freedom to get me interested. I used to pray for Uncle John to take me to Biggin Hill instead of Brands Hatch, both being equidistant from where we lived. But no – it was always down the A20 in The Bomb.

In 1948 there were just over a million cars on Britain's roads. By 2016 there were thirty-one million; and the devastation wrought by this ungoverned proliferation has changed the country irrevocably. This was semi-officially foreseen. In 1963, while I was still at university, the Buchanan Report on urban transport planning was published: a report so pertinent and readable it went into Penguin paperback the following year.

> It is impossible [wrote Sir Colin Buchanan] to spend any time on the study of the future of traffic in towns without at once being appalled by the magnitude of the emergency that is coming upon us. We are nourishing at immense cost a monster of great potential destructiveness, and yet we love him dearly. To refuse to accept the challenge it presents would be an act of defeatism.[29]

He went on to make some predictions that today seem miserably accurate as year by year traffic speeds in Britain's cities become ever slower while a single accident on a motorway can cause a tailback stretching many miles, sometimes trapping drivers for hours. Pollution in cities can daily reach, and frequently surpass, levels the WHO classes as lethal, especially to children and the elderly:

> The problems of traffic are crowding in upon us with desperate urgency. Unless steps are taken, the motor vehicle will defeat its own utility and bring about a disastrous degradation of the surroundings for living. ... Either the utility of vehicles in town

will decline rapidly, or the pleasantness and safety of surroundings will deteriorate catastrophically – in all probability both will happen.[30] ... Distasteful though we find the whole idea, we think that some deliberate limitation of the volume of motor traffic is quite unavoidable. The need for it just can't be escaped. Even when everything that it is possible to do by way of building new roads and expanding public transport has been done there would still be, in the absence of deliberate limitation, more cars trying to move into, or within, our cities than could possibly be accommodated.[31]

Unfortunately, and as we all know, the 'deliberate limitation' of motor transport has been firmly resisted by every British government in the last half-century. We foresaw it all and did nothing. Each government has, unopposed, contributed to the unplanned national plan of not only giving the private car clear priority over public transport, but its environment over that of human beings. *Lector, si monumentum requiris circumspice*, as Sir Christopher Wren's son inscribed on his father's tomb in St Paul's. 'Reader, if you want a monument, look around you.' In the cathedral all is still magnificence. Outside in today's England Colin Buchanan's 'disastrous degradation' is everywhere apparent. Unless one makes a real effort, it is extremely hard to get away from the distant hum of a motorway or bypass, and often traffic noise forms a full-time background even at night, so central are motor vehicles to the modern economy, both in their usage and their manufacture.

The tsunami of vehicles on UK roads today effectively hides the fact that virtually none is any longer made by a British-owned company. This is ironic. Although UK factories are currently churning out 1.7 million of them a year, this hardly constitutes a *British* motor industry since the profits mostly go abroad, typically to investors in Japan, Germany, France and the United States. In fact, 56 per cent of the cars Britain currently makes are exported to the EU, the UK's supply chain being highly integrated with that of Europe. In blithe disregard of environmental factors, certain components can cross borders forty times during manufacture.[32] To judge from appearances, though, it is a healthy industry even if one threatened by a growing revulsion for diesel-powered vehicles and in Britain also by diminishing sales and fewer young drivers. In Britain's accelerating post-war output of vehicles, an equal deceptiveness concealed the imminence of the industry's eclipse by foreign competition. The roots of this downfall had in fact always been there to see, although the 'British and Best' jingoism that followed the war's endlessly rehearsed victories made them all too easy to overlook.

During the six wartime years manufacture of private cars virtually ceased while all factories were switched to producing military matériel: not just vehicles like tanks and lorries but aircraft and a vast range of other equipment. Since it was a command economy and almost no company could be allowed to fail no matter how bad its performance, any spirit of commercial competitiveness largely died out. When in 1945 the factory lines were reopened for private vehicles most firms returned only sluggishly to competing in the marketplace. At that time Britain's dire financial indebtedness and steel rationing meant there was intense government pressure to build vehicles primarily for export. This is why when I was a child the great majority of private cars on the roads were not merely British but still of pre-war vintage: Austin Sevens and Morris Tens that had been up on blocks during the war for lack of petrol, Humber Super Snipes that had been staff cars for the military, and in London those 1932 Beardmore taxis with an open luggage space beside the driver and a horizontally split windscreen like the Model T Ford's, whose upper louvre could be opened in hot weather. In that company my uncle's Bentley maybe didn't look quite as antiquated as it now seems.

Once the war was over, companies like Morris and Austin did have some new designs ready: in Morris's case the Minor, which was actually designed in 1941 by their talented Greek-born designer, Alec Issigonis. It went into production in 1948 despite the company's founder, Lord Nuffield, saying it looked like 'a ruddy poached egg'. The Morris Minor sold slowly at first but became so successful that by the end of 1960 it was the first British car to sell a million, and when manufacture ceased in 1971 1,619,658 had been built. This was despite performance so sluggish that a modern mobility scooter could have given a Minor a good run for its money. Most of those exported went to the ready overseas market of Britain's Dominions, colonies and former possessions. Yet this was often unintelligently done without modifying or strengthening the car's design to suit a particular market, the makers evidently assuming that motoring in tropical Africa or arctic Canada was much like tooling down to Basingstoke, with AA and RAC men patrolling on their motorbikes with sidecars full of spare fan belts. Stories soon came back of British cars simply not being tough enough to deal with the local conditions, quite apart from the often extreme difficulty of obtaining spare parts. Gaps in the overseas car market gradually opened up and were swiftly filled by sturdier vehicles from Ford, General Motors and Peugeot.

Britain did have one unequivocal export success in the Land Rover. Like the Morris Minor, this was also launched in 1948, but as a four-wheel-drive, go-anywhere, reliable and easily repaired utility vehicle. What was more, at £450 it was reasonably cheap since it was classified as a commercial vehicle and hence exempt from the purchase tax that had been introduced the previous year. Perhaps because during the war the Rover Company had built early jet engines for Frank Whittle and maintained close connections with the RAF, it was well placed to take advantage of war surplus materials. It built the corrosion-resistant bodies of its Land Rovers from a light but resilient alloy called Birmabrite: a mixture of magnesium and aluminium that was suddenly plentiful from thousands of scrapped aircraft. In this way Rover was to some extent able to sidestep the steel shortage. Also, for years the standard colour of Land Rovers was various shades of green because the company bought up cheaply a huge supply of the paint that had been used for aircraft interiors.

Rover also took advantage of its wartime experience with Frank Whittle to design its own jet engine and from 1950 produced a series of gas turbine-driven cars, beginning with the world's first: a modified Rover 75 saloon with the number plate JET 1. It had a top speed of 85 mph and a 0–60 mph time of fourteen seconds: both quite fast for the day (the Jaguar XK120 could manage 0–60 mph in ten seconds; the early Morris Minor took fifty-two seconds, although that was a bit theoretical since its top speed was only 58.7 mph). JET 1's chief drawback was its runaway fuel consumption, a characteristic of all early jet engines that severely limited the combat radius of first- and second-generation jet fighters. JET 1 could only manage six miles to the gallon, which made for expensive motoring even though the fuel was kerosene/paraffin and hence cheaper than petrol. The car also had a two-second lag in acceleration, which would have made it unpopular at traffic lights and a menace in overtaking. Rover's experiments continued into the mid-1960s when their gas turbine racing car did respectably at Le Mans. It had been a brave and thoroughly British experiment, but jet engines in domestic cars were an automotive dead end.

Land Rovers, however, were not. They were an immediate success both at home and abroad wherever ruggedness was prized over comfort and speed. They were particularly favoured by armed forces the world over. The only drawback was that Rover began to take this for granted and failed to update them quickly enough. Even though a 'posher' (i.e. halfway comfortable) version had been envisaged as early as the late 1940s, it was really only when overseas competition from other off-road vehicles like Toyota's equally successful Land Cruiser – which sold especially well in the Far East and Australia – that Rover was belatedly goosed into bringing out the first Range Rover in 1970. Their mistake was one not uncommon in British industry: that of complacency. Happy to go the easy route and keep churning out their Land Rovers with very little modification to either mechanics or styling, they were slow to spot the change in the market for better-off customers who wanted a more family-friendly vehicle without sacrificing off-road capability. That being said, Range Rovers quickly established a lucrative market for themselves.

Despite the increasing success of the Morris Minor and the Land Rover, by 1952 the American companies General Motors (which had owned Vauxhall since 1925) and Ford had between them taken 29 per cent of the British domestic market. This threatening trend led that same year to the merging of the two bitter rivals, Morris and Austin, together with several smaller companies, into the British Motor Corporation. BMC promptly commanded 40 per cent of the UK market and became the world's fourth largest car company. At the same time German car production was increasing, overtaking that of France in 1953 and then Britain's in 1956. In that year BMC had fifteen different models on offer, ranging from Rolls-Royces to Morris Minors, but little that was really new. The company seemed mesmerised by the success of the Land Rover and the Minor, together with that design's various offshoots like the Morris Oxford and ultimately the Morris 1000 Traveller. This last was a half-timbered absurdity, a poor man's shooting brake for the would-be tweeds-and-green-wellies set. Resting on one's laurels is as recognisably British as the Morris Minor itself, the syndrome being detectable across the entire spectrum of national life, and BMC became less and less competitive until 1959 when it introduced Alec Issigonis's Mini.

This best-selling and influential car is usually hailed as the automotive embodiment of John Bull: more quintessentially British even than toad-in-the-hole and a good deal more so than the House of Windsor. It was more British than even its makers knew in that, although destined to be produced in various versions and well over five million examples for the next forty years, it still managed to be a commercial flop because it was seriously underpriced. Ford famously acquired one and dismantled it down to the last nut, pricing everything, and discovered that BMC (who were not good at parts inventories) were losing a cool £30 on each one sold: a tidy sum given that the showroom price was £496 including purchase tax. I briefly owned a Mini myself in the 1960s and thought it then and now a nasty little tin box; but I was clearly in a minority. Besides, it was brilliantly and specifically designed to *be* a box, with a weight-saving bare steel interior and space-saving transverse engine. The reason for the extreme utility of the design – with its horrible cord-operated door latches, sliding side windows and instruments in the middle of the dashboard instead of in front of the driver – dated specifically to the Suez crisis of 1956: until Brexit the stupidest blunder with international repercussions that Britain had committed since the end of the Second World War. An immediate consequence of Suez had been the reintroduction of petrol rationing, which led to a rash of imported bubble cars from Italy and Germany (Isetta, Messerschmitt, Heinkel). BMC's two-door Mini was designed with such lean times in mind while contriving to project an image of Spartan fun that proved perfectly suited to the somewhat mythical swinging sixties. It swiftly killed off the bubble cars, which actually cost very little less than the Mini. For those who wanted a slightly more plummy version of the car and who couldn't afford a Rover there were always the Riley Elf and the Wolseley Hornet, both those old companies having been swallowed up by BMC. The Elf and the Hornet were merely Minis gussied up with such things as radiator grilles with badges and interiors with real carpets.

Meanwhile, my schoolfriend's father's Jaguar XK120 had been superseded by the XK140 and XK150. All three were excellent examples of British car design even if the original had been heavily influenced by a much-raced pre-war BMW. They duly gained a sporty reputation in the United States, though not for reliability. It was then that the phrase 'Lucas – Prince of Darkness' first began to be heard from owners exasperated by their cars' dodgy electrics. But such things seemed irrelevant when Jaguar's most eye-catching model of them all, the E-Type, first appeared in 1961. Its combined elegance, glamour and top speed of 150 mph gave the car a magnetic aura that attracted a knot of admirers wherever one was parked. London's King's Road on a Saturday in the early 1960s positively glittered with them. Even Enzo Ferrari was moved to call it 'the most beautiful car ever made'. By now the Morris Minor was obsolete, if still selling to the elderly, while the Mini and the E-Type were just beginning their dominance of two very different markets. What with all the other swiftly changing models of several different marques, one might have been forgiven for thinking the British car industry was doing well.

But behind the scenes it was faced with a problem similar to that which had dogged the aviation industry since the war. There were simply too many different companies making too many similar and unexceptional models and with too many variants of engines and components in the hopes of pleasing everyone. In short, both industries were fragmented and ill coordinated. In 1959 the Minister for Aviation, Duncan Sandys, published a notorious White Paper that led the following year to the forcible bundling-up of virtually all Britain's aero manufacturers into the British Aircraft Corporation. Similarly, the British Motor Corporation now viewed still further amalgamation as the only possible way forward. It was not alone, the already merged firm of Standard Triumph having existed for several years before it was bought by the truck and bus company Leyland Motors in 1960. In 1965 BMC acquired Pressed Steel, which was supplying all their car bodies, including those for Rover, Rolls-Royce and MG as well as for the still-independent Jaguar Cars Ltd. This was enough to oblige Jaguar to throw in its lot with BMC, which rebranded itself as British Motor Holdings. Three years later, in 1968, BMH merged with Leyland, which had already swallowed up Rover in the previous year. The now vast conglomerate became the British Leyland Motor Corporation, better known thereafter as BL.

These mergers and takeovers were characteristic of the times, bigger being seen as automatically better. Words like 'rationalisation' also conferred a spurious aura of careful deliberation on entities whose very size and disparateness in practice ensured the very opposite of business efficiency. The political pressure behind it all was unmistakable, since the City's financial jugglers were enthusiastic about what they called 'M & A'. Mergers and acquisitions, managed with due craftiness, could be made to shake free a good deal of cash. Mergers also effectively meant managers favouring the short-term interests of their shareholders and renouncing any long-term plans for growing their original businesses. The complexities were paralysing. BL now comprised nearly a hundred different companies making a great range of different things including refrigerators (via Prestcold, who had come with Pressed Steel) and sundry little firms making a zillion components that in 1974 would be swept under the umbrella of Unipart. No doubt the new BL boardroom offered its exalted members a grandiose view of the company bestriding the automotive globe. However, the chief drawback to such an unwieldy behemoth at once became only too apparent: that it posed overwhelmingly tricky management problems.

How was it possible to run such a motley agglomeration

smoothly? For one thing, the personnel of the various car companies thus forced together tended to remain loyal to their original, highly individual firms and did not at all relish having to share the same factory floor. (Cynics might see a certain parallel here with the forcible welding together of widely differing countries and cultures under an EU 'boardroom' in Brussels.) The absurdities at BL included former rivals now making cars that were identical but for the badge on the bonnet, yet with their old dealers selling them competitively. The Triumph 2000's deadliest rival was its identical twin, the Rover 2000. The Morris Marina locked horns with the Austin Allegro. The MGB challenged the Triumph Spitfire and vice versa. The only thing that might have saved such an arrangement would have been brilliant and incisive management. And as also in today's case of Brussels, it was precisely this leadership that was lacking. Worse, such amalgamations also exacerbated underlying political differences at the level of the workers' representation, with a multitude of unions with varying degrees of principled self-interest and ideological militancy able to command much bigger strikes and go-slows. These, together with worsening quality and production standards, were eventually to threaten BL's very existence. In 1975 the Labour government, faced with BL's imminent bankruptcy and consequent mass unemployment in its heartlands of support such as Merseyside, opted for nationalisation and desperate injections of public money as the remedy of last recourse. Not that BL was alone in its economic plight. The entire country's balance of payments was in such a disastrous state that the following year Britain would have to go on its knees to the International Monetary Fund for a bail-out.

Well before that point was reached, the predominantly right-wing British press had decided it was all the fault of the unions holding big manufacturers like BL and Ford to ransom. They were not alone among opinion-makers. Newspapers of every political stripe pointed out that the economy and even the country itself was now seriously endangered by Hamelin-like swarms of scurrying and malevolent Communists and Trotsky-ists plotting and gnawing away behind the national wain-scoting. How could any management hope to succeed once the concept of an honest day's work for an honest day's pay had been overtaken by an ethos of greed and feather-bedding that was espoused by a lot of work-shy ingrates duped by their Communist shop stewards?

The problem with seeing Britain's industrial problems of this period as entirely the unions' fault is that these sorts of social upheaval were not confined to Britain but in one way or another affected the whole of the Western world. The New Left politics in the Europe of the 1970s were largely those of the post-war baby-boomers who had reached or passed studenthood and were adopting social causes such as civil rights, women's libera-tion and anti-imperialism generally. With the well-publicised violence of the more extreme gangs such as Germany's Red Army Faction and Italy's Brigate Rosse, a strong sense of the old order needing to change was everywhere in the air, even if its violent overthrow seemed hardly likely. Even Britain had a wacky paramilitary equivalent in its secretive and very right-wing GB 75, apparently led by an ex-army general. Margaret Thatcher's ambition to smash unionised industry, which was to climax in her confrontation with the miners in 1983–4, led many commentators (and especially motoring correspondents) to ascribe the main cause of the British motor industry's demise to its union problems as the symptom peculiar to the British Disease, almost as though no other European country was suffering from such things as strikes and shoddily made cars. Italy in the seventies seemed perpetually paralysed by strikes, while many of the period's Lancias and Alfa Romeos were celebrated rust buckets. Germany, too, had its strikes, especially in the steel industry, and not only in the Ruhr.

True, the unions could indeed be pesky. But what people chose to overlook then – and today forget or simply don't know – was how abominable and often downright dangerous factory working conditions could be in those largely pre-robot days. In 1967 a young sociology student in Liverpool, Huw Beynon, decided to do his fieldwork on the assembly line at Ford's Halewood plant on Merseyside. He was given shop floor access and gradually won the confidence of both workers and shop stewards. When his *Working for Ford* was published in 1973 it caused a sensation among middle-class reviewers, the author being roundly condemned for transcribing the opinions of 'foul-mouthed' workers, four-letter words and all, and for having apparently indulged in 'a prolonged love affair with a group of militant Merseyside shop stewards' (as even the *New Statesman* put it). Yet the book rapidly became a classic, its honesty being transparent and its accuracy vouched for by the workers themselves. As at Ford's pre-war plant in Dagenham – which with its own smelter and wharf and vast car compound on the Hornchurch marshes had grown to be practically a self-contained city with a life and economy of its own – everything at Halewood was organised around the assembly line. The original Henry Ford had, of course, pioneered this method of production, since when he and his son Henry II had fine-tuned it to the last detail with each individual job timed to the second. The line was God. It was kept moving at an inexorable speed determined by the foreman and in accordance with the current needs of the market.

> *They* decide on *their* measured day how fast *we* will work. They seem to forget that we're not machines, y'know. … They expect you to work the 480 minutes of the eight hours you're on the clock. They've agreed to have a built-in allowance of *six minutes* for going to the toilet, blowing your nose and that. It takes you six minutes to get your trousers down.[33]

Nothing – not a man's injury or even death – was allowed to hold up production:

> They wouldn't stop that fucking line. You could be dying and they wouldn't stop it. If someone was hurt the first thing the supervisor

thought about was filling the job. He'd start doing the work before he made sure the bloke was all right. I tell you, you could have been dying and they wouldn't have bothered.[34]

This was soon proved to be true:

> We were in the locker room before the shift had started and he collapsed with a pain in his chest. He went an awful colour but then he reckoned he was all right. We went down the stairs on to the shop floor, walked across to the line and he collapsed again. Y'know – flat on the floor. His face was an awful grey colour. We all rushed round him like and the buzzer went. The line started. The foreman came across shouting 'get to work ... get on the line'. And there we were, sticking things on the cars and he was lying there. He must have been lying there ten minutes ... dead. In front of us.[35]

It is a measure of how hard things were in the Liverpool area (as elsewhere in Britain's industrial heartlands) that men with acute cardiac and other serious medical problems dragged themselves to work at all, so great was the fear of being jobless. But even to normally healthy men the work was often exhausting, whether physically or mentally. Beynon recounts the daily complaint of how soul-rottingly *boring* work on the line could be: repetitious, mindless, utterly trivial. Small wonder that all sorts of dodges and jokes were invented to relieve the inhuman daily tedium, and equally small wonder that the outcome was frequent lapses in the quality of the uncaringly built cars that came off the line.

In short, the sort of atmosphere that in the 1960s and 1970s predominated in the factories producing the overwhelming bulk of Britain's vehicles was in general resentful and conducive to neither quality nor consistency of output. As Beynon's book made clear, the demarcation between *Us* (blue collar shop floor) and *Them* (white collar management) was like the line drawn in the sand between two tug-of-war teams. As time went on boredom and mulishness turned easily to vandalism and sabotage, with outright theft as standard practice. This was certainly not peculiar to Ford factories. In 1997 the journalist Richard Littlejohn gave an interview for one of *Jeremy Clarkson's Motorworld* programmes and reminisced about living within the aegis of British Leyland:

> You could get anything for any car in Birmingham for the price of a pint. I remember when we moved there in 1977 we went house-hunting and eventually we bought a house from a guy who worked at the Castle Bromwich paint factory. And the house was painted British Racing Green. There was an Allegro tobacco living room and an aquamarine metallic Montego silver bathroom. Everything had been nicked out the paint shop.[36]

Brand-new engines and gear boxes disappeared from stores and the anarchy and demoralisation at BL's Longbridge plant soon attained mythic proportions. Until late 1977 BL's Chairman had been Lord Stokes. In November that year the feisty South African businessman Michael Edwardes took over in a last-ditch attempt to turn things around. Desperate measures were clearly needed. As Jeremy Clarkson said later, 'In the first six months of Michael Edwardes' reign there were 357 stoppages at Longbridge alone. People only ever went to work to sleep or nick things.'[37] Nor did the cars on which BL was pinning its hopes inspire much confidence. Clarkson described as 'idiotic' that the Marina and the Allegro, 'two awful cars from the same company', were competing against each other. This opinion was endorsed by the late Derek Robinson, 'Red Robbo' himself. (By a curious coincidence his death at the age of ninety was announced as I was writing this very paragraph.) As convener, the man had many years' experience of engineering matters: he had been working at the Longbridge plant since he was fourteen. In interviews he occasionally singled out the Austin Allegro as epitomising so much that was structurally wrong with the cars he and his workmates had to build. This was a design whose aerodynamics were better when the car was going backwards than when it went forwards; and although it was popular in the UK in the seventies, by 2008 it had been voted Britain's worst-ever car.[38]

It was a disaster from the start, the Allegro. It had all sorts of faults, not least the linkages which were horrendous. And the design was wrong. But that was what we had to make. And we got a philosophy, particularly under [Lord] Stokes, that we did all our testing *after* we sold them, on the roads. The customers did it for us.[39]

Oddly enough, complaints similar to Robinson's were likewise made about the aircraft Britain was producing at the time, both military and commercial: that in order to save time and money after crippling delays, too few prototypes were built and too little time allotted to ironing out their less catastrophic design flaws before they were passed to their customers, who then gradually uncovered their shortcomings for themselves. Apart from that, though, Robinson's resigned sentence 'But that was what we had to make' neatly encapsulates so much that was wrong with the management of British industry in that period. The workers themselves, most of whom were not stupid and understood a good deal about all aspects of the cars they were making, were progressively demoralised by *knowing* that the cars they were producing were mostly wrong for the market and often sub-standard. Worse, they also knew that in the opinion of management their views were worthless and would never be listened to. Tony Benn, who from 1975 to 1979 was Secretary of State for Energy, took this very point when interviewed about BL years later. 'They were the people who made the cars. I mean, take Derek Robinson, for example: he had worked in the industry all his life. And then you bring in managers from a business studies course who'd got a degree in business management but who couldn't mend a puncture in a motor tyre – and you speak about the people who *made* the cars as the problem?'[40]

How could such a reversal of ordinary horse sense be anything other than bad for morale? In the same TV programme an ex-BL man described a Marina that had been left incomplete when a strike was called. Once the strike was over, 'the car went out with no trim on one side. Others hadn't been correctly wired up. Certain things worked, certain things didn't. If you put the indicator on all four flashers went or the horn blew.'[41] One brand-new car was returned with a dent in the bodywork that had been caused during assembly. Someone had simply slapped in some filler before the car was sprayed but that had now fallen out, leaving an unpainted crater. Similar casual ad hockery was demonstrated on the MG lines at Abingdon following a change in US regulations stipulating that car headlights had to be at a certain height. 'They just put blocks under the suspension mounting to bring it up, and then that spoiled the handling.'[42]

A lack of proper quality control before the cars left the factory was clearly down to bad management, as was a particularly ludicrous failure to foresee a major problem with the production of the new Austin 1800. At the last moment it was discovered that the car was just too wide to fit into the enclosed bridge that spanned a main road and linked the two halves of the Longbridge works. To get around this it was necessary to load the incomplete and still unpainted cars onto open transporters on one side of the road, take them through a gate, cross two lanes of traffic and drive a quarter of a mile down the road in all weathers and possibly even with salt on the road before going through another gate where they could be unloaded again. It was inconceivable that such a thing could happen at a factory of one of BL's German or Japanese rivals. Managerial ineptitude on this sort of scale was damaging enough to BL's reputation at home and abroad even without the constant strikes that bedevilled this and other industries at the time. It is scarcely surprising that morale was low. Yet as Harry Irwin, the Transport and General Workers' Union representative on the BL board, said: 'If the workers were convinced that management were focused on getting new orders into the factory doors, you'd be amazed at the transformation that would follow.'[43]

Michael Edwardes did his best to bring about that transformation even though from the first it seemed an impossible task. The Ryder Report, an investigation of BL by the head of the National Enterprise Board, had been submitted to Tony Benn in March 1975. It told everyone in awful detail what they already knew: that BL had outdated machinery, terrible industrial relations and appalling management. As Edwardes later put it, British Leyland was:

> a classic management case-study: ageing models, declining market share, highly publicised disputes and strikes, chaotic individual bargaining arrangements involving 17 different unions across 50 factories, no consensus on the Board, a strategy based on the unachievable Ryder Plan and a world image so damaging that the company craved only for silence, which it didn't get.[44]

But the Labour government was over a barrel. BL was going to cost an estimated £2.8 billion over seven years to put right. If the government refused to cough up, the company would close with the loss of over a million jobs and no British government – let alone a Labour one – could contemplate that for a second. In the ten months before Edwardes took over, the strikes BL suffered had left it with losses of a quarter of a million vehicles and so short of cash that from November 1977 it was impossible to pay the men's wages without emergency funding. Nationalised industry or not, it was useless turning for additional help to the government which, with a hung parliament, had problems of its own. Besides, Edwardes had not yet had a chance to draw up a corporate plan, and there was no point in trying to extract money from anyone without a plan to show them. Eventually, at the Treasury's urging, the banks grudgingly stumped up a minimal bridging loan to add still further to BL's prodigious overdraft.

BL's new Chairman also discovered that there was not even a proper breakdown of cost information model by model, making it impossible to keep any sensible accounts – as had been proved by the chronic underpricing of the Mini. It was obvious not only that managerial heads would have to roll since 'we had a classic case, on a massive scale, of faulty executive appointments', but that BL's entire structure was wrong. From the first, Edwardes was at one with the workforce in disliking the company's corporate centralism under which the old names like Austin, Morris, Land Rover, Jaguar, MG and Rover 'were being subordinated to a Leyland uniformity that stifled enthusiasm and pride', their names not even appearing in BL's organisation charts. There were only factory names like 'Solihull Plant' (which was Rover) and 'Abingdon Assembly Plant' (MG).

Edwardes' reorganisation of BL took three years, during which time it was mostly touch and go. By the end he had got rid of more than 90,000 employees – a good proportion of whom were managers – and even poached some replacement managers from Ford. He also noted a critical shortage of senior engineers capable of managing the engineering effort. Meanwhile, the morale of BL's British-based distributors and dealers was so low that Renault took to chartering aircraft to fly selected individuals over to France for a few days' wining and dining and encouragement to jump ship. Hard decisions were taken, such as the closure of the Triumph TR 7 factory at Speke and its transfer to Coventry, as well as the axing of MG sports models chiefly because the US market was uninterested and without it there would be no economies of scale in making the parts that were specific to them. Indeed, by the summer of 1979 BL was losing around £900 on every MG sold in America.

Perhaps the best publicised of Edwardes' travails was his protracted fight with the unions. In May 1979 Margaret Thatcher had taken office as prime minister after Britain's notorious Winter of Discontent when 1.5 million public sector workers were on strike across the UK. She certainly saw a major part of her mandate as curbing the unions. In September Edwardes delivered his completed Recovery Plan to BL's union leaders, explaining that it was more of an ultimatum. Either they and their members accepted it or the entire company would go bankrupt within a month and every last one of them would be out of a job. In November this was put to the employees. Eighty per cent of them voted, of whom 87.2 per cent were in favour of the Plan. Almost at once a plot led by Derek Robinson to sabotage it was 'unearthed'. (This was the word Edwardes used when his account was published in 1983, although it was disingenuous. It has since been revealed that MI5 had a mole planted in Red Robbo's union who had been able to keep the government and Edwardes himself informed of its every move.) Robinson was a long-term Communist Party member who never forgot that his primary loyalty lay in promoting the interests of the Amalgamated Engineering Union members he represented. However, most of the British media ignorantly lumped him into the same 'Bolshie' category as certain other union firebrands like Alan Thornett at Cowley. This was a mistake since it confused two very different forms of politics. Thornett, as a member of the Workers' Socialist League, was a Trotskyist and ultimately more interested in bringing about the Revolution that would lead to the overthrow of the United Kingdom. Robinson, on the other hand, was a typical CP member in his savage disparagement of 'the Trots' and their premature talk of revolution. His own opposition to Edwardes' Recovery Plan was based on a Marxist-Leninist conviction that everything the bosses did was a way of doing down the worker. He elaborated this position in a printed pamphlet whose argument was premised on keeping jobs at all costs, noting that 'in other industries like Upper Clyde Shipbuilders work-ins and occupations have been necessary to prevent closure. If necessary we shall have to do the same.' This led to Margaret Thatcher and her Secretary of

State for Industry, Sir Keith Joseph, insisting that Robinson be sacked, otherwise BL would not get the £450 million they were asking for. Edwardes duly dismissed Red Robbo, which in turn led to a partial walkout at Longbridge in his support. The strikers were promptly given an ultimatum: return to work or consider yourselves sacked.

Since the majority of the workers were by now convinced of BL's parlous state and that they were fighting for their very employment, they returned. Even as Robinson was calling for his own reinstatement Edwardes went on TV to give a summary of Red Robbo's thirty-month stewardship at Longbridge: '523 disputes with the loss of 62,000 cars and 113,000 engines, worth £200 million'.[45] On 20 February 1980 14,000 workers voted against Robinson's reinstatement with only six hundred voting for it. It had taken ninety-three very damaging days to resolve the crisis, by which time other threats to the company's survival were prominent, one of which was the value of sterling. This had recently soared in the wake of Margaret Thatcher's election, making BL's balance of payments still more impossible, to the point where Edwardes was claiming the company was losing £4 million a week 'even when we're not on strike'.

Although in the already quoted TV documentaries both Jeremy Clarkson and even Derek Robinson claimed that the blame for the demise of Britain's indigenous car industry lay equally with its clumsy historical mergers, its management and the unions, Michael Edwardes himself was perhaps unexpectedly a good deal less equivocal:

I could offer many other explanations; but as relevant as they are, none is as fundamental as the fact that management over a number of years lost their will to manage. Britain and the world blamed the unions, and turned their backs on British Leyland products. But the real blame lay with management, for they failed in their duty to manage. 'Management' is not an automatic right, it has to be earned. It is a duty, and if it isn't fulfilled it lets everyone down: employee, fellow manager, customer, supplier, and shareholder.[46]

If Edwardes' patient but draconian measures did result in a somewhat fitter and leaner British Leyland, the company was not indefinitely proof against the prevailing Thatcherite ideology, and in 1986 it was renamed the Rover Group and privatised, albeit with a 'golden share' proviso that stipulated there could be no takeover bid until 1990. In *Car* magazine in 1995 James Ruppert wrote that 'given the way we built, marketed and serviced cars in the 1970s and 80s, our indigenous industry deserved to die'.

Ten years later it did. In 2005 the last of Britain's home-owned volume car production came to an end when the MG Rover Group went into administration. The Morris, Austin, MG and Wolseley names were sold off to China's Shanghai Automotive Industry Corporation. Vauxhall remained a subsidiary of Opel until March 2017, when General Motors sold both to the huge French group PSA that owns Peugeot and Citroën. Thus, in common with the products of most of the UK's other industries, its mass market cars finally vanished into foreign hands for as much cash as the asset-strippers could raise. This demonstrated the exact conformity of Britain's prevailing economic ideology with Oscar Wilde's definition of a cynic as knowing the price of everything and the value of nothing. Rolls-Royce owned by BMW? Bentley owned by Volkswagen? How did we allow that to happen? I am thankful old Uncle John – a Desert Rat in the Second World War as well as a lifetime Conservative – is no longer around to see what his country's tireless mismanagement has achieved in his absence. At least his ancient 4½ litre Bomb remains British to the core, somewhere down under.

How to sum up this collapse? While admitting that the true history of British cars is complex and includes some justifiably world-famous examples of engineering and design genius, the motoring correspondent James Ruppert wrote that the reason we don't make British cars any more can be bleakly boiled down to 'because we built mediocre cars badly, good cars indifferently and, worst of all, offered cars that no one else in the world was really interested in'.[47] In its breezy way this judgement is perhaps too harsh, given that there are plenty of older British motorists with happy memories of their Vauxhall Wyverns, Lotus Cortinas and MG Sprites. But in essence it is probably correct. It is a shame.

The history of another British industry famously beset by strikes and bad management goes back centuries before cars or even steam power were ever dreamed of. The story of British shipbuilding dwarfs that of cars to a flash in the pan. Cars are simply consumer durables we once made for a century or so. But for hundreds of years the products of Britain's shipbuilding yards steadily made and defined Britain as a political entity and eventually as the world's first superpower. At first sight it seems unlikely the ailments that put paid to Britain's comparatively short-lived car marques could have anything in common with those that in a few short decades were allowed to end an industry representing centuries of national significance. Yet it was so, minus only shipbuilding's major Achilles heel of hubris, which was less of a problem in the post-war car industry. With two American car companies operating in Britain from before the Second World War, British car manufacturers could never completely forget that the foreign takeover of another British marque like Vauxhall was always a possibility, even though it was often easy to overlook that both it and Ford were ultimately answerable to corporate head offices on the far side of the Atlantic. (They shared this honorary Britishness with Woolworths, the demise of 'Woolies' in 2009 seeming to many like the death of a national institution, for all its American ancestry.)

By contrast British shipbuilders had had it all their own way for centuries, unchallenged – as they saw it – until it was all too late.

5.
Shipbuilding

'Whoever commands the ocean, commands the trade of the world; and whoever commands the trade of the world commands the riches of the world; and whoever is master of that commands the world itself.'

—JOHN EVELYN, *1674*

Swan Hunter's penultimate tanker dwarfs the terraced houses of
Leslie Street, Wallsend in 1975. *Tyne Pride* would go through four
name changes before she was broken up in Bangladesh in 2005.

Of all British industries, shipbuilding is by far the oldest and most resonant. An absolute prerequisite for any island race, the ability to construct seagoing vessels was the mainstay of our nationhood for a thousand years, with a good deal of Shakespearean and other literary invocation to prove it. Guff about the heart of oak (the title of the Royal Navy's official march) referred to the tough heartwood of timber 'rift sawn' at an angle across the grain for maximum strength and by extension referred to the hearts of the press-ganged 'jolly tars' who manned the ships made from it. It was also a nod to the ancient forests that until medieval times still covered much of Britain and were then steadily felled to feed a thousand small shipyards scattered around the coasts and estuaries. In due course maritime expansion and the acquisition of Empire and trade routes led inevitably to periodic clashes with rival nations that had similar intentions – principally France, Spain, Portugal and the Netherlands. Occasional wars led to improved design and construction methods for Britain's wooden warships that gave England the world's most powerful fleet even though in several encounters (for example, in the Napoleonic Wars) emerging victorious was often a close-run thing and by no means guaranteed. Still, as the 1760 words to 'Heart of Oak' have it, 'Britannia triumphant, her ships rule the seas' was generally true from then on.

What tipped the balance unequivocally in favour of Britannia's continued dominance of the world's oceans in the nineteenth and the first half of the twentieth centuries was industrialisation, the mastery of steam and the development of the iron steamship. Built in Bristol and launched in 1843, Brunel's SS *Great Britain* represented the start of a new era, the maritime equivalent of Henry Ford's first Model T. By far the biggest ship of its day, it was also the first iron ship with a screw propeller to cross the Atlantic. Thereafter, British shipbuilding retained a technological world dominance that was to last for over a hundred years. One consequence of this was the increasing concentration of the nation's shipbuilding in a comparatively small number of yards on water deep enough for launching iron vessels: Barrow-in-Furness, Belfast, Birkenhead on the Mersey, Tyneside, Portsmouth, the Clyde. Rail access to plentiful supplies of coal and iron was essential. Also essential were abundant labour and – in due course – steel. In the late nineteenth century the world's largest steelworks was at Barrow. Boatyards lacking railheads and manpower were often forced out of business unless they carried on building in wood for a specialist market, such as crafting immaculate teak-decked steam yachts for wealthy Victorians.

For a century and throughout two world wars, Britain maintained the world's most powerful navy and merchant marine and as late as 1948 was building just under half the world's tonnage of ships. At the end of the nineteenth century Britain's shipbuilders and marine engineers were without peer in terms of efficiency and innovation. Thanks partly to the invention of the Bessemer converter steel steadily replaced iron in ship construction, a technology that gave Britain a further useful lead over rivals. British innovations in propulsion (such as triple- and quadruple-expansion engines) ensured that the lead remained. In 1884 Charles Parsons invented the modern steam turbine and in 1897, having installed one in a small purpose-built experimental craft, the *Turbinia*, he cheekily showed it off uninvited at Queen Victoria's otherwise stately Jubilee naval review at Spithead. It whizzed about, chased in vain by a picket boat that the *Turbinia* evaded easily – as well it might, since it was then the fastest boat in the world, with a top speed of over 34 knots (a fraction under 40 mph). It stole the show and was a brilliantly calculated advertisement for steam turbines, which in due course the navy began to adopt. Just how sensational this speed was at the time can be judged by the world's first water speed record for a conventional motorboat, which was set six years later by Dorothy Levitt at 19.3 mph.

However, this somewhat triumphalist account conceals periods when Britain's dominance looked like faltering, especially towards the end of the nineteenth century when facing challenges from Germany and the United States. Although maritime supremacy ensured that British shipyards built over 60 per cent of the world's merchant tonnage, the Royal Navy was slow to keep up with the rapidly growing German fleet and there was a 'naval scare' in 1909 when it appeared that the Germans were outbuilding the British. This spurred a panicky increase in the output of dreadnoughts and especially of submarines, which the Royal Navy had initially disdained as a disgracefully underhanded way of waging war and only began to take seriously when they saw how many the Germans were building. By such efforts the Royal Navy caught up. Even so, during the First World War it could never have defended both the United Kingdom and the Empire and it was sheer luck that none of Britain's overseas possessions came under serious attack. Thanks to the Anglo-Japanese alliance of 1902 we were effectively relying on the Japanese navy to protect Singapore, Hong Kong and a dozen other Asian possessions, not to mention Australia and New Zealand. Had Japan sided with Germany (as it was to in 1940) we would probably have lost great chunks of the Empire and with them the war. It was a good illustration of how flimsy some of the links really were that held the Empire together.

Following the war, the 1920s and 1930s were a time of comparative stagnation in world trade and the global output of ships was virtually halved. The 1929 Wall Street Crash led to the Great Depression in Europe when entire British shipyards had no work and several went out of business. Perhaps the most significant example of this was the closure of Palmer's yard at Jarrow on Tyneside in 1934. Two years of unemployment and poverty later, it led to the Hunger March by two hundred half-starved Jarrow workers who walked all the way south to Westminster to hand in a petition at the House of Commons. It was received but never debated. However, the marchers gained a good deal of public sympathy and their dignified pilgrimage did much to boost the cause of the left and trade unionism generally. Its images and echoes probably contributed substantially to the Labour victory in the 1945 General Election.

Yet most British shipyards managed to remain in business even during these lean times simply by dint of having a monopoly of the country's immense home fleet as well as a healthy slice of foreign commissions. Privately owned, most shipbuilding companies had been in the same families' hands for generations and had acquired their own ways of working that afforded particular sources of pride. As a result they tended towards a dogged conservatism of attitude. Such a way of doing things had, after all, provided them with a very comfortable income from as far back as they could remember. The drawback was inevitably that of complacency: of not being amenable to new and more efficient techniques or having the flexibility to adjust quickly to changed circumstances that now were suddenly forced upon the entire industry by yet another war.

It is hard to imagine that the subsequent labour disputes in Britain's shipyards did not gain significant muscle from the Jarrow affair. One of Britain's treasured myths is that during the Second World War the workforce was imbued with a positively Stakhanovite spirit of selfless overproduction, whether down the coal mines or in the aircraft factories and shipyards. Dunkirk and the Battle of Britain promoted the image of the nation pulling together in the face of a deadly enemy and this was certainly what the Ministry of Information's propaganda proclaimed with its British equivalent of America's 'Rosie the Riveter' posters exhorting women to work in industry

('Women of Britain! Come into the Factories!'). Especially during the Battle of the Atlantic in 1942, when the merchant fleet incurred such terrible losses that for a while Britain's very survival looked doubtful, most people took for granted that the shipyards were hives of industriousness, clattering ceaselessly by day and night with the staccato gunfire of riveters and flashing with arc welders in heroic efforts to keep Britain fed and Our Boys supplied. A glance through the Ministry of Labour and National Service's strike charts is enough to dispel any such fantasy. More working days were lost through strikes each year between 1942 and 1945 than had been in the last full peacetime year of 1938. The British Disease was well in evidence – so much so that a later historian could write: 'even a total war for survival had failed to remedy in British management and the British workforce that smug, stubborn conservatism of outlook and method that had been first identified a century earlier by Cobden and Lyon Playfair, and documented by royal commissions from the 1870s to the 1920s'.[48]

Being a newspaper coinage, the British Disease is an ailment not to be found in any medical lexicon and its symptoms vary according to the whim of the journalist. In general, though, they include strikes, stoppages, go-slows, exorbitant pay demands, equally absurd pay settlements, dysfunctional supply chains, loss of market share leading to contraction and mergers, lay-offs, and back to strikes, stoppages and pay demands all over again. Where shipbuilding was concerned strikes and labour difficulties had been familiar as a recurring problem ever since

Victorian times. This was chiefly because iron shipbuilding had inherited a workforce with membership of craftsmen's guilds that represented the sundry different skills involved in building traditional heart-of-oak wooden ships. Carpenters, joiners, shipwrights and caulkers still had work but now they were joined by boilermakers, platers, riveters, sheet metal men, pipefitters, anglesmiths, winchmen and the rest, not to mention welders and electricians in due time. Merely making a ship's ventilators might involve seven different crafts. Demarcation disputes could become nit-pickingly foolish and hold up a new ship for weeks and even months, and this remained true even in – *especially* in, as it turned out – wartime. One might have thought that any halfway competent yard management would urgently have met with union leaders and between them thrashed out workable agreements over demarcation and 'dilution' problems before the entire yard and the war effort were crippled.

Too often, though, 'halfway competent' turned out to be wishful thinking, as did a notion that patriotism or even pragmatism might trump union intransigence at a time of national emergency. In 1942, when there was a particularly desperate need for new warships and cargo vessels to replace those sunk by U-boats, many of Britain's shipyards were beset by the often elderly yard owners' complacent devotion to the pre-war status quo as well as by labour stoppages caused by demarcation disputes. The craft unions were leery of the introduction of any new technology that threatened future manning levels and their own traditional skills. Like true Luddites their instinctive response was to block it. The Amalgamated Engineering Union and the Boilermakers' Society banned members of the National Union of Railwaymen from working in any shipyard even when they had the appropriate skills, while the Electricians' Union at one shipyard refused to work with a non-union electrician and threatened to strike.

In August 1944, the time of the climax of the Battle of Normandy, the boilermakers had taken their objection to semi-skilled men operating new flame-cutters at Vickers-Armstrong [naval yard] to the point of refusing to work on any material processed on the new cutters unless these were operated and controlled by their members. They had done so even despite the setting-up of a Court of Inquiry and a personal reminder from the First Lord of the Admiralty about the urgency of the war work now being paralysed. The boilermakers only lifted their ban in December 1944 because the company took the semi-skilled men off the new flame-cutters and suspended the operation of the cutters for the time being.[49]

Here, 'flame-cutters' referred to oxyacetylene torches being used to perform tasks such as cutting the heads off rivets in order to remove damaged steel plates from a ship's hull under repair. The gas torches could also be used for welding and as such were viewed by riveters as a new and threatening technology. In this particular case the men returned to the time-honoured method of whacking the rivet heads off with cold chisels and hammers: a noisier, more tiring, slower and altogether less efficient method

even as German torpedoes were sending hundreds of thousands of tons of vital supplies to the bottom of the Atlantic.

That such industrial stupidity could cause a four-month
standstill of crucial work in time of war was bad enough. What
could be far more galling at a personal level was the widespread foot-dragging in the repair docks that the crews of
cargo vessels could see for themselves when they returned to
their home ports. These were often men whose convoys had
miraculously survived an Atlantic crossing under sustained
attack and who were still haunted by the experience of seeing
torpedoed ships' crews drown in seas of oil or flame. One ship's
officer told a reporter of a visit he and a government official
had paid to a dry dock in Liverpool to see how the urgent
repairs to his ship were progressing. It was not the first time
the officer had been there so when he and his companion went
aboard and could see no workmen he led the way downwards
through various decks until finally, in the very bottom of the
hold, they came upon a group of men sitting around a brazier.
'What they're supposed to be doing, I don't know,' he admitted
later to the official. 'They're never working when I see them.'
Afterwards when they were walking back through the dock the
government man said satirically, 'Just take a look as we walk
round and see if you discover anybody working.' He added that
he visited such yards from time to time and the sight made
him almost weep. He estimated that only one in ten workers
was actually doing anything.[50] The client for 1,951 of the 2,525
ships completed during the war (i.e. over 77 per cent of the

entire construction programme, including more than half the merchant vessels) was the Admiralty; but even it was unable to exercise control over the workers despite unofficial strikes being illegal.[51] It is worth remembering that such men were excused call-up by being classified as performing essential war work. All the same, such apparent lack of patriotism and conscience was also a measure of how marginalised some workers felt not long after Jarrow. Thoroughly disaffected and alienated from mainstream British society as they saw it (as represented by the administrative south), many were well read in Socialist literature and considered the war as having nothing to do with them. Rather, it was an irresponsible adventure the ruling classes of Britain and Europe had brought upon themselves, and serve them right.

Such stories contain in microcosm most of the main causes of British shipbuilding's subsequent demise. A management still essentially Victorian in attitude; a poorly educated workforce cut off from all decision-making, full of belligerent class grievances and fears that easily led to union militancy; resultant low productivity at critical moments; outdated practices and yard facilities – they all contributed. In the first four years after the war there were clear signs of impending doom even though Britain went back to building over half the world's tonnage of ships, just as it had before the First World War. Despite its wartime losses Britain still had the world's largest merchant shipping fleet and by law its owners were not allowed to go shopping abroad for their ships even had they wished. New vessels were urgently required to replace those lost or damaged in the war and the order books of the nation's yards were reassuringly full. As yet there was only limited international competition, especially from former enemies like Germany and Japan whose industrial infrastructure had been severely damaged.

However, in the general post-war boom between 1950 and 1958 the world's shipbuilding output trebled and it became obvious that rivals like Sweden were emerging even as West Germany and Japan were swiftly recovering and setting up newly modernised shipyards. West Germany was soon building more tonnage for export than Britain and by 1953 Britain's supply of the world's tonnage had sunk to 36.6 per cent. In 1956 Japan overtook Britain as the world's leading shipbuilder. If this was humbling it was also scarcely surprising since not only were most British yards slow to modernise but increasing industrial unrest was already taking its toll. Strikes held up production and fatally damaged the yards' reputation for completing orders within budget and above all on time.

One example will suffice of how disaster could follow intransigent stupidity. On Clydeside in the autumn of 1955 Cammell Laird was building a banana ship, SS *Leader*, for an American customer. The insulation in the holds required aluminium sheeting to be fixed to wood, and demarcation disputes at once erupted involving three separate unions. The sheet metal men drilled the holes in the aluminium in a separate shed in the yard and they now objected to the joiners drilling any further holes in it once it was mounted on to the wood panels aboard the ship. To them it was immaterial that the metal was married to wood and required further drilling to be installed: it was still metal and it was therefore their job to drill it. Cammell Laird's management, which had awarded the joiners a monopoly of drilling once the panels were aboard, evidently thought it best to cancel their agreement. The joiners promptly went on strike, as did the sheet metal men.

This was in September 1955. The strike dragged on until the new year, by which time it had become a national scandal headlined in a *Daily Mail* article of 13 January 1956. Twenty million dollars' worth of shipyard contracts were on hold while five hundred woodworkers had downed tools over an argument with a hundred metalworkers about who should drill holes. 'Laughable indeed,' said the *Mail*, 'if you have not studied your industrial history of the past few decades. But shipbuilders all – management and men alike – can never banish from their minds the ghosts of the lean times.' This emollient aside, hinting at memories of Jarrow, rather overlooked the reality that jeopardising contracts in this way practically guaranteed a return of the lean times.

Meanwhile, the exasperated vice-president of the American steamship company whose contract was being held up protested to Cammell Laird that three months' delay to his ship would cost him $360,000 and suggested the unfinished hull should be towed to Holland or Germany to be completed. The Ministry of Labour wrestled with the TUC; the General Demarcation

Agreement of 1912 was invoked and mulled over; the strike continued. The *Sunday Graphic* of 1 April 1956 then interviewed William White, the president of the shipping company that had ordered the SS *Leader* and also a second vessel from Hampdens, another Cammell Laird shipyard at Birkenhead. He calculated that delays to both vessels had already cost his company half a million dollars. He was quoted thus:

'The way I feel now, I wouldn't spend another nickel building ships in England. I don't ever want to hear of Birkenhead again. ... Nobody ever gave a damn whether we got the ship or not, except us. All we got was excuses from the company, always more excuses, and fine words from the politicians. Listen to this – it'll kill you.' [The President of the Board of Trade, Peter Thorneycroft, had just described the strike as 'deplorable and reprehensible']. 'Dig that: *deplorable and reprehensible* ... ALL I WANTED WAS A SHIP AND ALL I GOT WAS A LOT OF FANCY GRAMMAR. This isn't the first time we've had a raw deal from Britain. In January 1951 we placed an order for two shallow-draught ore carriers of about 8,000 tons with the Burntisland Company [on the Firth of Forth]. In May 1952 we placed exactly the same order with some Swedish yards. What happened? One Swedish ship was delivered 21 months after signature of contract and the second, 26 months after signature. The British ships took 36 months and 52 months.[52]

From the mid-1950s the story of British shipbuilding became one of precipitate decline. Today the UK is left with a handful of yards building the very few combat vessels the Royal Navy can any longer afford. No government has yet had the nerve to shop abroad for those even though it would almost certainly be quicker and cheaper to do so. The navy's tankers, however, are now built in South Korea. When in 2013 BAE announced the closure of its Portsmouth yard it represented the end of more than five centuries' shipbuilding there: the birthplace of the *Mary Rose* and the port probably more closely associated with the Royal Navy than any other in Britain.

This abject collapse – which effectively took place within a mere twenty years or so – occurred partly because of intermittent global economic downturns that affected everyone, not to mention strengthening foreign competition. Swedish shipyards were particularly admired in the 1950s and 1960s for their progressive technology and good labour relations, but even they were not immune and the rest of Europe's shipyards were equally affected, although they did not collapse. True, it is hard to see how Britain, with its already ailing shipyards and labour troubles, could ever have competed successfully with the far cheaper and faster production lines of South Korea and Japan. Mainly, though, the collapse of British shipbuilding was the result of such a compendium of home-grown errors as almost to transcend industrial ineptitude and become a parable of national failings. As one ex-civil servant put it, '[T]he withering of the shipbuilding industry was a rusty template of decline replicated subsequently with variations across swathes of other industries.'[53] It is certainly as illustrative a case of galloping and then terminal British Disease as afflicted any other of our now defunct or moribund industries.

One of the major – and entirely predictable – sources of trouble was the failure to change old-fashioned ways of working and embrace new technology. The basic construction of ships involved the joining together of steel plates as a skin to cover an already assembled skeleton in a shipyard berth. Ever since Britain had pioneered iron and then steel ships in the nineteenth century, the method used for joining plates to frame had been by riveting: at first by hand and then mechanically. As we have seen, this was to be superseded by welding, which offered enormous advantages not only in terms of ease and speed but in achieving a better hydrodynamic finish to a hull. Instead of tens of thousands of domed rivet-heads each setting up its own turbulence in the water, welding could offer an altogether smoother profile that in turn led to better performance and fuel economy.

Even before the Second World War some British yard owners had accepted that welding was the way forward but were unwilling to face the inevitable union ructions over new demarcations. Shipyard workers with centuries of highly successful craft traditions behind them were conservative even by their countrymen's overall standards. By 1939 both Sweden and the United States had identified welded ships as the future of shipbuilding. This turned out to be timely because within three years the wholesale destruction of Allied shipping in the Atlantic made imperative the mass production of replacement cargo vessels in the shortest possible time, and thus the Liberty ship was born in the United States. In a sense its construction was the maritime equivalent of the assembly line in that whole sections were prefabricated away from the berth then brought by cranes to the berth and welded together. Shipyards found that semi-skilled workers could soon be trained in welding and assembly and eventually 2,578 Liberty ships were built. Their standardised design was not very aesthetic (Admiral Emory S. Land described the ship as 'a real ugly duckling') and nor were they always impeccably built, some being notorious for bad handling and a few suffering catastrophic hull failure quite without the aid of the German navy. But they fulfilled a purpose, although as the war progressed and the U-boat campaign intensified the Liberty ships were superseded by the faster and bigger Victory ships that sensibly were also designed with a view to forming the basis of a merchant fleet once the war was over.

If ever there was a wake-up call for British shipyards after the war, the example of the Liberty ships and their rapid construction ought to have been it. The methods of building that the American shipyards had pioneered offered savings in both steel and time. By assembling a long series of a single design, workers became faster the more familiar they were with the task: a learning curve already well established in the motor industry as well as in the wartime mass production of aircraft. After the war both the United States and Sweden adopted these procedures and between 1946 and 1949 these two countries alone built most of the 264 all-welded vessels produced worldwide, of which Britain built a mere seven. However, it was not just the British workers' resistance to welding that slowed things down. Modular construction also required shipyards to be considerably redesigned, with berths enlarged to house the separate assembly bays and a new system of overhead cranes to transport the sections to where the complete hull was welded together. It would anyway have been an opportune moment for British shipyards to modernise at least one of their berths because most were showing distinct signs of obsolescence despite the patchy acquisition of new kit such as oxyacetylene torches. Their general layout remained the same as it had been before the First World War and most of the cranes were equally old, some of them still steam-driven. Yet the company owners (most of whom were of the same vintage if not decrepitude) evidently saw no reason to change a set-up that, as far as they were concerned, was tried and trusted. Least of all did they want to close a yard for the wholesale and massively expensive reorganisation that the assembly-line method of ship production would require at exactly the moment when their order books were bulging.

This was the point at which a canny government might have stepped in with a planned modernisation scheme in stages, perhaps subsidising a few yards at a time to close and refurbish while the rest carried on building their orders. But the war had ended and with it the command economy, and not even the Labour government had the nerve to force private yard owners to shut down temporarily and make the necessary investment. It was now that British shipbuilding finally succumbed to the increasing lameness brought about by its own success. Ironically, the one thing that had been instrumental in its global dominance was that the world's biggest trading nation had relied on the world's biggest merchant fleet, which in turn was owned by British shipping companies who naturally always ordered their vessels from British yards. For the last hundred years this handy symbiosis had meant the shipbuilding companies enjoyed regular and plentiful orders from home before having to consider orders from abroad. That this situation remained undiagnosed by shipyard owners as a potential weakness rather than a strength reveals the extent to which complacency had swamped whatever business instincts they might once have had. Competition from abroad for this mass market was something they had long overlooked or discounted as a serious possibility. German, French, American or Italian shipyards might have built a few fast passenger liners between the wars like the SS *Hamburg*, SS *Normandie*, SS *Washington* and SS *Rex* to challenge RMS *Mauretania*, RMS *Queen Mary* or even the *Titanic*'s old sister ship, RMS *Olympic* for the lucrative transatlantic routes and the glamorous Blue Riband for the fastest crossing. But this had been seen as acceptable competition at the top end of the market. Foreigners (in their view) just didn't have a century's experience in churning out the thousands of cargo vessels that, like maritime lorries, daily carried the overwhelming bulk of the world's goods. Glamour and prestige were all very well on the transatlantic passenger routes but the real money lay in cargo vessels...

How true this was soon became apparent as world trade began to pick up again. Maybe wholesale modernisation and restructuring of Britain's shipyards and work practices might have saved the day, but this possibility was complicated by a variety of caveats, some of them technical. One of these was that the metallurgical consequences of welding were not yet fully understood, except that it was known to set up different stresses in steel from those caused by riveting. The structural failure of some Liberty ships during the war had been a notorious warning. Almost a third of them had been afflicted by cracks in the deck and hull plates and in the case of three ships these were catastrophic enough to cause the entire ship to split in half in mid-ocean. The instinct had been to blame inexperienced welders, but it turned out that the weakness was caused by an unsuspected design flaw. It took an engineering professor at Cambridge University, Constance Tipper, to discover the cause. A metallurgist and crystallographer, she found that the grade of steel used to build the ships became brittle on prolonged exposure to the low temperatures of the North Atlantic. Because the plates were welded together cracks could propagate across the weld, often over very long distances, something that could not happen with individually riveted plates.

On learning this, less open-minded shipbuilders doubted whether welded ships might after all herald the future. It was obvious there was much more to be known about the materials and the correct techniques for assembling them. Evidently two principal problems needed to be surmounted: those of distortion and flaws. Overall distortion can occur in a metal structure being welded because of the localised intense heat being applied, and preventing as well as rectifying this can add significantly to the costs of construction. Flaws in the welding, especially those of two surfaces being incompletely fused together and with consequent concealed cracks, make such areas potentially weak under stress.

To more progressive – mainly foreign – yards this was simply a new technology that needed to be mastered because it offered clear advantages. Nor did such challenges daunt a British aero company like Bristol, whose Type 188 high speed research aircraft being built in the late 1950s was skinned with stainless steel, welding which required the painstaking development of entirely new techniques. Most British shipyards, however, had always prided themselves on bespoke if traditional construction: each ship was a named individual, perfectly tailored to her fleet owner's requirements. The idea of churning out whole batches of identical ships, no matter what the economic advantage, did not appeal. Nevertheless, welding did slowly take over until by 1960 welders outnumbered riveters in British shipbuilding by three to one.[54] In most yards, though, other kinds of modernisation such as new cranes were introduced only gradually and in piecemeal fashion. Thus uneconomical construction methods led to British ships being more expensive than those of their competitors. Only in the three major yards where much of the

Admiralty's work was done (Harland and Wolff, Swan Hunter and Scott Lithgow) was modernisation more thoroughgoing.

Over and above all this, though, most British shipyard owners of the day must stand collectively condemned for a serious want of imagination: a failure to work out something that by the mid-1950s was unignorable. This was that the newly modernised shipyards in the Far East paid their workers significantly lower wages than their militant British counterparts and could now churn out perfectly good standard cargo vessels quicker and far more cheaply than any yard on the Clyde. This being so, building merchant ships in the UK for foreign fleets was surely a doomed enterprise. Had the owners really bothered to think like businessmen they might have considered that now was the time to move into building more specialised or upmarket types of vessel such as cruise liners that, with their oak panelling and fitted cabins, were well suited to traditional British craftsmanship. But that would have meant the industry's contraction and rationalisation, not to mention deciding who had the right to bore holes. In 2013 Sir John Parker, the former chief executive of Harland and Wolff, conceded that the industry had missed an opportunity, although admittedly he was looking back only as far as the Thatcher years:

One of my big industrial disappointments ... is that I failed to persuade the government of the day that there was a big future in building cruise ships. Whoever bought run-of-the-mill bulk carriers or tankers drifted to the lowest-cost country. So how you survived in higher-cost countries was by building more sophisticated ships like cruise ships. I saw that there was going to be a lot of growth in cruise ship building ... [a]nd nearly twenty-five years on, these forecasts would have underestimated the demand.[55]

German and Italian shipbuilders had made the same calculation much earlier and got it right. Today both nations have yards that build cruise vessels and private yachts for oil sheikhs, Russian oligarchs and the like, some of these 'yachts' being substantial oceangoing ships. The result of the British yards' half-hearted approach to modernisation back in the 1950s and 1960s was that production levels remained stubbornly the same, while those of foreign yards – principally in Japan, Germany and Sweden – rose steadily. Worse still, the yard owners seemed not to have taken account of the changes taking place in global shipping. Motor ships were now the norm, and burgeoning markets everywhere for cars, generators and construction machinery were causing a worldwide increase in the demand for diesel fuel and petrol, which in turn required oil tankers of rapidly increasing tonnage. The economics of size also meant that cargo vessels were getting bigger, especially ships like bulk ore carriers and, in time, container ships. Again, most British shipyards were ill-adapted to make the changes needed to build ships of widely differing sizes and type. They had, of course, built motor ships and tankers before the war, although proportionally fewer than had foreign yards. Even so, by 1939 the Anglo-Iranian Oil Company, the forerunner of BP, had its own fleet of 93

British-built tankers. But after the war it was foreign yards that increasingly dominated the market for bigger ships. In the ten years between 1948 and 1958 Britain's share of the global output of new ships of all types slumped from 50 to a mere 15 per cent.

One of the arguments traditionally used to defend this lamentable record is that immediately after the war shipbuilding, in common with every other British industry, had to contend with the strict rationing of steel and other construction materials. In its desperate need of foreign capital the Labour government imposed allocations in accordance with each industry's predicted requirements. In any case only businesses that exported more than 75 per cent of their production were eligible for steel supplies. Not only that but, as mentioned earlier, British merchant fleet owners were forbidden by measures such as the Exchange Control Act of 1945 from having their ships built abroad even if they could get a more favourable price (a restriction that was lifted in 1951). Meanwhile, the shipbuilding industry calculated it could realistically produce 1.75 million gross tons of new ships per year, which would require 900,000 tons of steel plate: figures it repeated in 1953. Defenders of the industry have claimed it was starved of steel at a critical juncture. In reality, its notified requirement for that quantity of steel in 1953 had been met years earlier but the yards' combined output never remotely approached their projected tonnage of new ships, remaining obstinately stuck at a level that clearly reflected what they anticipated would be the requirements of the British merchant fleet owners, which was little different from the pre-war level. Evidently they never thought seriously of expansion by increasing their foreign orders. Any claims of a shortage of shipbuilding steel were thus not based on fact.

Also detectable in this abrupt downward turn was the legacy of the 1930s' Great Depression that had sent shipyards like Jarrow's out of business, thrown thousands of men out of work and forced entire families into conditions of abject penury. Part of the reason why British shipbuilders had not embraced a policy of growth in the global shipping boom following the Second World War was their conviction that such booms were always followed by slumps, and heavy investment in expansion would always turn into a liability as they tried to pay off the bank loans when business was stagnant. No matter how sympathetic and understandable its origins, this attitude was once again a rationale for the short-termism that underwrites so much of Britain's approach to industry. It surely speaks more of national psyche than it does of logic: after all, it is equally true that sooner or later slumps have always given way to booms. This, however, is a form of optimism that to British industrialists, who struggle to survive without the government backing that so many of their foreign competitors get, seems never to outweigh the perceived risks of investing in the future.

In 1964 the new Labour government instituted the Shipbuilding Inquiry Committee to find out what could be done about the industry. In time its chairman, Sir Reay Geddes, was due to report but before he could do so one of the best-known yards on the Clyde at Govan, the Fairfield Shipbuilding and

Engineering Company, went into receivership in the autumn of 1965. Since 1960 seven Clyde shipbuilders had already closed and because the Labour government was particularly sensitive about maintaining its support in Britain's dwindling industrial heartlands Fairfield's impending demise caused much anxiety in Downing Street. Faced with their imminent redundancy, the Fairfield workers agreed to accept a deal whereby the company's assets were bought from the receiver for £1.06 million (of which half was advanced by the government, £400,000 was private capital and £200,000 came from the unions) and a new company set up. Only two members of the new Fairfield board of directors were shipbuilders; the rest came from other industries. It was quite a radical scheme and forced through improvements to the yard's organisation and management that even the industry acknowledged were overdue. This immediately caused ill feeling in the rest of the industry because most of the other surviving shipbuilders were deeply opposed to the idea of government-backed bailouts for private yards that failed, on the self-interested grounds that preventing other companies from going out of business further diluted their own chances of getting what little work there was.

When it was published, the Geddes Report only further emphasised and enumerated the industry's already well-known failings. Accordingly, the Labour government had a rethink. Instead of giving financial assistance to individual yards it switched to a policy of merging them. This was in line with the pattern already established in the aircraft and motor industries:

when in doubt, nationalise and *merge*. The most immediate drawback was already familiar from those other industries. Fiercely independent family companies with roots that went back deep in the nineteenth century (a few even earlier) suddenly found themselves forced to amalgamate in groups tied to particular regions such as the Clyde. They were now also told to concentrate on the market for bulk carriers and oil tankers.

Apart from the resentment this policy caused and the rift it further widened between industry and government, it predictably failed to result in any increased share of the rapidly expanding world market because for the same old reasons productivity remained stubbornly at its previous level. In the new groups the enforced changes in working practices and management disrupted even the modest previous levels of output and yards began losing money hand over fist. Groups in Belfast and Birkenhead began to fail, as did Upper Clyde Shipbuilders. UCS was formed in 1968 by the amalgamation of five failing but major shipbuilders on the Clyde, including Fairfield. By 1971 it was clear that it, too, would have to go into receivership. Prime Minister Edward Heath was already embarrassed by having just had to make an exception to his electoral promise to stop refloating 'lame duck' companies with taxpayers' money by doing exactly that for Rolls-Royce. He now refused to do the same for UCS which, although seriously strapped for immediate cash, did have a full order book. A group of young Communist shop stewards, of whom Jimmy Reid and Jimmy Airlie swiftly came to national prominence, led not a strike but a 'work-in' to finish the contracts the yard had already signed. This action earned them nationwide publicity with saturation TV and newspaper coverage, not least because the shop stewards preserved strict discipline by telling their workers at mass meetings that there was to be 'no hooliganism, no vandalism and no bevvying' in order to prevent the usual accusations of workshy and 'bolshie' unions. It earned Reid, in particular, a good deal of support nationally, and enough sympathy when UCS was forced into liquidation to oblige Edward Heath to relent and keep it going in 1972 as Govan Shipbuilders.

Such were the desperate measures taken in the face of an unstoppable decline that was only partly due to the chaos following the yards' enforced reorganisation into groups. In the interim the bulk carriers and tankers the world market wanted had grown still larger, and the groups' medium-sized shipyards could not cope, although Harland and Wolff, Swan Hunter and Scott Lithgow did make further changes to enable them to tackle orders for these increasingly gigantic ships.

At that point, as if to prove that the industry's instinct for short-termism was bitterly justified, OPEC's Arab oil producers triggered the 1973 oil crisis by punishing the countries it blamed for having supported Israel during the Yom Kippur War in October that year. Britain was one of the embargoed nations. Within months the price of oil had quadrupled and produced a global downturn in trade that temporarily killed the market for new oil tankers as well as for ships of all kinds. British shipbuilding declined still further until the government turned to the remedy of last resort: nationalisation. This had actually been a Labour Party commitment in its manifesto for the February 1974 General Election and, including aerospace, it became the Aircraft and Shipbuilding Industries Act. But it only did so in the teeth of fierce parliamentary opposition that climaxed in the House of Commons on 27 May 1976 when the Act was passed by a single vote and the shadow Industry Secretary, Michael Heseltine, famously snatched the Mace off its stand and menaced the Labour front bench with it.

But by now shipbuilding was too enfeebled to resist and was forcibly wheeled into intensive care wearing the new corporate ID tag of British Shipbuilders to match that of the equally new British Aerospace, BAe. Unfortunately, shipbuilding proved to be beyond resuscitation. BS's organisational structures, like the yards themselves, were not equipped to tackle the latest trends in global shipping: container ships and cruise liners. Nor could it compete on price. In the words of a senior civil servant, BS was '[m]issing out also on the fundamental changes in working practices and supplier relationships that were enhancing the efficiency of Japanese, and then South Korean, shipbuilders. And the beriberi of decline spread to suppliers – steel, motors, pumps, valves, steering gear etc., and in turn through the component supplier network, leading to further layoffs and pretexts for militant action. And so on.'[56]

Yet Britain could not afford to let her oldest industry collapse completely, mainly because the Ministry of Defence insisted that some yards and their workforces had to be kept viable in order to build naval vessels. In desperation yards began trying to build things of which they had no experience or real understanding, such as oil rigs. Predictably, this was another disaster with the loss of great sums of public money. By 1979, after ten years of massive government funding, British Shipbuilders was still launching the same old annual 1.2 million gross tons that the industry had been launching since the war, only now its share of global production had fallen to 1.5 per cent. It was hardly a surprise when the incoming Thatcher government decided to privatise the naval shipyards and sell off the others, knowing full well that their chances of survival in the prevailing global economic downturn were virtually nil. The Secretary for Transport, Kenneth Clarke, must have realised that putting them up for sale was a death sentence intended to finish off as many insolvent and difficult yards as possible. In this it was effective.

Sunderland's last shipyard, North East Shipbuilders Ltd, would close in December 1988 but not before a Geordie, John Lister, went to Japan as Chairman of British Shipbuilders to ask if they would come and do an audit of NESL. A greater turnaround in the fortunes of a once proud, centuries-old industry can scarcely be imagined. A Japanese team duly arrived and after inspection concluded that much of the company was indeed competitive: the quality of the equipment as well as the skills of the workforce – notably the welders – were good. What was less good was the actual flow of the work. The audit mentioned 'too much walking', 'blocks standing unfinished and idle', 'too many different activities in a confined area'. Bad management, in short. The final conclusion was damning: NESL was taking nearly three times as many man-hours as Japanese yards to build comparable ships, and at 30 per cent higher cost.[57] As a footnote, the business magazine *Look Japan* reported in March 2004 that Mitsubishi's Kobe shipyard could build a 60,000-tonne container ship in *two months* from start to finish. Following by now traditional mass production methods the bow section, engine section, crew quarters and other blocks of the ship were built at nearby sites and assembled at the shipyard itself. Each block weighed between 1,000 and 5,000 tons and when brought together any discrepancy in tolerances always turned out to be less than one centimetre.

As with the car industry, it is hard to see how the idea of jobbing-in managers who had business degrees but no previous experience of the specific industry could have helped ship-building, other than perhaps by urging it to seek different markets and build different ships. On the other hand it was clear that existing managements, who had probably been in the business all their lives, must to some extent have succumbed to the inertia of custom. Certainly their yards often reflected this, where until the 1970s it was still possible to see a foreman wearing a traditional bowler – as opposed to hard – hat. For some reason Britons have always tended to overvalue their own management skills even though time and again one industry after another has demonstrated their inadequacy. Years ago – most likely in the 1980s – I remember watching an episode of the long-running BBC TV programme *Tomorrow's World* that focused on Britain's strike-torn car industry. A group of British managers (probably from Ford or British Leyland) was taken around a car factory in Scandinavia that must have looked to them like the shape of things to come. They admired the computer-aided design and manufacture, the generally unfactorylike clinical conditions, the atmosphere of calm efficiency, the nodding robots and impressive output of gleaming cars rolling off the line. Where they jibbed was at seeing a production meeting with shop-floor workers and managers sitting around a table in conditions of complete equality, the managers listening to the workers' advice on a variety of technical and procedural matters. It was evident that the British visitors were not ready to countenance a degree of participation that allowed workers to take actual decisions about certain aspects of their job that they obviously understood better than did the managers: the exact point Tony Benn would trenchantly make when interviewed at Longbridge years later. The programme left one feeling wistful for the sort of equable harmony of an enterprise where few if any lines were drawn between worker and management. Instead of opposition, everyone's energy and skills could be directed at making the business run more productively: another of the benefits of a practically classless society and in Britain's case something of a pipe dream.

The death in intensive care of Britain's oldest major industry was nationally mourned. Its decline had been too obviously irreversible, the symbolism too unavoidable after centuries of patriotic bawling about Britannia ruling the waves. Just as the tips of the old girl's trident disappeared beneath the surface for good, modernisation did belatedly catch up with her and beginning in 2009 six different shipyards, many of which were hundreds of miles apart, built the nine modules of the Royal Navy's new aircraft carrier HMS *Queen Elizabeth*. They were welded together in Rosyth. Never mind that this behemoth of the twenty-first-century electronic battlefield reportedly runs on the antique software of Windows XP. There she is, and British yards built her: the biggest ship the navy has ever had. 'Merely a large convenient naval target' was the Russian defence ministry's dismissive opinion. As the embodiment of Britannia, though, she is more like a tired old street-walker given a final bout of cosmetic surgery before venturing forth in a merciless world with the advice not to loiter beneath bright lights.

There is still the demise of Britain's merchant fleet to consider because it also threatened the survival of Britain's merchant seamen, for long considered the world's best-trained, both competent and disciplined. Most copies of my boyhood weekly *Eagle* and monthly *Boy's Own Paper* contained advertisements for joining the merchant navy as an apprentice, with tempting promises of a life of adventure on the world's high seas and qualifications in various kinds of engineering, navigation and radio that would guarantee one a well-paid job in civvy street if ever life on the ocean wave palled. I always took heart from the promise that no exam results were required and one might be accepted on interview alone. I was confident of being able to pull that off with a spiel about the excitement of far horizons and the challenge of keeping Britain's lifeline trade routes open to the farthest reaches of the Empire (which even then was being dismantled with unseemly dispatch). The mere knowledge that at least the merchant navy was there as a fallback employer if all else failed was very reassuring, as was the BBC World Service's weekly merchant navy programme I would listen to on short wave radio in South East Asia in the 1970s.

That career option began closing off in the eighties when British-owned ships were permitted to register in countries that had few regulations and paid their crews a pittance. The result is that today, two-thirds of what remains of Britain's merchant fleet sails under flags of convenience and has two-thirds fewer British officers. Furthermore, this position will not change for the better after Brexit since of all the EU member countries Britain offers its merchant sailors the least protection, their numbers having dropped from 90,000 in the 1970s to just 19,000 today. The United States protects its maritime industries by insisting that any ship working between US ports must be US-built and -crewed. Many other countries do likewise. Not the UK, however, where British-registered ships now account for a mere 0.8 per cent of the global total. It is all part of our ingenious economic strategy to win the race to the bottom: our one remaining industrial plan that is absolutely guaranteed success.

6.
Defence

*'The higher up decisions are made, the worse they are likely to be.
The higher up money is spent, the more likely it is to be wasted.'*

—SIR ANTONY JAY, co-writer of *Yes, Minister*[1]

The remains of XN728, an English Electric Lightning F.2A, sold for scrap in 1983 after Cold War service in Germany. The cockpit section has since been saved and is being restored.

There is a single minor respect in which the fate of British shipbuilding resembles that of British cars, in that there is a comparatively small but lively segment of the remaining industry devoted to the bespoke building of expensive leisure craft. In addition to about fifty sailing yacht builders in the UK there are some famous builders of motor boats. These range from outboard models for water-skiing and beautifully hand-crafted sports runabouts by Cockwells, to Hunton's express cruisers with two cabins and a top speed of 70 knots, and Sunseeker's 155 with its provision for twelve guests and eleven crew and a range of 4,000 nautical miles. This last, like so many boats these days, has forsaken all vestiges of a traditional nautical look and has the styling of a training shoe; or, come to that, the styling of most modern cars. This is a good example of convergent evolution and is equally reflected in the look of space ships in SF films: all jagged streamlines layered into an aggressive snarl.

Apart from that, the tiny handful of big British yards that survive mainly to build the Royal Navy's savagely diminished fleet prompts speculation about the future of all three of the country's equally shrunken armed services, and with it that of the defence industry itself. Despite rare and notorious instances of exotic poisons such as polonium and Novichok nerve toxins being used to settle old scores with individuals, the Cold War is long since over and the topic of Britain's defence is constantly debated against a background of wrung-out budgets, diminished ability (or even need) to project power abroad, and its increasingly disputed role in the UK's economy. Much hinges on the eternal struggle between anxious military forecasts for the next thirty years and the current chancellor's panic over next year's budget.

Yet Britain's defence industry remains one of the very few of our original industries that is left still generating export revenue in quantities serious enough for it to get real government backing. To that extent it is something of an anomaly, and the historical reasons for its survival are worth looking at, especially because, like any other industry, it has been plagued from time to time by strikes, economic downturns, bad management and embarrassing scandals.

In a previous book I attempted to give an overview of the fate of Britain's once-dominant aircraft industry.* The story has much in common with that of our other vanished enterprises. With the defeat of Germany in 1945, Britain briefly became the world leader in jet aircraft technology and production. At that point, had the politicians and service chiefs been more realistic and thinking straight, they ought quickly to have slimmed down what was not only Britain's biggest industry, but one still geared to wartime mass production. We could then have concentrated on our global advantage in the new turbojet technology. Above all, we ought to have left the whole sector of long-haul civil aircraft to the Americans, who had a huge advantage over us in this field, mainly for reasons of their own geography as well as our enforced wartime abandonment of civil designs.

* *Empire of the Clouds* (Faber, 2010).

Such a complete rethinking of our priorities and the industry's consequent reorganisation would admittedly have been a very tall order. Apart from anything else we lacked France's ironic advantage of needing to rebuild an entire aviation industry from scratch. What greatly aided the French endeavour was not just concerted government planning and investment but strength in at least two academic disciplines in which Britain has always been weak: strategic analysis and long-term technology forecasting. This, together with the French government's firm restructuring and financial backing of its aero industry, plus its invaluable ability to rely on a technologically literate civil service, explains why today France can independently make and sell abroad its fourth-generation Rafale fighter while Britain can no longer independently design and build any aircraft much larger than a glider and can only be a partner in the international consortium that designed and makes the Eurofighter Typhoon.

Back in 1945 our aero industry, like the car industry, was hydra-headed and comprised some twenty independent – mainly privately owned – companies each heading in the direction it thought best while competing with most of the others. Because of the size and importance of the RAF the ambition was to land a lucrative contract with the Ministry of Aircraft Production. There was no real attempt at national coordination and neither was there a serious effort to work out the longer-term implications of the new post-war world order in 1945. This was promptly revealed by Whitehall's confident prediction that, thanks to our much-touted first-generation jet fighters, the Gloster Meteor and de Havilland Vampire, no new fighter aircraft would be needed for either the RAF or the Royal Navy until 1957. Within two years the drawing of the Iron Curtain across Europe and the effective outbreak of the Cold War showed the magnitude of this miscalculation, which seems to have been based solely on a victor's hubris and pure wishful thinking. Many aero companies spotted the error and went ahead anyway with a mass of new designs, some of which were highly inventive. The overall result was a grossly inefficient duplication of effort and the waste of vast sums of money and talent, out of which only a bare handful of potentially first-class aircraft emerged (like the Hawker Hunter) and many (such as Gloster's E.1/44, nicknamed 'the Gormless' by its test pilot, Bill Waterton) that ought never to have left the drawing board.

Many of the major UK airframe and aero-engine companies like Vickers, Bristol and Rolls-Royce also produced a wide range of military equipment that went well beyond aviation. Their various divisions and plants were also supplying the army and the navy with tanks and scout cars, ships, weaponry of all sorts including gun-sights, artillery and missiles, and also communications and radar equipment: in short, the whole gamut of military hardware. Once the Cold War threat had become obvious even to Whitehall such companies competed to meet the various services' urgent requirements as put out to tender by the new Ministry of Defence.

There is probably no manufacturing sector that so readily engages pungent public opinion as the defence industry, whether it is making weapons for our own defence or for sales abroad to improve our balance of payments. We shall start with the home market, where the fundamental object of defence procurement is to furnish Britain's armed forces with the best equipment available for a given budget and within a certain time in order to defend the realm for the foreseeable future. That is how the taxpayer understands it. Since the taxpayer foots the bill it is not surprising that stories of grotesque delays, huge cost overruns, equipment failures and shady deals involving international corruption have increasingly merited headline treatment.

This is, of course, a familiar story the world over. The more scary they can claim the external threat to be, the more service chiefs everywhere tend to treat public funds as a bottomless bran tub of goodies. Whether these scandals really have become more frequent in Britain recently is a moot point; but there is little doubt that in today's economic and political climate such stories are likely to be covered more keenly than ever by the media. However, not being privy to the arcane world of procurement, most people (and indeed most journalists) have little understanding of the often Byzantine political and technical complexities that lie behind it, over and above the ordinary incompetence, stupidity and miscalculation common to warring departments in bureaucracies the world over.

Major scandals that hit the headlines have the cumulative effect of eroding public trust in Whitehall's competence while encouraging scepticism about the ability of the armed forces to defend the country, to say nothing of muddying the reputation of the defence companies on which we rely. I can still recall a scandal from 1964: that of Ferranti for their part in supplying the radar and guidance systems for the Bristol Bloodhound surface-to-air missile, as revealed in the official report on the affair by Sir John Lang. The Bloodhound was an excellent missile of considerable technical sophistication. It sold overseas as well as providing defence with sixteen RAF squadrons at our V-bomber and fighter bases until the collapse of the Soviet Union in 1991. However, shameless overpricing by the company led to its chairman, Sebastian de Ferranti, reluctantly agreeing to pay back £4¼ million – provided he was first given a guarantee that there would be no future discrimination against his company (the *nerve* of the man!). This deal was brilliantly attacked by Harold Wilson in the House of Commons when he revealed that Ferranti had actually made a profit of £5,772,964 – or 82 per cent – on its declared costs: a vast sum in 1964 (upwards of £100 million at today's value).[59]

The contract had been on a cost-plus basis, i.e. ascertained costs plus a percentage profit: a common type of contract but one with an inherent tendency towards overspend since it relies on the company's own word as to how much it has spent. In the nervous climate of the Cold War, public opinion was severely critical of the then Minister of Aviation, Julian Amery, as well as of the RAF and Ministry of Defence for not keeping better tabs on their contracts, given that the nation's security was at stake. Sebastian de Ferranti's response to Wilson's attack was an equally spirited tirade against 'rotten politicians', protesting in the aggrieved tones of an honest man deeply wronged that '[I]f you accept a risk contract and if you deliver the equipment on time, and export it all over the world against international competition, you will be knocked on the head for doing so.'[60] At the time, most people seemed to agree that while many politicians were indeed rotten, in this particular case MPs had done the right thing by exposing the equal rottenness of arms manufacturers who hoped to conceal an 82 per cent profit from the taxpayer. (Ten years later in September 1974 Ferranti, thanks to ongoing mismanagement, would have to be rescued financially – ironically, by Harold Wilson's new National Enterprise Board, who removed both Ferranti brothers, Sebastian and Basil, from their executive roles. Even the further expenditure of a good deal of public money did not prevent the company going into receivership in 1993.)

To avoid a repetition of this sort of gross profiteering, government and industry spent the next four years devising an agreed method of pricing non-competitive government contracts to give the contractor a reasonable (or 'fair') rate of return. This was established in 1968 as The Profit Formula for Non-Competitive Government Contracts, and is still in use. The problem, of course, is that there *is* no way of guaranteeing a fair price for a project that will probably take years to complete and may entail work beyond the edge of what is technologically feasible at the time the contract is signed. Yet if cost-plus contracts can easily lead to overspending, so too can fixed-price development programmes, and for much the same reason: it is extremely difficult to negotiate a fair price for unforeseeable problems and consequent delays in delivery. Ongoing experience with the Lockheed Martin F-35 fighter in all its variants demonstrates how relevant this is where a new advanced aircraft is concerned. This still incomplete programme has already become notorious as the single most expensive military weapons system in all history.

More than forty years after the Ferranti affair the axing in 2010 of BAE Systems' Nimrod MRA4 maritime patrol and attack aircraft aroused even greater uproar in Britain. It was bad enough when it was belatedly revealed that the project was some £790 million over-budget and more than nine years late. It was worse when BBC photographers in a helicopter managed to obtain pictures of brand-new aircraft being chainsawed into scrap at Woodford behind hastily rigged canvas screens, like fallen horses being put down on a racecourse. Public scepticism was still further intensified when the full import of that year's Strategic Defence and Security Review sank in: that Britain, an island nation, was now left without any maritime patrol aircraft for the foreseeable future since no replacement had yet been ordered. Were the people in whose hands the defence of these islands rested even vaguely capable of doing what they were paid for? asked various newspaper correspondents. Come to that, what sort of official accounting could possibly have permitted that degree of budget overrun and almost a decade in time slippage?

This last is a good question since Ministry of Defence contracts have long contained a fierce 'time clause' (technically, Standard Condition SC14) stating that if the contractual deadline is not met, the MoD is entitled to terminate the contract without compensation, recover payments already made, buy elsewhere and charge the defaulter any costs incurred. Yet despite this clause's fully legal status the MoD has seldom invoked it. Why? The Challenger II tank finally entered service in the British Army in the summer of 1998, two and a half years later than the deadline stipulated in the contract. Parliament was told that this delay had cost the MoD £37 million but that under a provision called 'Liquidated Damages' Vickers were penalised a maximum of £3 million. Taxpayers were obliged to forfeit the remaining £34 million they were legally owed.

Mere pocket money, as it turned out. By 2007 the first of BAE Systems' 'Astute' class submarines was already five years late and £1.5 *billion* over-budget. Never mind – it's only the public's money. Similarly, companies that supply kit that fails when in service ('Astute' submarines, Type 45 frigates, the army's initially appalling SA80 rifle and Bowman communications system, Short's Tucano T.1 trainer aircraft) are theoretically liable for their product's performance, which must be 'fit for purpose' under the terms of the Sale of Goods Act (1979) for up to six years after delivery, and under the Latent Damage Act (1986) for up to fifteen years after the cause of the failure is identified.

So: does the MoD consistently follow up such legally sanctioned avenues for clawing back some of the taxpayers' money? Will it be dunning BAE Systems for the full cost of maintaining ships it built at public expense but that don't work properly?[61] And why should an averagely cynical member of the public scoff at the very suggestion? One answer is that it has long looked as though Britain's defence budget exists far more as a political expedient to prop up British industry and save jobs than to defend Britain, a state of affairs that successive scandals seem only to confirm. It is indeed sobering when a former MoD Director of Contracts could write in 2000:

> It is important that the Public Accounts Committee should be able to judge to what extent MoD officials can be held to blame for the disastrous commercial and military consequences of the secret political defence procurement agenda to support British industry pursued by successive British governments.[62]

This quasi-official claim that a clandestine policy exists that rates defending the nation as less important than defending its industry is hardly reassuring, hinting as it does at the supremacy of pork barrel politics over national security. Still, that was in 2000. In 2014 the Defence Reform Act came into force and with it the new independent SSRO (Single Source Regulations Office). The job of this office is to monitor the amount of profit the MoD awards for contracts undertaken by a company at its own risk. However, an authoritative independent source has described the SSRO as reporting that 'new regulations have failed to curtail incidents of overcharging' and 'UK defence companies that continue to charge the MoD unnecessarily for goods or services will be "named and shamed" in a January report' (i.e. the Regulations Office's compliance report of January 2017).[63] No such naming and shaming took place then, although SSRO officials told Shephard Media that 'contractors' conformity to the regulations had been "poor" and the attitude of many – both within defence companies and the MoD itself – was that such previously-unregulated overcharging was simply a means of doing business'. This admission by both the defence industry and the ministry that overcharging was the accepted norm was bad enough; but claiming it was unregulated was outrageous. It was simply that the regulations had seldom been applied, and virtually never in their full force. In May 2016 the SSRO did recover £1.3 million from Rolls-Royce over marketing costs and an 'overstatement of the risk of future cost variation' as part of a deal to support the RAF's Hawk jet trainers.

The cosy relationship enjoyed by government and industry in defence matters extends to the senior ranks of the services as well, as a popular British journal has recently made plain:

For decades MoD officials and top brass who had influence over contracts (that were perpetually late and over-budget) found their commercial acumen was valued by the big companies that had benefited from those contracts.[64]

It may be a sign of the times that it no longer seems noteworthy to either the services or Westminster when retiring senior officers doff their uniforms, don suits and take a well-salaried seat in the boardroom of the very company they were lately negotiating with; but to the general public it looks bad, just as it does when ex-prime ministers parlay connections and expertise made in office into great fortunes immediately on stepping down. High-ranking officers' intimate knowledge of their service's requirements may well be invaluable to industry, but many feel such a move to be improper. After all, they were trained, have been paid and will be well-pensioned entirely from the public purse; and there is something graceless about converting that privilege into private loot, quite apart from the security aspects and clashes of interest.

One of the inherent problems in procuring any major new piece of kit is that so many opinions need to be sought, but with no guarantee these are wise or even well-informed. Mention of the RAF's Hawk trainers provides a case in point. By the late 1960s the RAF urgently needed a new jet trainer to replace the Folland Gnat T.1, which was inadequate to prepare pilots for fourth-generation jet fighters. The appropriate 'desk' or team in the Operational Requirement department had drawn up the specifications for an aircraft that in 1968 became the Hawk. While it was on the drawing board an absurd debate broke out between Hawker Siddeley's design team at Kingston and RAF staff officers in MoD over whether an Angle of Attack gauge should be included among the Hawk's instruments: absurd because by then all front line fighters had the gauges as standard. An AOA gauge tells pilots exactly when their airspeed falls below stalling point, regardless of the aircraft's weight or attitude in the air. In flying circles there's an old adage that 'airspeed equals life': that is, if you let your speed drop too far – typically when approaching for landing – and you stall, the chances are pretty good that you will die. In the days of the early jets it was soon discovered that swept-winged aircraft could be particularly susceptible to low speed stalls (and some even at high speed), so by the late 1960s AOA gauges in the cockpits of fast jets were thought of as indispensable rather than merely desirable extras.

Given that Gnats had been used since 1965 to train pilots to graduate to the much trickier Harrier Jump Jet, and given that AOA gauges were absolutely essential for the Harrier, let alone for any future fast jets, it was beyond question that the new Hawk trainers should have them as standard equipment. Indeed, by then it was plain that *every* aircraft – military, commercial or private – ought to have one. Hawker Siddeley certainly fitted one to their first Hawk for flight testing.

However, it quickly became clear this view was not widely shared in RAF procurement circles, most of whose older pilots had probably never used an AOA gauge and were evidently sceptical of these newfangled gadgets. They themselves had trained quite happily on propeller-driven Chipmunks and Harvards and even straight-winged Jet Provosts without ever understanding academic and arcane stuff about the importance of their angle of attack. Traditional basic instruments plus the seat of their pants had told them everything they thought they needed to know about flying; so though they were drawing up the specifications for an aircraft capable of near Mach 1 performance the RAF's Operational Requirement department duly omitted the Hawk's AOA gauge.

Meanwhile, at Hawker's Kingston factory the Hawk's design team were so insistent their new trainer needed one they actually offered to install AOA gauges as a matter of course and swallow the extra cost: an act of generosity by a supplier practically unheard of in the annals of procurement. All three of the Hawk project's test pilots – Andy Jones, Jim Hawkins and Hawker's Chief Test Pilot at their Dunsfold airfield, the late Duncan Simpson – insisted the instrument be fitted. Nevertheless, the RAF staff officers in MoD rejected this offer on the grounds that it would incur a financial penalty. When challenged to explain how a free offer might cost the RAF money, the response came that because the installation included two cockpit gauges, their associated wiring and also the sensor vane on the aircraft, the kit would impose a servicing penalty on the RAF throughout the life of the aircraft. Chris Roberts, who did the vast majority of the Hawk 200's development work and would himself become Chief Test Pilot at Dunsfold, remarked much later that this was a bit like telling BMW not to bother putting anti-lock brakes on your new car because you couldn't see the point of them and were worried you would have to pay for the spares when they went wrong or wore out. In his professional view the decision to skimp on AOA gauges disadvantaged almost forty years of the RAF's fast jet pilot training until the introduction in 2009 of the new Hawk T.2, which has the gauges as standard.

> All those pilots that have been passed onto fighter OCUs [operational conversion units] without any AOA experience have had to learn it there – on an aircraft that costs many times more per flying hour than a trainer. I instructed on the Harrier OCU and teaching the use of AOA was a waste of expensive flight time; yet until the pilots got a grip of AOA control we couldn't send them solo. The MoD just could not see that converting pilots to AOA management at flying school was going to save buckets of money more than the cost of maintaining a cheap system.[65]

Not all manufacturers are as scrupulous as Hawker Siddeley were in this instance back in the early 1970s. The late John Farley (who in 1978 succeeded Duncan Simpson as Chief Test Pilot at what by now was BAe) observed that the writers of specifications for a new aircraft or piece of military kit often have neither the requisite engineering education nor the experience.

> The junior and middle-ranking officers told to put a specification together are often only in the job for a year or two before being posted on in the normal way of the military. So how can they learn the job? ... The manufacturer can easily run rings round such service officers. This can result in some manufacturers who operate a bad culture being able to manipulate the spec. to get

work or research funding that may well not be in the interests of the service. ... Things may have improved a bit since the 70s and 80s regarding spec. writing but certainly not with inter-service rivalry. In my opinion the way the three services act in their own interests to increase their share of the defence budget rather than consider what is best for the UK as a whole is disgraceful. It results in an enormous waste of intellectual horsepower and time in the MoD.[66]

Unfortunately, there is nothing new about such rivalry. It certainly pre-dates the creation of the RAF, going back more than a century to the outbreak of the First World War when the army and the Admiralty competed with each other for Treasury funding which could result in the Royal Flying Corps (which was part of the army) and the Royal Naval Air Service having to compete for the best aircraft. When Sopwiths came up with the world's first and highly effective triplane fighter, their entire output had already been contracted by the RNAS. Consequently, no RFC pilot ever flew one in combat, much to the army's chagrin. Such rivalries are not peculiar to Britain, of course, and USAF/USN/Army squabbles have occasionally become incandescent. Not even a state of war can guarantee the cessation of such inter-service hostilities. What is strange is that after a hundred years no agreed way has yet been found of laying these issues entirely to rest. In the UK the hope is that for increasingly desperate economic as well as strategic reasons the gradual amalgamation of capabilities under the Joint Forces Command, together with NATO forces' collaborative programmes and the doctrine of 'interoperability', will steadily erode such ancient demarcation disputes while offering economic benefits.

As Britain's industrial capabilities have shrunk there has been an increasing tendency to shop outside for its military kit. Buying in equipment from abroad has its own hazards and is bound to entail some loss of sovereignty, as in the contentious case of Britain's four Trident-carrying nuclear submarines that cannot launch one of their (American) missiles without US permission and codes. So much for the independence of our deterrent. The late Admiral Sir Raymond Lygo gave another example of this, saying that the problem with buying a foreign-built missile or system is that you never quite know if it's going to work or is exactly the same as the one equipping the seller's own armed forces. This is important because the seller may vary its guidance or fusing system so as to make it susceptible to jamming at certain wavelengths. It is difficult to discover this when you buy a weapon unless you open it up, which is probably forbidden under the seller's industrial property rights or else the unit is security locked and the codes by which it functions cannot be accessed. This was a problem in the Falklands campaign where the Royal Navy had fifteen surface-combat ships armed with Exocets but lacked a home-grown missile capable of shooting down the Argentinian Exocets that were doing such damage.[67]

Buying in its aircraft is, of course, now the norm for the UK. Britain's ability to design, build and produce its own military or civil aircraft in production runs that are also big enough for export and to turn a profit (always our indigenous aviation industry's weakness) has long since collapsed. This means we have to resort to buying off-the-shelf – as in the case of the nine P-8A Poseidon maritime patrol aircraft belatedly ordered from the United States in 2015 to replace those sawn-up Nimrods – or else to collaborative ventures typically involving several European consortia as partners, as with the Airbus A-400M transport (an aircraft that itself went billions over-budget and was years late). That Boeing was able to base the Poseidon on the airframe of its 737-800 airliner neatly illustrates the enormous advantage the US aviation industry enjoys in having a wide range of existing aircraft that can be repurposed without the need to design something from scratch and tool up completely new production lines. Only very occasionally did Britain manage to pull this trick off, with the Avro Shackleton maritime patrol aircraft containing the ghost of the wartime Lancaster bomber until its retirement in 1991, and the late Nimrod embodying the last vestiges of de Havilland's Comet airliner.

One problem that afflicts virtually all modern military kit is that its cost has risen hugely to reflect an equally rapid growth in technological sophistication and complexity. For obvious reasons the instinct of customers everywhere is to want a piece of kit that is as flexible as possible. This trend is especially evident in aviation, where new combat aircraft are expected to be 'platforms' for a variety of potential roles, munitions and missiles, with the latter able to hit targets far beyond a pilot's line of sight over the Earth's curvature. They are also expected to have 'suites' of electronic countermeasures against enemy radar as well as intelligence-gathering or monitoring abilities. Such things demand enormous onboard computing power with a host of back-up systems. In addition, the aircraft may well be expected to operate from impromptu airfields and even from ships, which requires short-take-off and -landing ability.

The trouble with such multi-role kit is that in trying to be all things to all men it runs the risk of not doing any one thing outstandingly well. Sheer complexity also greatly increases the likelihood of encountering unforeseen technical problems in development and manufacture, with inevitable cost and time overruns and the probability of unfavourable press stories and official investigations. And once the kit is deployed, the sheer fact of there being so much more to go wrong also makes it likely that the equipment will spend much of its time out of commission, being repaired. Modern air forces have long become accustomed to a high proportion of their aircraft being 'hangar queens', spending far more time being repaired than airworthy. Yet there is a further aspect that is proving just as problematic, and that is the changing nature of warfare.

The comparative simplicity of the Cold War, when one side competed with the other for advances in rapidly developing technologies such as jet aircraft, radar and missiles, made the procurement of military hardware almost straightforward. Then, it was largely a matter of leapfrogging the opposition, which was either known or realistically guessed to be on much the same course. Today's scene is infinitely more problematic, with asymmetric warfare much more common and with the ascendancy of nations such as China and India to the status of world military powers throwing even the US and Russia off-balance as the erstwhile lone superpowers. It was always clear that 'procurement' could never be restricted just to the bureaucratic framework within which new matériel for the armed forces is ordered, built and delivered. It also had to contain a large measure of futurology: an attempt to predict how warfare itself might evolve and, particularly in Britain's case, the country's foreseeable role in world affairs and its probable budgetary constraints.

In the wake of recent political developments that role seems ever more in doubt, with the budgetary constraints still tighter – and all the more so following the decision to replace the navy's Trident submarines. The Lockheed Martin F-35 Lightning II aircraft is also a good example of how the wisdom of an Operational Requirement, when drawn up, can come to seem more debatable by the time – maybe even twenty years later – that a modern combat aircraft finally trickles into squadron service. Because of their complexities in so many different fields, aircraft generally take longer than other forms of weaponry to develop and induce to function to their required specification. One obvious consequence of this, apart from the virtual impossibility of completing a contract within budget, is that when eventually a new aircraft or other complex piece of kit enters service it is likely to be well on the way towards obsolescence. Indeed, more recent development of asymmetric, unconventional and UAV (drone) warfare, not to mention a new generation of radar and missiles, must throw into question the very role of enormously expensive piloted combat aircraft. The RAF's new Lockheed F-35B's much-touted reconnaissance fit may well have a momentary advantage over that of any known drone or even satellite, but recent rumours suggest there will soon be Russian and Chinese electronic countermeasure systems able to mislead or neutralise it. And, true to the drawbacks of buying foreign mentioned earlier, the RAF will not be able to modify any of their new jets' electronics.

Yet the whole issue of defence spending is affected by more than mere budgetary constraints. It does not help that the current public mood in Europe – and even in President Trump's United States – is one of increasing scepticism about military competence in general. Confidence that there could ever be simplistic military solutions to unreadably complex politico-cultural and sectarian confrontations overseas has been still further eroded by their frequent association with procurement scandals of one sort or another, often involving blue-chip companies. In 2006 Britain's Serious Fraud Office suddenly dropped an investigation into allegations that BAE Systems had maintained a slush fund that successfully influenced members of the Saudi royal family to change their minds about buying weapons from France. Four years later BAE Systems was fined

$400 million by the US Department of Justice in connection with the ongoing and notorious Al Yamamah deal with Saudi Arabia that originally dated from the mid-1980s. Nothing so decisive was achieved in the UK, where the National Audit Office's 1992 report into the deal was suppressed and remains so: the only such report not to be released. Then, in 2017, Rolls-Royce agreed to pay the enormous sum of £671 million to avoid prosecution by the Serious Fraud Office, the US Department of Justice and the Brazilian authorities for corrupt practices over a twenty-four-year period from 1989. This version of British justice is evidently permitted an aerospace company, when it is doubtful if any ordinary citizen could buy his or her way out of being prosecuted for fraud.

A collective media sigh goes up whenever such cases hit the headlines. Unfortunately, the moral high ground from which the sigh issues is also a bottomless bog of hypocrisy. As ever, the British economy desperately needs exports, and making the tools of war has long been one of the country's few remaining major industrial sectors, aerospace alone currently earning up to £32 billion a year (although not all of that is armaments).[68] Indeed, one could argue that it is the arms industry perhaps more than any other that best preserves the inventive standards and traditions of British engineering, research and technical expertise (the 'cutting edge', in company-speak). This, for example, remains a cogent argument for keeping Britain's three remaining naval shipyards in business. If they were to be closed down in a fit of parsimony or moral disgust, not only a source of the nation's income but a whole body of engineering skills and know-how would disappear, just as it already has in the case of our ability to build a nuclear power station or an aircraft, or even to electrify a railway line efficiently. As the bitter experience of the 1980s has made plain, it is all too easy to abolish industries but nearly impossible to revive them after second thoughts. It is always too late. Machine tools have been sold or scrapped, workshops broken up, factories bulldozed for 'business parks', company records casually dumped in skips and the skilled teams with priceless knowledge have retired or been snapped up by foreign companies.

As our foreign arms deals become known to the public, so follow the inevitable public expressions of moral disgust. After all, the world's five largest arms exporters – US, Russia, China, France, UK – are also the five permanent members of the UN Security Council with its supposed primary agenda of maintaining world peace, so a certain irony is bound to pervade the issue. Yet if now we complain about the profits Britain makes from being a merchant of death, we surely have only ourselves to blame for allowing such exports to become so crucial to our economic survival. Britain has been in the forefront of this trade for centuries. Indeed, other than the remains of shipbuilding and fishery, making weapons and military kit is arguably our oldest remaining industry. In 2016 the annual report of the UK's DSO (Defence and Security Organisation) shows £6 billion worth of arms sales for that year: some 9 per cent of the global market. Viewed over the previous ten years,

Britain emerges as the world's second-largest arms dealer after the United States. As this has become an economic sector we dare not do without, we ought surely to drop the pretence of being shocked when recently a collection of memos released by the National Archives showed that Margaret Thatcher's minister for defence procurement, Alan Clark, was ecstatic when Saddam Hussein invaded Kuwait in 1990. On 19 August he wrote her a memo marked Secret in which he said, 'Whatever deployment policies we adopt I must emphasise that this is an unparalleled opportunity for DESO [the Defence Export Services Organisation: an earlier version of today's DSO]; a vast demonstration range with live ammunition and "real" trials.' Such it proved; and it did indeed lead to closer UK defence ties throughout the Gulf States, a lucrative relationship that continues to this day.

Even as Clark was writing his memo, the Matrix Churchill affair was brewing. Matrix Churchill was a Coventry machine tool company that, with the full knowledge of British intelligence and selected ministers in Thatcher's government including Alan Clark, had illegally supplied Saddam Hussein with the equipment to make such things as artillery shells. When in the early 1990s the story broke, Matrix Churchill's four directors were put on trial. It soon became apparent that Clark's Ministry of Defence had itself been advising the company on how to disguise their application for export licences. Clark famously admitted under oath that he had been 'economical with the *actualité*' and the case collapsed. In 1996, in the aftermath of the damning Scott Inquiry into the affair, Clark retrospectively glossed this by saying truthfully, 'I was not responsible for morality – that was for others.'

A good deal of public posturing went on, especially on the left. It was as though what had happened was somehow unprecedented, even though any averagely cynical citizen probably assumes this sort of thing is commonplace. The Matrix Churchill affair may have added a little impetus to the wave that carried the first Tony Blair government into office in 1997. Before that, and doubtless in order to offset the cynicism, Robin Cook as shadow foreign secretary wept a judicious crocodile tear or two to remind the British public of why it was all so awful.

> It matters because we armed Saddam Hussein in private, and the machine tools we supplied helped provide some of the shells that were fired at British troops. It matters also because Parliament was deceived over this, and you can't deceive Parliament without corrupting the democratic processes and the democratic rights of the British people. And thirdly, it matters also because the businessmen who sold these machine tools were put on trial by a government which has approved the export of those machine tools, and that of course corrupts the justice system on which we all depend.[69]

In short, it is always appropriate to affect moral distaste whenever we discover afresh that the weapons trade commonly involves connivance, bribes and kickbacks – in short, corruption

– as well as death. In July 2017 the High Court naturally decided that the UK had acted lawfully in granting export licences to UK firms selling arms to Saudi Arabia even though the Saudi bombing campaign in Yemen probably breached international humanitarian law. What else could the court have done? There *is* no way of fighting a 'humanitarian' war, least of all when battle-fields occupy cities: the very concept is nonsensical. A govern-ment may cover itself legally by insisting on as many safeguards and end-use certificates as it likes when selling bombs or rifles to an overseas customer, but it perfectly well knows there are myriad ways of circumventing such official precautions and it can never guarantee how the weapons will be used. Besides, of what use are non-nuclear bombs and guns unless dropped and shot? No doubt the many well-meaning supporters of the Campaign Against the Arms Trade also rightly complain about ruthless cutbacks in the NHS and Britain's public services; but they must realise the two stances are not at the moment compatible.

This issue has always been contentious and riddled with hackneyed irony as, for example, when British pilots conduct air strikes in the morning and in the afternoon British volunteers with Médecins Sans Frontières help patch up the victims. When as secretary of defence in 1966 Denis Healey announced the setting up of the DESO's forerunner, the Defence Equipment (Overseas Sales) organisation, he said:

While the Government attaches the highest importance to making progress in the field of arms control and disarmament, we must also take what practical steps we can to ensure that this country does not fail to secure its rightful share of this valuable commercial market.[70]

What 'rightful' means in this context is not entirely clear. However, when nearly thirty-six years later, in 1994, John Pilger asked Healey what he felt about this earlier statement, Healey admitted:

I don't feel all that happy about it. But remember that this was at the time when the Cold War was really at its height. There was an enormous amount of arms sales by the Soviet Union all over the world in the hope mainly of getting political advantage. But for me the main thing was to reduce the unit cost of British weapons by selling some of them abroad.

Such sales, being British rather than Soviet, were evidently not for 'political advantage'. Still, the Cold War era when Ministry of Defence deals with private companies could be hidden behind a smokescreen calling it 'restricted information on the grounds of national security' ought to be long gone. Procurement and sales are simply a vital part of the economy that, like any other, demands rational decision-making combined with as much transparency as possible. In *Yes, Prime Minister* Sir Humphrey Appleby, effectively speaking for the entire civil service, cheerfully admitted, 'The purpose of our defence policy is to make people *believe* Britain is defended.' This remains true both for potential enemies and for Britons. As Britain's military might has steadily dwindled, so governments and defence spokesmen have increasingly relied on trumpeting the military's counterpart to the civilian myth that Britain is open for business: the equally risible claim that Britain 'punches above its weight'. This is largely dependent on a historical status dating back seventy years: that we are a nuclear nation and have a permanent seat on the UN's Security Council. Both these things are usually abbreviated as our having 'Top Table' status – an odious phrase originating in public school and Oxbridge college dining halls. The plain fact is that the United Kingdom is well on the way to being militarily, as well as politically, irrelevant. Awful irony also lies in store for anyone old enough to remember those post-war schoolboy jokes about Italian tanks with one forward gear and thirty-three reverse, or the Bolivian navy with fifty-four admirals and a couple of balsa rafts on Lake Titicaca. Currently, Britain's Royal Navy can with difficulty field some nineteen major surface ships (destroyers and frigates) and has thirty-three admirals each costing some £110,000 per annum.[71] Even if one adds in ten nuclear-powered submarines, the admirals still outnumber the ships.

When enough Britons stop believing their country is defended, their scepticism is likely to embrace the rest of our outmoded system of government. Post-Chilcot and post-Brexit Britain carries little credible global clout in any sector, fatally handicapped as it is by well-publicised military, financial and political failures. To these can be added social failure in the shape of a disgruntled majority of citizens beset by falling incomes and living standards. Britons seem unlikely in the future to want to give priority to Great Power pretensions the country can no longer afford in preference to decent housing and the medication and education of their children – unless, of course, the press barons conduct a concerted campaign to increase national panic over some dastardly foreign threat.

Worse still for Britain's economic and military future, there is reason to think that the kind of warfare we seem to expect – and for which we so expensively continue to buy new old-fashioned hardware (jet fighters, aircraft carriers, submarines and the rest) – is already outmoded. As Tim Robinson, editor of the Royal Aeronautical Society's magazine *Aerospace* observed, 'Today, any self-respecting teenager would consider a two-year-old mobile phone an antique; yet the West's most modern jet fighter, the [Lockheed] F-35, first flew a full 17 years ago.'[72] (And it is still not yet in RAF and RN squadron service, he might have added at the time.) In the first place, asymmetric warfare in which costly matériel is expended against cheap targets quickly becomes prohibitively expensive for the results gained. The US-led coalition fighting in Syria and Iraq has regularly fired £54,000 missiles from aircraft costing £30,000 per flying hour in order to destroy a single battered Toyota pick-up belonging to ISIS. This scarcely represents half a century's advance in tactics over the asymmetry of the war in Vietnam, when the United States kept up a massively expensive campaign of bombing North Vietnam, Operation Rolling Thunder, that lasted three years and eight months and devastated vast tracts of countryside without leading to victory or even preventing the Viet Cong's flow of bicycle-borne supplies down the Ho Chi Minh Trail. In both cases the fallacy lies in the primitive idea that killing the adherents of a belief will prevent it from spreading, and that the highest-tech equipment comes with built-in magical properties that can achieve this.

In the second place, in July 2017 London's Royal United Services Institute (RUSI), a strategic think-tank with international backing and reputation, recommended that the British government should shift its focus away from attack systems and instead concentrate on research, innovation and 'adaptive technologies' (what US defence mavens now refer to as the Third Offset) where the high-tech frontier is now firmly in commercial rather than defence hands. RUSI's conclusions were that future wars are far less likely to require set-piece engagements of the old kind than they are to involve cyber warfare and attacks against communications and navigation systems. Why bother to fire expensive missiles even at an aircraft carrier like the new HMS *Queen Elizabeth* when for a fraction of the price you can take aim at a country's crucial IT infrastructure and its economy and cause paralysing damage? Even an enemy on a shoestring budget could in theory plunge an opponent into a depth of social chaos undreamed of by any conventional means short of all-out nuclear attack. Maybe the idea that software is the new hardware will put the arms industry out of business more effectively than any

Campaign Against the Arms Trade ever could. If so, campaigners might rejoice; but it is a grim prospect for the British Exchequer.

An earlier version of this chapter appeared in the RAF Historical Society's *Journal*, 'Cold War Air Systems Procurement' (2017).

7.
Motorbikes

'Drunk on the wind in my mouth,/
Wringing the handlebar for speed,/
Wild to be wreckage forever.'

—JAMES DICKEY, 'Cherrylog Road'

'Rollie' Free, aerodynamically stripped, breaks the US motorcycle speed record in 1948 at 150.313 mph. The 'HRD' logo is clearly visible on the tank of his Vincent Black Lightning.

The story of the motorbike industry's post-war decline and fall is perhaps as representative a British saga as any. Being less sprawling than the car industry, whose accretion of smaller companies making not just auto-mobile parts but unrelated things like refrigerators eventually rendered it baggy and even incoherent, the motorbike industry's component bones formed a much smaller skeleton and are consequently easier to exhume and identify. As in the case of cars and boats, it is pleasing to be able to point today to its small-scale reincarnation in the form of some high-quality new models, albeit for a more restricted and better defined market. Unlike other industries (power generation, civil aircraft, bicycles) that were allowed to collapse with scarcely a whimper of public regret, the demise of the old motorbike industry in 1983 did provoke some national breast-beating. However, most of the limited serious debate about the causes was side-tracked into wrangling about union activity even though that was not a primary factor in the demise until comparatively late, if then.

A peculiarity of motorcycles is – as the cliché has it – that they tend to be bought rather than sold. This was undoubtedly true between, say, 1920 and 1970, with the majority of machines being bought by younger men who generally understood them, who kept up with fashion as much by word of mouth as via advertising, and who certainly knew what they wanted. With that sort of market it is possible to see how an industry might need to rationalise and concentrate itself, but not how it could fail completely. And yet fail it did.

At that time the relationship between young man and machine was at least as old as the century. From pre-First World War days there was often a considerable overlap between the various kinds of machinery to which mechanically minded youngsters might be attracted. Thus the young Geoffrey de Havilland used to ride his home-built motorbike to the field where he taught himself to fly the aircraft he had himself designed. This was all part of a new technological and industrial trend that was to change the world as the internal combustion engine relegated steam power to history. As soon as the basic design of early petrol engines became established at the end of the nineteenth century there was no lack of inventive youngsters to see their possibilities. Compared to cumbersome steam engines the new motors were small, self-contained, and had a terrific power-to-weight ratio. Young men were soon fitting them into contraptions of their own making, principally to see how fast they could go, whether on land or in the air. A home-designed and -built engine took the Wright Brothers' Flyer into the air for the first time in 1903. By the First World War several pilots were skilled enough mechanics to modify their own aircraft's engine in order to improve its performance. A young Royal Flying Corps pilot, H. R. Davies, had been an apprentice with the AJS motorcycle company before the war. He was twice shot down and while interned in Germany decided to make his own motorbikes after the war. This he did, starting HRD Motors Ltd in 1924. More of him later.

Even today this impulse towards 'home-grown' mechanical enterprise is by no means wholly extinct. At its lowest, garden-shed, level it typically involves teenagers bolting scrap motors to almost anything with wheels including mobility scooters, prams and skateboards. The American humourist Dave Barry once went for a spin on a lawn mower to which its owner had fitted a turbojet helicopter engine. Probably the apogee (in every sense) of weekend tinkering was posthumously established in 2017 by that year's winner of the Darwin Awards, a jocular prize given to an individual who has managed to select him- or herself out of the human gene pool, usually by heroic stupidity. This particular individual was an American who got hold of a JATO (jet-assisted take-off) rocket designed to enable heavily laden transport aircraft to get airborne from short runways. He bolted this to his Chevrolet Impala and fired it up on a desert road with a long straight that ended in a slight rising bend past a cliff face. The Arizona police later deduced that 'the automobile remained on the straight highway for about 2.5 miles (15–20 seconds) before becoming airborne for an additional 1.4 miles and impacting a cliff face at a height of 125 feet leaving a blackened crater 3 feet deep in the rock. Most of the driver's remains were not recoverable. It has been calculated that he attained a ground speed of approximately 420 mph.' Thus passed another of the lads: an inventive breed daft enough to try anything to see what will happen. His were the same immortal longings that well over a century earlier had induced the young Henry Ford to mount an immense 19-litre engine on a bare chassis with no rear suspension and primitive steering. In January 1904, only twenty-six days after the Wright Brothers' first flight, Ford pushed his machine to a new world land speed record of 91.37 mph.

By comparison the earliest motorbikes were both sedate and unreliable. The world's first mass-produced bike was German: Hildebrand & Wolfmüller's 1894 model. But Britons were not far behind. As a matter of fact Triumph Engineering had started business in the previous year, to be quickly followed by Royal Enfield, Norton, BSA and others. A random list of British firms founded before the First World War that became household names and lasted for several decades would include AJS, Villiers, Ariel, Brough, James, Matchless, Singer, Douglas, Francis-Barnett, Raleigh, Scott, Humber, Velocette, Panther, Sunbeam, Rudge and many others. Not surprisingly, several of the earliest companies (such as Raleigh and Rudge) had started out as bicycle makers and began a sideline of fitting the comparatively novel internal combustion engine into their strengthened cycle frames. Military use during the First World War spurred motorbike design into becoming more rugged and reliable, and from the 1920s road and competition machines began to proliferate. For obvious reasons of price and utility they tended to be bought by young men strong enough to pick them up when they fell over, able to carry out roadside repairs and unworried by exposure to the elements as well as to quantities of oil. Even though by the 1930s there was a handful of women like Florence Blenkiron competing in motorbike sporting events, it had long been made clear that motorbikes were not considered suitable for women:

It seems that the fact of a girl being a rider of a motor cycle immediately labels her as being 'mannish' – admittedly an unpleasant
characteristic – uninterested in frocks and frills, careless of home
life, and devoid of any desire for women friends.[73]

Indeed, an almost superstitious taboo seemed to operate
against females working in or even coming into contact with
the industry: a visceral feeling that it could only bring bad luck,
like a woman boarding a Scottish fishing smack even today. In
the late 1930s Norton made it clear that it would not employ
women in its Birmingham factory because to do so would compromise existing standards of craftsmanship.

This being Britain, the idea also persisted until well after
the Second World War that motorcycles were a predominantly
working-class form of transport. Rare exceptions were colour-
ful riders like T. E. Lawrence, who died when he came off his
Brough Superior in 1935 and was wilfully déclassé since although
he could mingle with heads of state and the aristocracy he was
serving incognito in the RAF as an enlisted man. Twenty years
later the equally helmetless seventeen-year-old GPO telegram
delivery boy named Terry who breezily misjudged a bend and
came through our garden fence on his BSA Bantam was *exactly*
our idea of a motorcyclist. We sat on the lawn with Terry while
my mother stuck Elastoplast on him and he laughed. He
smelled of Vaseline hair tonic. Both boy and bike were merely
grazed; the fence was a write-off.

The reach of the Empire and then the Second World War

made British motorbikes a familiar sight throughout much of the world. In the post-war 'export or die' drive it was clear that the better marques had great foreign sales potential, not least because they were already widely distributed and understood and spare parts were usually available or locally reproducible. While in Egypt for a year in 1976–7 I was surprised by the sheer number of interwar British bikes still being ridden, many in immaculate condition. Others belonged to tradesmen who had cobbled together a sidecar of their own design in which to keep their tools and other gear. It was exactly this type of bike I bought and rode back to England from Alexandria: a BSA M20 military model from 1938 with a heavy, home-made sheet-metal sidecar like a lockable coffin. It had old girder-type front forks and a single-cylinder 500cc engine that only once needed attention on the journey, and that while sedately thumping its way along an interminable German autobahn.

The 1950s and 1960s represented a period when it was still definitely a buyer's market for British motorbikes, especially in the United States. They could hardly have had better visibility there since the three most macho film actors of the period became indelibly associated with them. Marlon Brando rode a Triumph Thunderbird (rather than a Harley-Davidson) in *The Wild One* in 1953; two years later James Dean took up racing his Triumph Tiger immediately after filming *East of Eden*; and in 1963 Steve McQueen's stunt double famously jumped his Triumph Trophy to freedom in *The Great Escape*. This sort of exposure was a marketing man's dream, and even as late as the latter half of the 1960s the UK's largest dollar-earning export industries were reputed to be whisky and motorcycles. With such a well-established market presence, together with passionate rider loyalties, it might be thought that the British motorcycle industry could hardly go wrong. It was full of brilliant engineers and designers, many of whom had begun as apprentices after the First World War and had risen in their companies to be chief designer and even in a few instances to managerial positions, although most preferred to remain on the shop floor or in their drawing offices, dreaming up the new engine or styling that would revolutionise the company's fortunes.

Alas for that. A combination of appalling mismanagement, personal rivalries, union intransigence and sheer stupidity was to bring this lively industry to its knees in little more than twenty years. The stupidity was already in evidence within a year or two of the end of the Second World War, when it would not have taken a genius to work out that countries with high industrial competence like Germany and Japan were likely to benefit from their recent military defeat in that they could start afresh in modern factories with brand-new machine tools and manufacturing techniques. It was both foolish and hubristic of British bike companies to take for granted that their own products would have no serious rivals for decades, if ever, presumably while the market magically stayed the same. Victory in war evidently made it easy to forget that several famous British marques had some German ancestry. The founder of Veloce Ltd of Birmingham that went on to build Velocettes until 1970 was German by birth. The founder of Triumph Engineering back in 1893 had been a young German who had emigrated to Coventry and maintained close links with subsidiary companies in Germany between the wars. Triumph knew perfectly well how good German bikes were. It would also be conveniently forgotten that BSA's bestselling Bantam light motorbikes were originally a German design whose plans were ceded to Britain in 1945 as part of the spoils of war.

Thus it was already obvious by 1948 that with the big financial boost from Marshall Aid German industry in general would swiftly be rebuilt. Since making motorcycles is a light industry and the Germans had their own history of first-rate marques and experience to draw on, it might also have been easily deduced that they would quite soon challenge British bikes. German motorbikes of the recent war were already famous for their innovative design and rugged reliability: machines like BMW's R71 of 1938, the slightly later R75, and Zündapp's KS750 flat twin. The R71 was soon copied by the Soviet Union as the Ural and is still produced in Russia today, just as in China there is a model based on the German original. One could hardly wish for better proof of an outstanding utility design; wise Britons in the industry would have done well to consider that a sound tradition plus fresh thinking and tooling might soon help resurgent manufacturers, not merely in Germany but in Italy and Japan as well.

Some, like Bert Hopwood, did foresee trouble. He had started out as an apprentice engineer with Ariel Motors in 1926 and for years maintained one of the industry's prickliest relationships with the equally talented design engineer Edward Turner. In 1930 Turner became famous as the designer of Ariel's celebrated Square Four engine. Both men were to move independently from company to company and, despite a certain grudging respect for each other, frequently fought like cats when they coincided. After the war Hopwood moved to Norton, where in 1948 he designed the Dominator, and then to BSA, where he produced the Golden Flash of 1951. In due course both he and Turner ended up at Triumph. In 1998 Turner would be posthumously and memorably described as 'Triumph's Mr Toad',[74] while Hopwood also had his critics for his 'Black Country dourness'. Although both men exhibited engineering genius, the industry contained others of equal talent but who never wrote their memoirs, so they remain largely unsung. By Hopwood's retirement, when he came to write the autobiography that doubles as an insider's history of the rise and fall of Britain's motorcycle industry, he was far enough removed from 1945 for hindsight to have further sharpened the focus of his already acerbic view of what went wrong. He wrote: 'Quite frankly, I do not understand why the so-called businessmen who were then running the British motorcycle industry did not work this out for themselves [i.e. the inevitability of German and Japanese resurgence] and stop fiddling with the yearly up-dating of ancient merchandise.'[75]

Hopwood's cantankerous tone was mainly that of exasperation, for by then he not only had a lifetime's view of the collapse of so many great companies but also the memory of several machines he, Turner and others had designed that might have turned a company's fortunes around had they not been cancelled by an indifferent management while still at prototype stage. Nor was he wrong about British manufacturers' preference for revamping and tweaking their old successful designs instead of coming up with radically new machines to keep pace with the growing foreign competition. In 1952 the German company NSU produced their 'Max' bike. Hopwood described it as having superlative performance: 'a handsome machine with a brilliant 250cc engine of unusual design and a frame which was manufactured basically from two huge pressings flash-welded together in a matter of seconds'. As an engineer he knew that to introduce such innovative production techniques into the British industry would require a bomb – or at least a complete change in thinking, partly at shop-floor level but mainly in the boardroom. He also knew this was not likely to happen.

> What shocked and disappointed me then, and to this day leaves me
> with a great feeling of despondency, was the complete unawareness
> of the chairmen and other top executives of the British industry.
> They did very little to prepare for the intensive competition which
> was so obviously threatening to obliterate us. Almost everyone at
> board level seemed to be asleep; and on the rare occasions when I

had the opportunity of discussing the situation with people of this stature I was upset by the self-satisfaction and feeling of lethargy which seemed to exist.[76]

Still worse for him was watching the gradual shift towards people he scorned as 'academics' trying to run motorbike companies. It was soon to become a commonplace in the industry that many managers and board members knew nothing whatever about engineering or motorcycles, and even appeared to have scant interest in them. It was the beginning of the idea which today has acquired the status of holy writ, that being a manager is a professional qualification obtained as part of a degree course at a university or business school and it matters little what the company to be managed actually does. Current wisdom apparently sees no difference between managing a company that makes marmalade and managing Network Rail. In neither case is a knowledge of – let alone enthusiasm for – citrus fruit or rolling stock of any particular relevance. Once again, it was exactly Tony Benn's point about the management at Longbridge. To someone like Hopwood this way of running a motorcycle company made no sense whatever. Such people, he wrote, 'were instrumental in opening the floodgates to newcomers who were as much at home in our industry as would be a horse doctor in the sphere of human brain surgery'.[77] After all, he himself was a man who in the morning could show an apprentice how to grind in an exhaust valve; then after a canteen lunch begin drawing a set of exquisite engineering plans for an entirely new

engine; and in the late afternoon describe to the sales department the particular market he was designing that engine for
and the exact niche it was intended to fill. His frustration
with managers and board members who could see no point in
changing a successful but ageing design mounted steadily and
he would quote Alf Child, a big motorbike distributor in the
United States with whom he set up a deal for BSA. According
to Child, 'Trees die from their topmost branches down to their
roots, and it is the same with business', a piece of rough-hewn
wisdom that many a British industry would have done well to
bear in mind before it was too late.

This was certainly true at the BSA group of companies from
the early 1950s, where the topmost branches of the company
tree carried a good deal of dead wood. Since 1940 the group's
managing director had been Sir Bernard Docker, in essence a
City banker and playboy. His second wife, Norah Collins, was
the Lady Docker whose name became a half-scandalised, half-
envious byword for vulgar extravagance in the otherwise aus-
tere post-war years. Sir Bernard, who was Norah's third trophy
husband, owned a large private yacht and was also chairman
of the Daimler Company Ltd. This was technically Britain's
oldest car company, having been founded in 1893 before BSA
bought it in 1910. By 1948 Daimler was ailing, largely because
the extreme-luxury limousines it had always sold to the world's
wealthy and aristocratic were now perceived as old-fashioned in
those straitened times. Worse, in 1950 the British royals deserted
the marque for Rolls-Royce after half a century's patronage of

Daimler cars – and this when pub savants claimed that true aristocrats bought Daimlers and only common nouveaux riches bought Rolls-Royces. Much the same trope can be heard today denigrating Ferraris for a supposed association with overpaid footballers.

Daimler's image clearly needed a boost, so between them Sir Bernard and Lady Docker designed several glitzy show models opulently decorated with gold stars, gold plating, ivory dashboards and zebra skin upholstery ('Mink is too hot to sit on,' as Norah helpfully explained). She would then glide around town in these one-off Daimlers, thoroughly enjoying her mission to *épater la bourgeoisie* and restore the marque's public image. As she herself put it, 'We bring glamour and happiness into drab lives. The working class loves everything I do', thus showing how much she had in common with Imelda Marcos, who frequently said the same thing about the impoverished Filipino peasantry she dazzled. As any Greek tragedian could have guessed, the Dockers would quite soon come to grief. Apart from being on the board of BSA, Sir Bernard was also on that of the Midland Bank. In 1953 he and Norah were investigated for infringing Britain's strict currency restrictions by smuggling money out of the country in order to gamble at the casino in Monte Carlo. The Midland Bank, who had been trying to get rid of him for some time, did not even wait for the investigation to finish and dumped him from its board for 'absenteeism'. In 1956 he was also finally ousted from BSA.

In some ways the Dockers epitomised much that was wrong with Britain's post-war attitude towards business. It was a time that believed titles and glitz in the boardroom easily outranked genius on the shop floor. This fitted well with a widespread attitude common to the City and boardrooms throughout the land that industry was a sort of grubby sub-species of trade, and while regrettably necessary it didn't need to be taken too seriously. Industrial premises had occasionally to be visited in grim districts of even grimmer towns, but a few hours' slumming could soon be offset by a round of golf at Sunningdale, a couple of days on a good trout stream or grouse moor, and dinner at the Mirabelle. This was not true of all company directors, of course, many of whom made heroic efforts to see their firms prosper; but the predominant ethos was undeniable. The complacency was often extraordinary, as was the appearance in company boardrooms of the same old titled rogues, very few of whom had much knowledge of or interest in the companies they headed. As a journalist in London I remember buying a copy of Andrew Roth's *Lord on the Board* when it came out in 1972 and marvelling at the aura of sinecured layabouts that hung over the boardroom lists he had painstakingly compiled and cross-referenced. Roth exposed a whole network of freeloaders, among whom a minority of hard-working and knowledgeable people struggled to keep their companies afloat.

Meanwhile, at Whitehall level, the Department of Trade and Industry sought in vain to find a reliable way of predicting that a company was heading for the rocks despite its own optimistic book-keeping. One day a civil service researcher spotted a correlation between imminent failure and the award of honours to the company's board. His boss later quoted the formula in his memoirs:

> *A knighthood for the CEO means the knacker's yard within four years; and if the Chairman and CEO both have knighthoods, within three years.* This is a formulation that has offered many a wry smile as British companies have passed into oblivion with benighted bosses cashing in share options and picking up their compensation packages. More recent history suggests a variation: elevation to the Lords presages complete catatonic failure of his eminence's erstwhile business. Perhaps the outstanding instance was the collapse of Dunlop [in 1985], whose board at the time read like a messenger's speech from *Henry V*. Recalling a lunch with some of the directors beforehand, one boldly asserted, 'We timed our rights issue to perfection, I thought' – another good anticipatory symptom that rigor mortis is setting in.[78]

Back in 1956, once Sir Bernard Docker had gone BSA's motorcycle division looked to be in a promising position. Not only had it swallowed up the Sunbeam, Ariel and Triumph marques but it had several machines of its own (such as the Shooting Star) that were selling well. By now Triumph bikes were dominant in the sports world, regularly carrying off the honours in the Isle of Man TT and races in the US. Consequently, they were much in demand as café racers: a quintessential buyer's market that needed little further advertising. The problem was that the new BSA division simply couldn't design or build enough new machines to satisfy it.

Part of the reason for this was a malaise that was to affect swathes of British industry once the mania for mergers had taken hold. As in the case of cars, the theory was that 'specialist management strength' would be greatly improved if small or promising but failing companies were taken over by larger entities. In this way the individual virtues of each, once added together, could be made to work for the whole, with corresponding economies of effort in such areas as marketing. In Britain this sort of amalgamation had been seen as a recourse for failing companies since the end of the nineteenth century. While in the United States mergers were viewed dynamically as leading to a fresh impetus for commercial success, in Britain they tended, in the words of the economic historian Peter Mathias, to result in 'desperate and half-hearted alliances apparently motivated more by a desire to preserve the status quo than to tackle markets more aggressively'.[79] As we have seen, at its most pronounced this fashion led to the forcible shoehorning of proudly individualistic companies, often still family affairs, into unwieldy monoliths such as the British Aircraft Corporation [1960], British Leyland [1968] and British Shipbuilders [1977]. At once these conglomerates proved exceedingly difficult to manage. Companies with a lengthy history of designing and making their own products suddenly found themselves having to share the same management – sometimes even the same factory – with companies that until a few weeks previously had been bitter rivals. Each had different ways of working, different hierarchies, different structures, different outlooks and often quite different and intensely loyal customers for their products. This was certainly true of motorcycles, where someone who was an Ariel rider would never have bought a Matchless.

The in-house split between the BSA's marques and Triumph was such that it was sometimes hard to believe they were part of the same group. As Hopwood was to remark,

> The two units were soaked with antagonism and continued to go their separate ways with not the slightest attempt being made, so far as I could see, to bring the situation back onto the rails. This state of affairs sprang directly from top management level, and Edward Turner in particular made it no secret that Triumph territory was sacrosanct. He flatly refused to allow any movement towards inter-company management collaboration, and it is not surprising that, given this sort of encouragement, a barrier of mistrust grew which was, much later, almost impossible to remove.[80]

Worse still, another unforeseen drawback of amalgamations of this sort was falling standards: the tendency of the best manufacturing units to succumb to the dispiriting downward drag of the worst. Given a thousand Victorian homilies about rotten apples infecting a barrel or mixing hot water with cold and getting tepid, it was odd that nobody had spotted this predictable 'lowest common denominator' syndrome as one likely outcome of such mergers. It was soon to plague the British car industry as well.

In 1955 Hopwood left BSA to join the Associated Motor Cycle group (AMC). This was made up of five famous marques: AJS, James, Matchless, Francis Barnett and Norton. In terms of high-performance racing machines Norton was AMC's answer to Triumph at BSA. Hopwood was proud to see that the Norton range was still powered by the 500cc and 600cc twin cylinder Dominator engines he himself had designed nearly eight years earlier, although he was also somewhat alarmed that they had scarcely been modified since. Even so, Norton had signed the brilliant young rider Geoff Duke, who won three world championships and numerous TT trophies on the company's machines. For many years the combination of Duke and Norton was famous worldwide, certainly in my Letts schoolboy's pocket diaries where most years there seemed to be a picture of a triumphant Duke in his one-piece leathers and pudding-basin crash helmet straddling a powerful machine with 'Norton' emblazoned on the tank. (The other crash-helmeted Duke in those diaries was the test pilot, Neville.)

Hopwood knew that while such publicity for Norton was valuable, most of their potential young customers were not in the market for high-performance big bikes. He tried to convince AMC's management that it was vital to produce a range of smaller capacity machines: 250cc and under. He knew from the sales of BSA Bantams and Triumph Cubs (and from those of the German NSU's Max) that there was a growing market for lighter motorbikes that appealed to younger riders because they were cheaper to run and maintain, and to their parents because they were less of a handful for their inexperienced teenaged sons. But both BSA and Triumph refused to develop new types, contenting themselves with periodically revamping the old designs. Hopwood pointed out that this tactic was doomed because youngsters always wanted new models. Not only that, but lighter bikes were also the way to go for foreign markets opening up outside the anglophone nations. In what was then known as the Third World where economies were improving it was easy to predict the need for a cheap mode of transport for people who were sick of walking or riding donkeys, who aspired to something quicker than a push-bike but who couldn't possibly afford a car. Yet the British motorbike industry had generally fought shy of producing smaller machines, believing that profits would be too meagre from what it saw as a limited market for cheaper bikes.

One notable exception was the Velocette company. This had remained staunchly independent and had concentrated on building excellently engineered and often innovative designs that included racing types with good pre- and post-war records. A measure of their market awareness was that as early as 1948 they produced their LE ('Little Engine') bike expressly designed for a new generation of riders who wanted a light, reliable run-about. It had a 149cc engine and its overall engineering was very advanced and included a shaft – rather than chain – drive. The disadvantage was that this level of sophistication made the bikes too expensive and they only sold well by being bought by over fifty UK police forces for local patrolling. Soon known as 'Noddy bikes', they were a common sight until the company went out of business in 1971, independent to the last. Not for Velocette the mergers that increasingly clotted together the rest of the industry. It was a sobering moment when I first noticed that British police had begun deserting not just their Noddys but their Nortons and Triumphs, too, in favour of foreign machines. The sight of coppers on Hondas and BMWs showed that yet another industry was on the way out.

The example of the Velocette LE shows it would be a mistake to think of Bert Hopwood as having been a heroic lone visionary. If he seems so now it is only because the majority of the industry in which he was working was foot-draggingly slow to spot opportunities and effect change. In Japan, early motor scooters like Mitsubishi's Silver Pigeon and Fuji's Rabbit had been on the market since 1946. In Italy a year or two later the first Vespas and Lambrettas appeared. To judge from their sales they satisfied a growing market for a cheap form of transport and their high-pitched buzzing soon filled Italy's city streets with an excitable, glamorous, even sexy note of independence with the promise of much more *dolce vita* to come. They quickly took their place as part of the street scenery in Italian and French films of the period (Fellini's 1954 *La Strada*, for example). Above all, girls as well as boys rode them, hair streaming and cotton dresses moulded revealingly by the warm Mediterranean breezes.

Then in 1956 two canny directors of Honda Motors toured Germany and were much struck by the popularity of mopeds such as NSU's 49cc Quickly, which had been selling briskly since its launch in 1953. It seemed to them that there was a mass market for such bikes. They returned to Japan and in 1958 Honda's first Super Cub was launched. This beautifully designed 49cc model was the beginning of a range that expanded over the next sixty years and has now sold well over sixty million examples to become the biggest-selling motor vehicle of all time.

In 1955, just before Hopwood left BSA, the company did concede that in view of the foreign mopeds being imported there might after all be a market for such economical commuter machines. They quickly produced a couple of their own: the 75cc Dandy moped and the 198cc Beeza motor scooter. Both were given the full razzmatazz press treatment in time for that year's Earls Court Show. After that, neither was seen or heard of again. This, too, betrayed a British habit not confined to the motorbike industry and equally noticeable (but with far more expensive consequences) in the car and aviation industries. This was to rush a new model into production with much fanfare in order belatedly to catch a market opportunity but without first having built several prototypes and tested them to destruction. Once the inevitable teething troubles, flaws and glitches normal to new types had been ironed out, redesigned and tested yet again, the new model might have been a marketable proposition. As it was, the Dandy was a nice-looking machine but in Hopwood's own words 'it suffered the loving care of a dozen or so "chief engineers", most of whom were obviously out of their depth'. The bike's persistent problems led to its being scrapped.

Another source of failure among British bike companies was in a way sadder because it was brought about by exceptional quality as much as by a failure to spot market trends. At the beginning of this chapter mention was made of the ex-RFC pilot H. R. Davies and the company he founded in 1924 as HRD Motors Ltd. This was bought in 1928 by Phil Vincent, a talented young designer with family backing, who then marketed a line of extremely well-engineered HRD Vincent bikes, most with large engine capacities. In 1936 the Vincent Rapide appeared: a 1,000cc V-twin capable of 110 mph that had all sorts of innovative features including a new type of suspension. This bike was considerably faster than nearly all other road machines of the day and was coveted by those strong-nerved riders who could afford it. During the Second World War Vincent, like most other motorbike companies, had much of their manufacturing capacity taken up making military equipment; but in 1948 it produced one of the most famous of all British motorcycles, the legendary Black Shadow. This was marketed quite simply as the world's fastest production motorbike. Capable of 125 mph in street form, in its Black Lightning racing version it could reach 150 mph. Admiring onlookers, by no means all of them bikers, would gather around a Black Shadow wherever one was parked. I can remember being late for a university tutorial in

1962 through gazing at one in Oxford's Broad Street. Its satanic all-black finish, giant speedometer and gleaming exhaust pipes marked it as an exceptional specimen of automotive genius and induced an emotion strong enough to cause the hint of tears that sometimes afflicts me when looking at particularly beautiful engineering – why, I shall never know. These days, rare examples of such Vincents change hands at auction for small fortunes.

The problem was that these divine machines were hand-built and didn't lend themselves to mass production. Consequently, they simply could not be produced fast or cheaply enough to satisfy what was, after all, a specialised niche market mainly for those yearning to dice with death. By 1954 Vincent was in financial trouble deep enough to become an importer for NSU Quicklys which promptly sold 20,000 in one year: a sales figure that made NSU revoke the licence and set up its own agency. The following year Vincent went out of business for good, leaving its comparatively scarce motorcycles to become collectors' items around the world. In a sense, theirs was a problem analogous to that of Rolls-Royce cars, which were also hand built and bespoke enough not to be capable of fast line assembly. The crucial difference was that the sort of people who ordered the cars were usually very much richer and more numerous than those who ordered Vincent's bikes.

At AMC Hopwood, now a director of Nortons, soon noticed another sign that the ploy of merging disparate companies was not likely to work, and especially not if the various managements stubbornly maintained their old ways of thinking. He had deliberately sketched a new twin-cylinder 250cc engine that could also be made in a smaller version, and he proposed this as something the Group as a whole might adopt throughout their various ranges of bikes. His immediate boss soon made it clear to him it was unthinkable that Hopwood, as a Norton man, should presume to concern himself with Group strategy. Surprised, Hopwood decided to go ahead anyway with his design, which had a one-piece cylinder unit. It was not long before he was severely rebuked with the information that 'most motor-cyclists love to spend their Sunday mornings taking off the cylinder head and re-seating the valves', and his design would make this impossible.

This epitomised for him how far out of touch the industry was with its customers. The weekend tinkerers were undoubtedly still there, but they were rapidly shrinking to a minority as motorbikes grew more reliable and the motorcycling public now included female as well as male riders of maintenance-free foreign mopeds and light bikes, all of whom had better things to do on their precious weekends than spend them crouched in freezing garages messing about with oil and spanners. No longer was the average motorcyclist resigned to doubling as a mechanic. He expected low-maintenance machinery that *worked*. 'Poor hapless little souls,' Hopwood observed of AMC's customers whose management evidently expected them to regularly skin their knuckles and enjoy it. 'No wonder they decided to "go Japanese".'[81]

And so on it went for the next quarter-century. As already noted, a handful of British bikes achieved fame and fortune in the US and on the racing circuits; but once Honda, Suzuki, Yamaha and Kawasaki began to flood the world's markets with stylish, fast, up-to-date and reliable machines that didn't leak oil all over driveways and garage floors, British bike ownership increasingly gathered about it a slightly diehard – even self-consciously 'butch' – air. It was a tribute to a few gifted designers like Bert Hopwood, many first-rate engineers, and the occasional director or board member who knew the business from within that British manufacturers still managed to produce some outstanding machines like the BSA/Triumph Trident, the Triumph Bonneville and Daytona, a 1,000cc Grand Superbike and a few others. But an industry so badly mismanaged was never going to be able to compete with the great range of comparatively inexpensive but sophisticated Japanese bikes expertly marketed with full after-sales backup (always a British weakness, as we soon discovered when we tried to sell our cars to the Americans). Good as they were, even the best British bikes retained a faint aura of rugged origins and uncertain maintenance when up against big BMWs that exuded a showroom air of German precision engineering. Italian bikes, too, had a stylishness about them and marques like Ducati, Gilera, Laverda and Moto Guzzi were backed by just as long a racing tradition as any of the British bikes. Indeed, Geoff Duke himself eventually defected from Norton to Gilera to win fresh racing laurels.

It should be noted that the success of the Japanese bikes was by no means all down to indigenous engineering brilliance. They greatly benefited from a technical breakthrough that had been made by Walter Kaaden, an ex-Nazi engineer who had worked on V-1s at Peenemünde during the war. After the war he devoted himself at home in East Germany to finding a way to make motorbike engines more powerful, supported by the racing team MV. In the words of his biographer, Mat Oxley,

> he became the father of the modern two-stroke, godfather of a thousand Grand Prix victories and a few million motorcycle sales. Using V-1 rocket technology, Kaaden ... made the two-stroke sing like a musical instrument, using resonance and harmonics instead of mechanical valves to create the most powerful internal combustion engines on earth. His 1961 MZ 125 race engine was the world's first – in cars or motorcycles – to make 200 horsepower per litre without supercharging. ... This was the know-how upon which Suzuki, and then Yamaha and Kawasaki built their reputations. The Kaaden-inspired two-stroke was thus a cornerstone of Japan's takeover of the global motorcycle market.[82]

Unable or unwilling to copy such radical innovation, the British motorcycle industry seemed in terminal decline by the early 1970s, fatally dishevelled by the series of mergers and 'rationalisations' it had suffered from the mid-1950s onwards, and now by increasingly disaffected union activity. Despite its complement of brilliant and far-sighted designers who had taken to heart the post-war edict of 'export or die' and could all too clearly see the threat of foreign competition, no company board ever fully got the message or summoned up the energy to provide vigorous and united leadership. One design engineer at BSA, Bill Morgan, later insisted that they had reverse-engineered Hondas, Suzukis and Yamahas as soon as they appeared and were fully aware of the improved design, higher-quality manufacture and performance – all of which could be matched, he said, but only by radical change within the industry with a completely new outlook, tooling and working methods. 'But' (summarising the attitude of the top management), 'they just weren't interested.'[83]

By the time of Edward Heath's premiership in 1970 Britain's general economic and social conditions were beset by rising inflation and unemployment. Government policies became increasingly desperate and confrontational. The Industrial Relations Act of 1971 was intended as a way of curbing the unions; and although the union militancy that climaxed in the Triumph workers' cooperative at Meriden is often viewed as having been the last straw, it ignores the veritable bales of chaff that had been gathering at boardroom level since the war and beneath which the motorcycle industry had progressively laboured. There is a good case for saying that much of the increasing union activity that so bedevilled British industry in the 1970s had to do with the workers' awareness of how badly their companies were being managed. It knocked the last vestiges of company pride out of them and surely contributed to cynicism. What was particularly stupid about the way things were handled in the motorcycle industry was that nearly everyone who worked in it at factory level was a fan of bikes, so there was an inbuilt devotion to the product (this was true also of the car industry, but to a lesser degree). From hearsay evidence everyone starting out, from apprentice mechanic to designer, was dead keen to build first-rate machines. But they progressively lost faith in the way their group was managed by directors and board members who apparently had little vision or interest in motorbikes and who paid themselves extremely well into the bargain. They might have drawn parallels between the way their industry was run and the way someone like Sir Owen Green ran his.

Owen Green was the managing director of BTR (British Tyre and Rubber), the highly successful conglomerate that was to swallow up Dunlop in 1985. In 1993 he published a diatribe in the *Daily Mail* against boardroom greed in which he famously said, 'How a director who has just had an 18 per cent rise dares tell his workers to show restraint and accept less than 5 per cent, I cannot understand. Can you work wholeheartedly for a company which accepts that sort of behaviour at the top?' Twenty years earlier, during the Meriden sit-in, this would surely have provoked cheers among the strikers. So would the already quoted and equally memorable remark made at the time by Harry Irwin. Irwin was a senior representative of the Transport and General Workers' Union on the board of the monolithic shambles that was British Leyland. He said: 'If the workers were convinced that management were focused on getting new orders into the factory doors, you'd be amazed at the transformation that would follow.'[84]

Bert Hopwood finally gave up on AMC, sick of the feuding between BSA and Triumph. Triumph's motorcycles were selling in ever fewer numbers although they still retained considerable cachet and loyalty, particularly as racing machines. The factory at Meriden, outside Coventry, had been Triumph's home since the war when the original factory in the city was destroyed in an air raid. In the motorcycling world it was a kind of Mecca. In 1964 the entire US International Six-Day Trials team went to Meriden in person to collect their race-prepared bikes. Among them were the actor Steve McQueen and the celebrated stuntman Bud Ekins, who had performed the famous fence-jumping trick on a Triumph in *The Great Escape*. At the very least the visit was a great photo-op. for the company. Yet by 1970 the industry as a whole was in a terminal mess with yet more mergers and remergers. The BSA group went bankrupt in 1972 and the remnants of its motorcycle division, together with AMC, became part of Norton-Villiers-Triumph, or NVT, under the chairmanship of Dennis Poore. After reviewing the books Poore announced that he would close Meriden in early 1974 and move NVT to BSA's old factory at Small Heath, Birmingham, making 3,000 of his 4,500 employees redundant. This immediately provoked the blockading of the Meriden factory by the workers. The sit-in and subsequent formation of a cooperative gained a fair amount of public sympathy as well as support by the new Labour government. The Meriden cooperative, trading as NVT, went on building 750cc Triumph machines. NVT itself ceased to exist in 1977 and the cooperative used government loans to rebrand itself as Triumph Motorcycles (Meriden) Ltd. By 1978 their Silver Jubilee Bonneville was the best-selling European motorbike in America. Other models followed, most selling decently but still not well enough to pay their way, hampered as they were by a strong pound that made them uncompetitive with comparable Japanese and Italian marques. A few years of further government bail-outs merely staved off bankruptcy, which finally came in 1983.

So ended ninety years of motorcycle building by Triumph Engineering, effectively the sole survivor of the many famous and not-so-famous companies that together had constituted the British industry. However, in 1984 the entrepreneur John Bloor bought the name from the Official Receiver and today the marque lives on successfully as an entirely new company, Triumph Motorcycles Ltd, with its factory at Hinckley in Leicestershire. Many of the old and resonant model names have been retained, but the bikes themselves are new throughout. In August 2017 Kane Avellano circumnavigated the world solo on his modern Triumph Bonneville, at twenty-three the youngest rider ever to do so. He covered 28,000 miles in eight months, keeping up a daily average of nearly 300 miles that surely testifies to a sturdy bike as well as rider.

As a final irony, one of the engine designs the present Triumph company adopted was a modular one that the late Bert Hopwood had kept urging to a succession of deaf ears in the directors' offices of the old Triumph back in the 1960s. 'What did I bloody well tell you?', one can imagine his shade demanding truculently.

8.
Nukes & Fish

(i) Nukes

'Normal human activity is worse for nature than the greatest nuclear accident in history.'

—MARTIN CRUZ SMITH

The second cooling tower taking shape at Calder Hall's No. 1 reactor in 1953. The coupling of the world's first commercial nuclear plant and a labourer with a spade somehow feels quintessentially British.

(p.252) Second Cod War, 1973. The Icelandic gunboat *Thor* collides with the British frigate HMS *Jaguar*, which sustained damage to her bows requiring dry dock repairs at Chatham.

Amid the stories of decline it is cheering to be able to recall just how superb so many of Britain's scientific and technological skills have been – as, indeed, some still are. As quoted in Chapter 2, the American business pundit Peter Drucker said that Britain ought to have been the world's economic leader in the post-Second World War era. Thanks equally to native inventiveness and the stimulus of war, Britain had emerged in 1945 with outstanding competence in pharmaceuticals, electronics, computing, aerospace and nuclear technology. Each of these fields had already reached, or just passed, the threshold of world-changing importance. All had attracted some of the twentieth century's greatest scientists, many of whom were themselves British. Alexander Fleming had discovered penicillin; Alan Turing made important advances in computing; Frank Whittle had pioneered the jet engine. Ernest Rutherford was hailed as the 'father of nuclear physics' as William Penney was of Britain's atom bomb.

Where atomic physics was concerned, the resounding breakthrough had been 'splitting the atom' for the first time. Two of Rutherford's students, John Cockcroft and James Chadwick, achieved this in 1932 at the Cavendish Laboratory in Cambridge. This and subsequent work on nuclear fission by the brilliant German radiochemist Otto Hahn and his colleague Fritz Strassmann had set scientists in Europe and America busily working out the implications. It was obvious that if fission could be tamed into a continuous process it could in theory yield prodigious amounts of energy. The next weighty discovery was also made in Britain, in March 1940. Under the spur of war two émigré scientists at Birmingham University made the theoretical leap whereby nuclear fission might be engineered to build an atomic bomb small enough to be deliverable by air. On the outbreak of war in 1939 Otto Frisch and Fritz Peierls had both elected to remain in England, or had otherwise been unable to return to Germany, and were head-hunted by the Australian professor of physics at Birmingham, Mark Oliphant. Their 1940 thesis, the so-called Frisch–Peierls Memorandum, was the first description of the critical mass of fissile material necessary to sustain a chain reaction and hence to build an atomic weapon.

The following month Britain's MAUD Committee, and then the joint British and Canadian 'Tube Alloys Directorate', were founded to investigate the possibility of building such a weapon, the conclusion being that it might be feasible as early as 1943. 'Tube Alloys' was a deliberately misleading code-name that hid one of Britain's most secret wartime projects. Its counterpart in the United States was the fledgling Manhattan Project to which William Penney was quickly seconded. At that time, of course, America was not yet an official ally and would remain neutral until the Japanese attack on Pearl Harbor in late 1941. At an unofficial level, though, there were regular exchanges of scientific information between Britain, Canada and the United States, as well as more physical shipments. As yet, nobody on either side of the Atlantic knew for certain whether Germany was working along similar lines; but given

Otto Hahn's worldwide reputation the worry was that Hitler might well have co-opted him to produce a German nuclear weapon. Oliphant mentioned his Birmingham colleagues' breakthrough to Penney in the US and in September 1940 the top-secret Frisch–Peierls Memorandum was simply handed over to Washington. Together with many other gems of British research it was sent as part of the Tizard Mission, later described by an American historian as 'the most valuable cargo ever brought to our shores'. The Mission was accompanied by John Cockcroft, who briefed his American counterparts and discovered that the Manhattan Project was not as far advanced as the British–Canadian Tube Alloys.

Soon several more British and Canadian nuclear scientists went to the US and worked on the Manhattan Project, with which Tube Alloys was quickly merged. It was taken for granted by everyone, and more than once formally agreed, that when the war was over the Project's participants would continue to pool their nuclear research. However, once Victory in Europe day had been celebrated in May 1945 and the US had dropped the first two atom bombs on Japan in August, it was clear that an entirely new era of warfare had dawned and Washington surrounded practically anything to do with nuclear science with near-paranoid secrecy. In September that year the British physicist Alan Nunn May was revealed by a Soviet defector as having passed atomic secrets to the Russians throughout the war. May was not himself a weapons physicist but he had done a good deal of work on ancillary nuclear subjects such as heavy water and had good contacts in the scientific community. Yet despite his having been a member of the Communist Party before the war, MI5 had cleared him to work on nuclear matters. Although the USSR had until so recently been a heroic wartime ally in the fight against Hitler, the sudden news of May's long-term commerce with the Soviets prompted considerable American mistrust of British security at a time when the outlines of the Cold War were already being drawn.

In 1946 the US signed the Atomic Energy Act into law. Otherwise known as the McMahon Act after the senator who sponsored the bill, it immediately prohibited the sharing of nuclear information with the nationals of any other country. These included even its former Manhattan Project participants from Canada and Britain, though with one notable exception. William Penney was allowed to stay on, probably because he was the scientist best connected with the inner circle of advisers on which the US military relied. He was therefore well placed to keep up with any progress made by American nuclear science.

In London the shock of betrayal by such a recent ally went very deep, especially since the Tizard Mission in September 1940 had freely presented Washington with British scientific discoveries of extraordinary value, even if the gift-giving had to some extent been forced upon London. At that time the Battle of Britain was being fought and the outcome was far from certain. The possibility of a German invasion was still very much present and the idea of Britain's newest scientific advances in such things as jet engines, radar and nuclear physics falling into Nazi hands was unthinkable. At the same time, what with all Britain's available factory and manufacturing facilities being concentrated on mass-producing the more humdrum machineries of war, there was no spare capacity properly to develop many of the secret projects. Apart from the Fritz–Peierls Memorandum the Tizard Mission's famous tin trunk included a sample of a new type of plastic explosive developed for the British Special Operations Executive (SOE) and a complete set of blueprints for Frank Whittle's jet engine. But the 'pearl beyond price' – as an American scientist was to call it – was the cavity magnetron that had been invented only months earlier by another two Birmingham University scientists. This was a copper disc little bigger than the pendulum of a grandfather clock that could generate microwaves of unheard-of power, enabling high-resolution radar as well as much greater accuracy for anti-aircraft guns. Not only did it guarantee the superiority of Allied radar during the war, but its long-term commercial value was to prove incalculable, since a cavity magnetron is still at the heart of every microwave oven.[85]

This background history is necessary to explain not just Britain's deep resentment of the McMahon Act, but how that measure was to determine the course of our own home-grown nuclear industry. Once the Act had cut us off from officially sharing any further atomic secrets with the United States, Britain took the fateful decision to go it alone. The possibility of using nuclear power to generate electricity rather than to make bombs had long been considered perfectly feasible. It was merely a matter of firing neutrons at rods of uranium fuel. This resulted in fission, to be kept at a controlled level by the use of a 'moderator'. The Manhattan Project had determined that neutrons move at roughly a fortieth of the speed of light – some seventeen million miles per hour – and they needed to be slowed down or 'moderated' in a reactor so as to provoke fission that would not become unmanageably hot. The still abundant energy thus generated could heat water to produce steam and drive turbine generators, exactly as would an ordinary coal-fired boiler. The advantage of uranium compared to coal is its efficiency. Thirty-three tons of it can produce as much energy as 2.3 million tons of coal or ten million barrels of oil. In short, here was a technology that seemed to offer almost unlimited cheap energy that British scientists were already well equipped to harness and the British economy badly needed as an alternative to laboriously home-mined coal and imported oil.

However, at a secret Cabinet committee in October 1946 the Attlee government decided that Britain had an even more urgent priority: the country must have its own atom bomb. National hubris clearly played the decisive role in this choice. As the foreign secretary Ernest Bevin said, 'We have got to have this thing over here whatever it costs... we've got to have the bloody Union Jack on top of it.' The project entailed secretly diverting a great deal of scarce money and resources. It also depended on William Penney returning to the UK with his unique knowledge of recent American progress in nuclear science. Well before the first British bomb was ready orders also went out to four of Britain's top aircraft manufacturers to design jet bombers capable of delivering it. Out of these the three future V-bomber types – the Valiant, Victor and Vulcan – were chosen and at vast expense eventually built, tested and put into squadron service. As the Cold War standoff intensified during the Berlin Airlift in 1948-9, Britain's strategic role in the nuclear defence of Western Europe as well as that of the United Kingdom was seen as essential. Washington viewed Britain's yet unbuilt nuclear-armed V-bombers as a vital part of Europe's defence, and even as the US was building up the bomber force of its own Strategic Air Command it leaned heavily on Whitehall to speed up the production of Britain's bombers and its bomb.

One might think that London's Ministry of Defence would have been justified in telling Washington that building a British atom bomb was out of the question unless the McMahon Act was immediately repealed and the two countries could go back to working together as they had a mere two or three years earlier. But the United States – and arguably the USSR as well – was now a world superpower. The global balance had shifted decisively and Britain, battered and impoverished, had decisively lost some of its pre-war status and bargaining power. In 1947 construction of a nuclear facility began at what had been a wartime Royal Ordnance factory, ROF Sellafield. This, like other factories making explosives, had been sited in a sparsely populated area in the far west of what was then

Cumberland as a protection against German bombing raids. Renamed Windscale Works, the facility was designed to produce fissile materials for Britain's atom bomb, chiefly plutonium. Two air-cooled reactors known as the Windscale Piles were built, of which Number One became operational in 1950. Number Two followed in 1951. In addition there was a reprocessing plant to deal with the spent fuel rods from the two reactors, which were of the type known as Magnox. They were specifically designed to turn uranium into weapons-grade plutonium-239.

Thanks to William Penney's leadership and the information he had been able to relay from America, Britain's first atom bomb was ready in 1952 and was successfully tested in Western Australia's Montebello Islands in October. It had been built so secretly that even some Cabinet members were in the dark. The incoming prime minister, Winston Churchill, commented with amazement that the more than £100 million (anything up to £13 billion at today's prices) spent on the project had so far managed to evade all parliamentary notice. Britain was now unquestionably a member of the world's most exclusive club, although the following month the US exploded the world's first hydrogen bomb: a great advance that revealed Britain was still several years behind in nuclear science. It was not until late 1957 that Britain exploded its own thermonuclear device.

Meanwhile, at Sellafield the world's first industrial-scale nuclear power station had also been taking shape. Named Calder Hall, it was opened by the Queen in 1956. The press had a field day with claims that 'a new atomic age' had dawned with 'electricity too cheap to meter', all thanks to British science and technology. Apart from the patriotic fillip to Britons' spirits, it gave the impression that they were about to get something for nothing. The general trumpeting effectively concealed the prodigious sums on nuclear research that had already been spent at Sellafield, and also that their real purpose had been entirely military and not civil at all. The wishful thinking of electricity 'too cheap to meter' was soon exposed. Since Calder Hall's air-cooled Magnox-type reactors had been designed to produce weapons-grade plutonium they turned out to be inefficient at generating electricity because among other things they produced steam at the wrong temperature. The system worked; but it never did feed the hoped-for amount of electricity into the national grid and nor did it come remotely close to amortising its cost.

However, although generating the nation's electricity was pre-eminently a civilian affair, anything to do with atomic or nuclear matters was still treated as though it were top secret military business. A revival of wartime 'hush-hush' secrecy surrounded even the Calder Hall power station. Thus when in October 1957 there was a fire in the core of Pile No. 1, considerably more radioactivity than news leaked out. Virtually nothing reached the UK press although the fire raged for several days and partly consumed eleven tons of uranium. A radioactive cloud of the isotope iodine-131 was sucked up the chimney and blown out across the country. What saved it from being an accident of Chernobyl-like dimensions turned out to be an afterthought: a last-minute modification that had been pushed through by John Cockcroft even as the two Piles were being finished. Suddenly alarmed, he had ordered special filters to be installed with great difficulty in a retro-fit at the top of the Piles' chimneys. These were mocked as 'Cockcroft's Folly' until the fire broke out and in its aftermath it became clear that only Pile No. 1's filter had prevented a catastrophic release of intensely radioactive particles. Even so, despite the radio-activity that gradually spread eastwards across the northern UK and eventually to the Continent, it was decided not to evacuate residents living downwind of the fire. Later, this decision was officially glossed as having been intended to avoid public panic, although in reality it was designed not to compromise the military-style secrecy that hung its own cloud over the Windscale reactors. Luckily iodine-131, although it can cause thyroid cancer, has a half-life of only eight days. However, it is easily taken up through the food chain, especially by graz-ing cattle, and for the next month all the meat and milk from downwind herds was banned from sale and impounded. Norman Nicholson's poem 'Windscale' described 'Where sewers flow with milk, and meat/is carved up for the fire to eat,/And children suffocate in God's fresh air.' Today the sealed Pile No. 1 is being slowly dismantled but is not due for complete decontamination and demolition until 2037. Since then no air-cooled Magnox reactor has been built anywhere in the world.

Meanwhile, Britain's boffins had moved on, having long been smitten with the idea of a breeder reactor. This seemed to be an impossibility, the nuclear version of a perpetual motion machine. It had been calculated that a core of plutonium-239 fuel wrapped inside a blanket of uranium-238 would 'breed' yet more plutonium, thus not only producing the heat to generate electricity but magically making more of its own fuel at the same time. By such miraculous means, they calculated, an almost infinite amount of electricity could be generated by a very finite amount of fuel. An experimental British fast-breeder reactor was built; but the enormous cost was only multiplied over several years as all attempts to get it to work properly failed, and once the project was cancelled yet more money had to be spent on trying to decommission it safely. Fast-breeder reactors have also been tried in the United States and elsewhere, but all have been failures – certainly commercially speaking – and have generally been officially rated as far too dangerous and unreliable. It all showed that in physics, as everywhere else, you can't get something for nothing.

Britain's second-generation reactor design for a nuclear power station rejected the original air-cooled model in favour of one optimised to produce electricity economically. There are really two main determinants in deciding the design of a nuclear power station. One is the kind of fuel to be used (for instance, natural as opposed to enriched uranium); the other is the choice of coolant. This latter is vital since if a reactor's core is allowed to overheat it could cause a runaway rise in temperature potentially leading to a meltdown and even to a radioactive release. For various reasons, including the lack of suitable supplies of enriched uranium,

British scientists turned down the water-cooled reactors that the Americans favoured and instead designed an Advanced Gas-cooled Reactor, or AGR, the type which today still powers virtually all of Britain's nuclear electricity generation.

By now the UK Atomic Energy Authority (UKAEA) was in control of anything nuclear, whether military or civil. This tended to restrict all decision-making to a hand-picked cadre of experts. The process was thus not just overcentralised but ridiculously secretive as well. As already noted in Chapter 3, Britain's AGR design was described by the economic historian David Henderson as 'one of the three worst civil investment decisions in the history of mankind'. This was a shame, since it was most carefully planned to be not just safer but more efficient since, unlike the other kinds, it could be refuelled without shutting the whole reactor down. In theory it could go on feeding electricity into the national grid without a break, meaning its electricity would be cheaper than any a coal-fired station could produce. Together with other technical advantages touted by the UKAEA, this gave Britain hopes that its AGR design had great potential for badly needed export orders. Meanwhile, five new power stations were ordered for the home market.

In the event, gas-cooled reactors turned out to be extremely troublesome. They proved difficult to build, even leaving out the way the construction of those first five twin-reactor stations in the 1960s and 1970s inevitably fell foul of the labour difficulties and strikes that were also plaguing other British industries.

The first to be ordered, Dungeness B, began building in 1965 and was supposed to be up and running by 1970. However, it was not until 1983 that it generated so much as a single watt because the design had proved prone to endless difficulties and breakdowns. During this period several of the other stations learned from Dungeness B and, having modified their design, were actually finished and running first. The cost of remedying the various problems, the redesigns and endless delays was prodigious and only really came to light in the 1980s when Thatcher's privatisation of the electricity companies necessitated some serious costing in order to establish their true market value. The embarrassing discovery of their grossly uneconomic prospects meant they had to be judiciously dropped from the sale and in 1995 were incorporated into British Energy. In 2009 Électricité de France (EDF) bought British Energy, including all seven of Britain's working nuclear power stations. Each had two reactors and to this day all bar one are AGRs: the design Britain hoped had great export potential but alas turned out to have none. The odd one out is a single Pressurised Water Reactor (PWR): today the most common design, globally speaking, and the one that generates the bulk of France's electricity in that country's numerous nuclear power stations. Yet again, such are the penalties of being a pioneer.

In April 2013 a document was published with the title *Nuclear Industrial Strategy – The UK's Nuclear Future*. It had a foreword signed by Vince Cable and Ed Davey, respectively the Secretary and Under-Secretary of State for Business,

Innovation and Skills. According to them, 'The UK was the first country successfully to develop, deliver and safely operate nuclear power stations... We can now look back on nearly 60 years of successful and, above all, safe exploitation of low-carbon nuclear power...' This goaded David Henderson into another of his pithy assessments:

> If a major policy initiative is based on a hopelessly distorted view of the past, this does not augur well. The above official assessment of the history of nuclear power in Britain is sheer fantasy. It is disturbing to reflect that the officials who drafted the text, as well as the two cabinet ministers who signed it, presumably believed it to be true.[86]

It is tragic that the McMahon Act should so unthinkingly have played into the hands of Britain's post-war desperation to retain its slipping powers, and doing so in such a way as to make the government opt in secrecy for centralised control of a new technology. Had it been able to draw on wider consultation with more and different scientists, not to mention MPs, planners and even public opinion, the outcome might have been different. (The same point might be made about de Havilland's obsessively keeping all its stress calculations of their Comet airliner in-house instead of getting RAE Farnborough to double-check their figures, which tragically turned out to be faulty.) But such were the times and Britain's reluctance to be open about civil atomic matters. Far less excusable was allowing this situation to continue for so long. Still more time has now gone by and today our nuclear generation industry is in the hands of foreign expertise. A retired British engineer who had worked at Sizewell commented in an email to me in 2014:

> [E]ven if the UK government can bring itself to create the right environment to enable new nuclear stations to be built, I doubt that the UK now has sufficient engineers with the appropriate experience for the project; all the ones I worked with have long retired, and their companies have all but gone. So the high-tech part of any new-build nuclear stations would now need to be implemented by foreign companies, who had more foresight than us. I'm sorry to rant on, but all we engineers share the same view about the demise of UK engineering and manufacturing, and with it the opportunities for export.

Well publicised accidents at reactors such as Three Mile Island (1979), Chernobyl (1986) and Fukushima (2011) have to this day affected the public acceptability of nuclear electricity generation. However, increasing numbers of people worried about the environmental effects of burning fossil fuels seem to feel that, since the technology of renewable energy (wind and tides, for example) may never be able to supply Britain's entire needs, nuclear generated energy regrettably remains Hobson's choice at least for the foreseeable future and despite the still unsolved and hugely expensive problems of decommissioning and radioactive waste disposal.

(ii) Fish

'This island is made mainly of coal and surrounded by fish. Only an organising genius could produce a shortage of coal and fish at the same time.'

—ANEURIN BEVAN

If a unifying thread in this chapter is that of Britain feeling itself obliged to give away priceless possessions to its political and economic cost, the case of the UK's decimated fishing industry is certainly no exception. Over the last half-century there has been a radical change in the nation's attitude towards the sea. No Briton who grew up in the Second World War was ever allowed to forget that we were an island nation. Never mind the Shakespearean quotations that peppered politicians' speeches, our dependence on the merchant navy's convoys for vital supplies of food and raw materials was constantly emphasised and made obvious by the very existence of ration books and coupons. Yet as the chapter on shipbuilding seems to imply, we must gradually have given up feeling that we are primarily and historically a maritime nation. That status has been yet further eroded by the huge growth in air travel and air freight, and finally rendered largely superfluous by the Channel Tunnel's dry-land connection with the Continent. Today, few Britons have much knowledge of or interest in the sea that stubbornly continues to surround these islands. It has become an irrelevance to them. Stories of increasingly urbanised children claiming that chicken nuggets grow on trees have recently been matched by others asserting that fish cannot possibly live in the sea otherwise they would drown. In both cases the children were not of primary school age but teenagers, so maybe after all it was simply proof of an admirable satirical streak. All the same, one wonders. Container ships that look more like floating office blocks and cruise ships that are shopping malls with cliff faces of windows (not even portholes) have abolished anything very nautical about modern sea-going. With their shops, cinemas, swimming baths, gymnasiums, game bars and video arcades such cruise liners are clearly designed to re-create the urban lifestyle without which their passengers evidently could not survive the inconvenience of being at sea.

Almost the sole exception to this trend is commercial fishing, which remains an industry no amount of health-and-safety edicts can make less inherently dangerous, nor one whit drier or warmer. Britain was probably the first nation to turn fishing into a fully mechanised industry by taking advantage of its lead in steam technology. In the late nineteenth century steam power was enabling fishing boats to travel further and faster to unfished grounds, independently of the weather, and to return quicker with the catch. Steam-powered winches aboard the vessels made it possible to deploy and retrieve much bigger trawl nets with larger catches from deeper waters. Once these were landed, steam locomotives from the port's railhead could deliver fresh (rather than dried or salted) fish overnight to towns and cities across the country. In this way, although Britain shared great areas of the seas around its shores with the fishermen of neighbouring countries, by the turn of the twentieth century it dominated immense fishing grounds out to considerable distances as if they had always been British by tradition and default. The next technological breakthrough was refrigeration: a great advance on the old 'livewell' system where cod were kept alive and fresh in tanks of seawater aboard fishing smacks. Refrigeration systems eventually became small and efficient enough to be used in railway trucks and the entire market for fish was changed with wet fishmongers now able to open shops throughout the land.

However, well before the nineteenth century was out the consequences of overfishing were apparent in fishing grounds around Britain and off the north-eastern United States. This had been noticed even before the coming of mechanisation; after it, total catches began falling alarmingly. As yet, not enough was understood about the reproductive biology of different species so no-one could reliably say when the various kinds of fish were ready to spawn, nor where they went to do so. Least of all did either scientists or fishermen know how to allow juveniles to reach reproductive maturity. Unlike with most animals hunted on dry land, a single catch might bafflingly contain yearling fish and others that were twenty years old.

At the growing signs of scarcity commercial fisheries became more politicised, with the traditional fishers of particular grounds defending them more or less aggressively against out-siders and rivals. That stocks could become depleted but then recover if a fishery was stopped for some reason was perfectly illustrated in the First World War when, thanks to German U-boat activity in the North Sea, Britain banned its own cod fleet from operating. At the end of the four years' hostilities the fleet sailed again and the catches were astounding. Not only were the cod now abundant but far bigger than they had been before the war. These bounteous harvests lasted a few years, but soon enough catches and the size of the fish dwindled again until by the middle 1920s they had shrunk to their pre-war levels. It is instructive to look at old photographs of cod fishers holding up their catch in the late nineteenth century. Some of the cod are as long as the men struggling to lift them are tall. Any supermarket shopper today can compare them with the minnows that now pass for fully grown adult fish.

Similar things were seen again after the Second World War when the British fishing industry got back into full swing. It was true that it was always small compared with the country's heavy industries; but it did employ hundreds of boats and thousands of fishermen and others dependent on the trade. Crucially, these tended to be in areas where fishing was the only source of employment and hence the industry could wield disproportionate political muscle when it came to election time, especially in north-east England and Scotland. By the 1960s Britain's deepwater trawling industry was the world's biggest. Based in Hull, it had a fleet of 150 that regularly suffered losses of ships and crew in icy northern waters. Safety measures were negligible, many trawlers being undermanned and without radios or medical equipment. In 1968 alone three boats were lost, together with 59 men. This tragedy led to a successful campaign by the men's wives – the so-called 'Headscarf Revolutionaries' – finally to introduce some basic safety regulations to a self-consciously macho, even fatalistic, industry.

Because the North Sea was fished by so many of the countries that bordered it, cod and other stocks were once again becoming depleted and many British trawlermen were driven further afield. Many had taken to fishing off Norway and Iceland; some, like the Hull fleet, had already been going to Iceland for so long they had come to consider it as practically their own territory. The Icelanders, who had always understood a good deal more than the British about conserving cod stocks and were careful to manage them sensibly, bitterly resented this and in the 1950s a series of skirmishes broke out between Icelandic coastguard vessels and British trawlers that culminated in the three 'Cod Wars' of the 1960s and 1970s, all of which Britain lost. Even at the time these seemed faintly absurd; but they were fraught with some quite acute political difficulties beyond the normal ones of occasional diplomatic apologies – as when all the windows of the British Embassy in Reykjavik were broken by stone-throwing mobs. At one point Iceland threatened to resign from NATO and declare a 200-mile zone that would have excluded all foreign shipping. Since this was taking place during the Cold War it immediately brought the United States into the conflict. Iceland was a vital part of NATO's strategic line that stretched from Greenland down to Scotland across the 'corridor' through which Soviet submarines had to pass in order to reach the North Atlantic. The US promised to open up its own markets to Icelandic cod and, because the Icelandic economy badly needed dollars, Reykjavik backed off and Iceland remained within NATO.

However, it continued to manage its own cod stocks with great skill, as it does to this day: so successfully, in fact, that ironically Icelandic waters are still the main source of British cod, pending the species' return to the North Sea in sustainable quantities.

At least the confrontations of the Cod Wars were straight-forward and out in the open. Britain was about to lose yet more of its fishing rights by outrageous political skulduggery. Back in 1964 Britain had co-signed the London Fisheries Convention that allowed vessels from the UK, Ireland, France, Germany, Belgium and the Netherlands to fish between six and twelve nautical miles of each other's coastlines. However, in early 1970 the original six Common Market countries suddenly noticed that a mere four nations controlled the overwhelming majority of Europe's fisheries. They were Norway, Denmark, Ireland and Britain, and all were applying to join the EEC. Not only that, but a United Nations treaty would shortly be coming into effect that would entitle maritime countries to a 200-nautical mile Exclusive Economic Zone around their shores. *Les Six* calculated that in this way the four countries would soon control over 90 per cent of all Western Europe's fish stocks. Thoroughly alarmed, they decided to draw up a quick 'common fisheries policy' before the four countries' applications could arrive, and present them with it as a fait accompli. This new CFP would supersede all previous conventions. Under its provisions all Europe's seas were to be designated as a 'common resource' to which all member states would be guaranteed equal access.

It was not until thirty years later in 2001 when Britain's Foreign Office files were released that it became clear exactly what a cynical stitch-up this had been. For a start, the 1957 Treaty of Rome had contained not a mention of a fisheries policy for the Common Market. There was merely a single reference in Article 38 to 'fisheries products'. Perhaps the most incendiary document to come to light in the archives was one written in French. It had been produced by the Council of Ministers' legal advisers in May 1970 and the lawyers emphasised that this was an 'extremely delicate' matter because, search it as they might, they could find nothing in the Treaty on which they could base a regulation granting all members 'equal access' to European fishing grounds. The Article 38 reference wouldn't do because it merely specified 'products' and not fishing activities. The lawyers desperately searched the Treaty for anything that could be made to apply and finally hit on Article 235, one of those usefully catch-all pieces of legalese that reads as follows:

If action by the Community should prove necessary to attain, in the course of the operation of the common market, one of the objectives of the Community and this Treaty has not provided the necessary powers, the Council shall, acting unanimously on a proposal from the Commission and after consulting the European Parliament, take the appropriate measures.

In other words, although seizing other countries' fishing grounds had never been one of the 'objectives of the Community', the

Six could decide to ignore their lawyers and use this Article together with some others that their legal secretariat had specifically ruled out in order to push ahead with a plan they perfectly well knew was technically illegal.

From the British point of view the real scandal is not only that the Foreign Office were well aware of this at the time, as a memo of theirs confirmed in June 1970, but that Edward Heath and his government were happy to accept this shameless move by the Six to appropriate Britain's fishing grounds. In February 1996 Heath himself, when questioned by the *Sunday Telegraph*, insisted that the whole thing had been entirely legal and had been authorised by Article 38 of the Treaty of Rome – an assertion he knew to be a lie. But by 1996 Britain's fishing grounds had long since been thrown open to what by then was the Nine, which included the biggest fishing fleet of them all, that of Spain. Like any politician constantly forced to defend a disastrous decision, Heath had clearly come to believe absolutely in his own falsehoods. The one applicant nation whose citizens in a referendum had thrown out their government's attempt to join the EEC was Norway, and their sticking point was precisely the idea that they would lose their own fishing grounds.

The release of these incriminating files under the Thirty-Year Rule revealed that as the implications of Britain's handing over its waters to a lot of foreigners dawned on its fishermen and their MPs, civil servants and ministers closed ranks in a deliberate attempt to conceal the way in which this fait accompli had been achieved. As the investigative journalist Christopher Booker wrote later:

> It was agreed right from the top [ranks of government] that we should not waste 'limited negotiating capital' on trying to save Britain's fishing industry and fishing waters, because they were viewed as a sacrifice worth making in exchange for the supposed wider benefits that Britain's membership would bring. Yet as a Scottish Office memo put it on November 9 1970, it was vital not to get drawn into explanations of what was going on or to admit what a disaster was in store for Britain's fishermen. The harsh truth was, the memo admitted, that 'in the wider UK context, they must be regarded as expendable'.[87]

And thus is Britain governed. Norway was revealed as a proper democracy, whereas Britons were deliberately kept in the dark and lied to by their own government in order that the prime minister could finally overcome General de Gaulle's repeated and humiliating '*Non*' and gain Britain's entry to the EEC. It is clear he was prepared to go to any lengths to get this and he stands revealed as the real initiator of the practice of giving away or selling off his country's patrimony that his successor Margaret Thatcher – and *her* successors in turn – were to continue with such enthusiasm.

Something not all bad might perhaps have come of this monstrous deceit had the EEC properly regulated Europe's fisheries so as to prevent overfishing and limit the gross environmental damage caused by ever-larger ships trawling ever-deeper waters. Far from it. For the next forty years the Common Fisheries Policy turned out to be a disaster that is only now with difficulty being corrected. On the advice of scientists who could often only guess at the size of various fish stocks, an annual Total Allowable Catch, or TAC, was set for different species. In practice this meant a total allowable *landed* catch since no amount of legislation could guarantee what might get swept up in trawl nets 120 metres wide and 15 metres high deployed at a depth of a kilometre or more. Anything other than the target species was deemed 'bycatch' and had to be thrown overboard. I witnessed this first-hand while aboard trawlers out of Peterhead and Fraserburgh in the late 1990s, and it was pitiful to see tons of perfectly edible fish – as well as inedible but important seabed species of sessile creatures – wrenched from the deep and chucked overboard dead to the screaming gulls wheeling in our wake. That this was allowed to continue for decades as ever-improving technology enabled ever-deeper swathes of destruction to be carved across Europe's seabeds was an environmental disgrace. It was likewise a political disgrace that the EEC did deals with impoverished African nations permitting European factory ships to hoover up the fish that were often the only source of sustenance the impoverished coastal dwellers had. The CFP further compounded its foolishness by ill-considered legislation designed to lessen the damage it was inflicting on European waters. Given the huge overcapacity of the EEC's fishing fleets, the main problem was simply that too many boats were chasing too few fish. Consequently, a limit was placed on the number of fishing vessels each member country could deploy, but without specifying their size. The predictable result was that fishermen took advantage of big EEC subsidies to swap their small boats for much larger ones designed to fish still deeper for untapped stocks. These were essentially factory ships fully equipped to fish for deep-dwelling species, with on-board processing and cold storage that enabled them to remain at sea for weeks at a time, and hopefully outside European waters.

What I remember best from those trips I made – the last of which went far into the North Atlantic, skirting Iceland – was how during the short day we appeared to have the heaving waters to ourselves while at night we seemed to be surrounded by lights that revealed the competition. 'Focking Spaniards', as our skipper kept saying. 'They've no bloody business up here. What's wrong with the focking Med where they belong?' Or else, 'Focking Russians. That one there's getting far too close. *Fit ye deen, ye bastard?*' he would yell at a swerving line of lights in the blackness beyond the steeply raked wheelhouse windows. 'They lost the Cold War and now they think they can bloody well sail anywhere scooping everything up in their factory ships.' By now the Cod Wars were history but it was clear a lively spirit of contentiousness still hung over these northern waters. One reason was that in 1982, when the UN Convention on the Law of the Sea came into force, Britain gained a 200-nautical mile

Exclusive Economic Zone (which, together with its various overseas territories like the Falklands, made it the fifth largest in the world). Its north-western boundary had been drawn from Rockall, a tiny granite tooth sticking out of the ocean 285 miles to the west of Scotland and representing Britain's furthermost outpost. However, in 1998 the United Nations disallowed Rockall as the UK's westernmost point because it is uninhabitable, with Atlantic waves often breaking right over it in winter storms. The UK's boundaries were then redrawn from St Kilda, an island off the Outer Hebrides some 150 miles further east. At a stroke the UK lost control of a huge area of ocean that immediately became international waters. Within weeks powerful Russian trawlers had taken up station and began intensively fishing a prime haddock stock off Rockall, to the obvious disgust of British fishermen like our skipper.

If his loathing of other nations was pungent for encroaching on what he evidently (if wrongly) considered as Scottish domain, it was as nothing compared to his opinion of Edward Heath: an opinion shared by his crew and everybody else I spoke to in Scotland's fishing communities. This was even before the release of the Foreign Office files provided chapter and verse for what had gone on behind the scenes. But it was already clear what Heath had done to their industry and livelihood. In those days he was still alive and it was impossible to repeat in print what my informants said for fear of libel action. But behind the more lurid accusations was a constant indictment: that of high treason. To have given away Britain's rights over waters it had jealously defended for centuries for a highly dubious political end and without consulting anyone was, in their opinion, worthy of having him clapped in the Tower to be followed – with any luck – by public execution. Anything less was far too good for him.

Such rants are doubtless cathartic even though their ostensible target has long been an Aunt Sally. More recent events have proved equally damaging to Britain's fishermen, and Westminster has been far more to blame than Brussels. Each EU country has fixed annual quotas of different fish species to do with as it chooses; but unlike other members the UK lets its fishermen sell off their quotas for cash. This has been exploited by the so-called 'slipper skippers' who would sooner toast their toes in front of the fire at home than go fishing. A single Dutch owned but UK-registered trawler, the *Cornelis Vrolijk*, owns 23 percent of the entire British quota.[88] Two-thirds of the rest are owned by three multinationals, leaving precious little for the small boats that are so vital to the tradition, economics and social life of Britain's ailing coastal communities. But Westminster cares nothing for that, aware only that the UK's fishing industry now accounts for less than half a percent of GDP and employs a mere 12,000-odd fishermen. It clearly finds our island status and historical dependence on the sea at best inconvenient and at worst an irritating irrelevance.

9.
Engineering

'… the kind of country that Britain has become: a country that has lost faith in its ability to design, make and build useful things, a country where the few who do still have that ability are underpaid, unrecognised, and unadmired.'

—James Meek, *Private Island*

The engine workshop at RAF Halton. The School of Technical Training was founded in 1919 and provided generations of apprentices and recruits with first-rate qualifications.

B ehind the demise of so much British industry in the second half of the last century lies a dense tangle of economic trends, political motives and social attitudes. As mentioned in Chapter 2, a complaint runs like a purple thread through historians' accounts as well as in today's newspapers: that Britain has never produced enough engineers, still doesn't, and anyway undervalues those it has. In order to examine this contention we need to return to that earlier chapter's somewhat simplified account of the two broadly differing versions offered by scholars, according to whether they take a 'cultural' or a 'scientific' attitude to British history.

A glance through the last two hundred years would reveal that even in the early nineteenth century, scientists of the stature of Sir Humphry Davy and Charles Babbage were already lamenting Britain's dearth of science education. Babbage even published a pessimistic book as early as 1830: *Reflections on the Decline of Science and some of its Causes*. In 1868 Lyon Playfair, a chemist who had trained on the Continent and was head of the science section of Britain's Science and Art Department – a subdivision of the Board of Trade – protested that 'the crying want for this country is a higher class of education for the foremen and managers of industry'. At casual first sight this might seem misplaced. After all, the roll call of inventors and engineers who had even then started or were pushing onward the Industrial Revolution is mainly of men (although not exclusively men) of world renown. A shortlist might include:

Thomas Newcomen, an ironmonger who developed the first practical steam engine (1712).

John Harrison, a self-educated carpenter who went on to invent the first marine chronometer that enabled navigators to establish their ships' longitude reliably (1759).

Abraham Darby III, a Quaker ironmaster who built the world's first completed iron bridge (1779), the eponymous and beautiful Iron Bridge in Shropshire: still standing and in daily use.

James Watt, whose steam engine of 1781 was the sophisticated improvement on Newcomen's and whose many variants were to power the Industrial Revolution.

Thomas Telford, the self-taught son of a Scots shepherd. His remarkable Pontcysyllte aqueduct (1805) is still the world's highest and still in use, as are many of his bridges.

Robert Stephenson was apprenticed to a mining engineer at fifteen and went on to build *Rocket* (1829), the world's first reliable steam locomotive.

Isambard Kingdom Brunel built the first tunnel beneath a navigable river, designed the Clifton Suspension Bridge, the entire Great Western Railway and the first transatlantic steam ships, of which the pioneering screw-powered SS *Great Britain* (1843) can be visited in Bristol.

Joseph Paxton, a gardener, designed the Great Conservatory at Chatsworth (1841), then the biggest cast iron and glass structure in the world, until he vastly exceeded it with his Great Exhibition 'Crystal Palace' in 1851.

Decimus Burton designed and built the exquisite Palm House (1848) and Temperate House (1862) at Kew Gardens, both of which still form the gardens' centrepiece.

Several of these individuals had precious little formal schooling but gained their practical knowledge from apprenticeships even if later they made their names in different disciplines. What they all had in common is that they were largely pioneers in their own fields, practical men with 'hands-on' skills often backed by remarkably little theoretical or academic knowledge. Most also demonstrated that, provided a citizen survived the usual diseases and hardships of the eighteenth and early nineteenth centuries, lowly social standing was not necessarily a bar to later success, although they might still have to contend with ingrained snobbery. When the chemist Humphry Davy invited the young Michael Faraday to accompany him on a continental tour in 1813 Faraday went as Davy's scientific assistant, for a while also acting as his valet. Davy's wife treated him as a menial, obliging him to travel on the outside of coaches in all weathers and eat separately with the other servants, to the point where Faraday became miserably depressed and thought seriously of returning to England and giving up science altogether.

Yet even as such men became celebrated in their lifetimes, anxious views were expressed that Britain ought not to have to rely entirely on the hit-and-miss, arbitrary manner in which a handful of exceptional individuals struggled to bring their inventions and discoveries to the world's attention. If people started out with a better education it would greatly increase the chances of any native brilliance being recognised and developed at an earlier stage. As water power gave way to steam and led to the growth of the great mills and 'manufactories' there were anyway more opportunities for the ordinarily skilled. There was an increasing demand for workers who could do more than keep boilers stoked and moving parts lubricated. They now needed to understand how the machines actually worked. By 1820 there were thirty-two factories in the Manchester area alone. These operated 5,732 power looms so there was an urgent need for men who could actually make the machinery for the rapidly expanding textile industry. Back in the eighteenth century this task had been performed by traditional craftsmen such as blacksmiths and wheelwrights, but their skills were hardly equal to building the complex and delicate power looms. Soon the need for skilled workers in the mechanical trades led to their formal training via more organised apprenticeships, but above all in mechanics' institutes.

The first of these institutes was established in Edinburgh in 1821, followed by others in Glasgow, Liverpool and London in 1823. These were started by local industrialists and wealthy benefactors, partly out of enlightened self-interest but also from a recognition that this new industrial era required an entirely different training and skills from those of largely agrarian occupations and would inevitably change the country and its economic future for good. Most mechanics' institutes also doubled as libraries and reading rooms since many of the young men who had deserted the land in favour of what they hoped would be a better living were curious about these new machines and eager to learn more about how they worked, to say nothing about the world at large. However, literacy was another matter and many needed basic schooling before they could take advantage of the library. The institutes spread mainly where Britain's industrial heartland was rapidly forming in the North and Midlands in towns like Glasgow, Barrow, Manchester, Leeds, Bradford, Newcastle upon Tyne and Birmingham. Although one or two were established in London and in West Country towns with shipyards such as Bristol and Falmouth, the outlines of a north–south divide were already becoming apparent.

Also becoming clearer was what can only be read as the determination of the English middle and upper classes to retain their near-monopoly of literacy, as can be seen from their evident reluctance until as late as 1870 to pass an Education Act that might have done far more than merely make schooling compulsory for working-class children aged five to twelve. As it was, seasonal absenteeism was commonplace in the dame schools run by local women who were themselves often barely literate. This was especially true in rural areas where children might be required to help with the harvest or simply act as bird scarers in newly sown fields. Even the most basic literacy was still very patchy in working-class mid-Victorian Britain and numeracy even more so. Yet as industrialisation and its inevitable book-keeping took hold, the need to be numerate as well as literate was becoming urgent. Whereas in the early days of industrialisation the factories and the canal system could be kept going by a comparatively small number of competent engineers, the rapid nationwide spread of the railways with their associated paperwork of inventories and timetables required an army of employees to be adequately literate and numerate. The railway companies and the factories also needed more and better engineers to furnish constant technical improvement. The nation's existing educational system could nowhere near supply them to the required level and official anxiety increased steadily as the century wore on and other countries that were rapidly industrialising – Germany in particular – began to pose a real threat to Britain's industrial and economic hegemony.

The mechanics' institutes proliferated and performed a great public service, but there was a limit to what could be achieved by the local benevolent societies and private individuals who founded them. What was urgently needed was a state education system that would provide at least basic literacy and numeracy to a point where a further, more specialised, training could build on them. It is almost impossible not to see a deeply ingrained class system as being behind the nationwide lack of properly educated engineers. Science in the abstract was to some extent catered for: Britain already had internationally famous institutions such as the Royal Society (founded in 1660) and the Royal Institution (1799). But these were academic forums for 'natural philosophers' to present new discoveries to each other. They were learned societies in which the educated classes could exchange ideas and discoveries. They were never designed to be educational in the ordinary sense and still less were they places for teaching technology to students.

By contrast the French École Polytechnique for engineers was founded in 1794. And even though pre-Bismarckian Germany was less a unitary state than a conglomeration of mini-princedoms, a nationwide network of technical colleges had been steadily growing there since the early nineteenth century. They offered a much more thorough grounding than did Britain's mechanics' institutes. The Berlin Technical Institute dated from 1821 and technical high schools were opened in Karlsruhe (1825), Dresden (1828) and Stuttgart (1829). Not only was there little of that standard in Britain but they could also capitalise on having students who entered with a better basic education. They steadily produced a cohort of youngsters with a working knowledge of both science and technology: youths who understood the principles behind engineering and were therefore potentially adaptable and mobile rather than being tied like apprentices to one particular type of machine or traditional way of working. It was their *theoretical* knowledge that made them flexible and able to progress to practical applications anywhere.

In Germany this was considered not just economically important but a vital complement to those who were more classically educated, the ideal being a modern Renaissance man like Goethe, equally at home in literature and science. Two separated and opposed bodies of knowledge – as in C. P. Snow's 'Two Cultures' – would have seemed to them deeply wrong-headed. Thus might a society be achieved that was progressive: both literate and numerate, academic and practical. Further education for school leavers was therefore given a high priority, especially in Prussia, where twenty-six trade schools were set up as well as technical colleges where adults learned to become foremen and managers.

At the apex of national systems for training *Technik* were the *Grandes Écoles* in France, and in Germany formidable university teaching departments in chemistry, metallurgy, physics and engineering which dispatched into industry a broadening stream of graduates. These were the men who were developing the sophisticated technologies that would supersede the simple machines and processes devised earlier by the British 'practical man'. As a consequence, this worthy pioneer was by the 1840s beginning to seem to British critics and foreign visitors alike a primitive, soon to be left behind. In 1842, for instance, a young French industrialist reported home that British managers 'do not at all understand the important theory involved in the [manufacturing] processes. ... In certain factories in Newcastle, for example, they do not even know how much coal each furnace burns.'[89]

Amongst the 'cultural' historians it is a common trope to contrast this all-round education that was available on the

Continent, and especially in Germany, with that in Britain. The implication is usually that Britain lagged hopelessly behind in such matters and it is small wonder that we were steadily over-hauled by our foreign competitors. This is not wholly wrong, in that Britain was undoubtedly slow in some respects, her governments generally being laissez-faire in outlook and non-interventionist by both ideology and indolence. At a local level, however, and apart from the mechanics' institutes, there were honourable exceptions to Britain's failure to organise a technical education to support what had already become the backbone of the nation's economy. The first of these was the Cornwall Polytechnic Society, founded in Falmouth by a Quaker in 1832; and the second the Royal Polytechnic Institution, founded in London in 1838. It is notable that neither was state funded; both were privately financed. The Royal Polytechnic Institution morphed in due course into the Regent Street Polytechnic of 1891 and in modern times into the University of Westminster. Both the Cornwall and the Royal offered free tuition. The Royal Polytechnic Institution was started expressly because its founders had woken up to the threat to Britain's economy of better-organised industrial competitors in Germany, France and America. All the same, two lone polytechnics in southern and western England were an inadequate resource for supplying engineers in the quantity and of the standard increasingly needed in the industrial Midlands and the North, even when added to the seven hundred-odd mechanics' institutes that existed by 1850.

It is indeed strange that this weakness in the British industrial system was not quickly remedied since it was not just scientists like Sir Humphry Davy and Charles Babbage who could see the root of the problem. Even *The Times* of 31 October 1854 could lament, 'This great commercial and mechanical country is governed by an official body comparatively ignorant of the mechanical arts.' Connoisseurs of the knuckleheaded immutability of Britain's governmental attitudes can skip the next 127 years to an early episode of *Yes, Minister* where exactly the same point can still be made with utter credibility, although it referred to chemistry rather than to engineering. A factory to make a compound called metadioxin is to be opened in a northern constituency that badly needs jobs, but its MP needs to assuage panicky rumours that it might be a dangerous substance liable to provoke foetal defects. Seeking reassurance, she calls on the minister responsible, Jim Hacker, with the senior civil servant Sir Humphrey Appleby and his assistant Bernard Woolley also present at the meeting. It swiftly becomes apparent that no-one has the first idea what metadioxin is, although the two ex-public school civil servants can readily parse the meaning of 'meta' in Greek. Nor can anyone say what 'inert' means, or even 'compound'. Hacker later recorded this in his diary:

> Suddenly, this all seemed awfully funny. None of us knew *anything* about the matter we were discussing. Joan, Humphrey, Bernard and I, all charged with a vital decision on a matter of government policy – and you couldn't have found four people anywhere in the

UK who understood less about it. I grinned, embarrassed, like a naughty schoolboy. 'We *ought* to know something about inert compounds, oughtn't we?'[90]

Of course this was satire. But it also depended on viewers knowing how well it described attitudes in Whitehall's upper echelons: a state of affairs impossible in France, for instance, where *Polytechnique* graduates are educated in a wide cross-section of mandatory scientific subjects.

Back in the mid-nineteenth century what seemed crucially absent in Britain was any governmental recognition of the importance of *technology*, as meaning the application of theoretical science to industry. It was even stranger that none of Westminster's capitalists seemed to realise that without being able to turn discoveries into products that could be sold at a profit, mere pioneering was of no economic benefit. This was bleakly illustrated following the discovery of synthetic dyestuffs (briefly alluded to in Chapter 2). In 1856 the brilliant eighteen-year-old chemist William Henry Perkin was trying to synthesise quinine, then the only treatment for the malaria that plagued so much of the expanding British Empire. He failed in this but in so doing accidentally discovered the first organic aniline dye, a deep purple colour later named mauveine. Given that its main raw ingredient, coal tar, was readily available in England and that other aniline compounds might in theory be synthesised to produce different colours, and given also that Britain was home to the world's largest textile industry, this discovery should instantly have been flagged up as a vital advance that could finally make that industry independent of the animal and vegetable dyestuffs which had to be unreliably and expensively imported from all over the world.

Perkin did patent what he called his 'Tyrian purple' and even opened a factory to make it. However, it was German industry that went on to discover and develop the vast range of aniline dyes of which mauveine was merely the first, an irony being that to do so it had initially to import supplies of coal tar from England. In 1863 a factory to make aniline dyes was started near Frankfurt, later to become Farbwerke Hoechst (still later Hoechst AG). In 1865 the Badische Anilin- und Soda-Fabrik also began making aniline dyes from the coal tar that was a by-product of a gasworks it had set up to supply street lighting. It was soon producing dyes in a great profusion of colours, forming the basis of an industry that today has made BASF the world's largest producer of chemicals. A footnote to this story is that in the First World War the dyes for the British Army's khaki and the Royal Navy's blue were imported from Germany.

The discovery of aniline dyes was unlike almost all previous inventions and discoveries in that it was not a refinement or development of an existing technology: it was pure organic chemistry being used to make completely new compounds. At that time Britain lacked what Germany so conspicuously had: a body of well-trained chemists who were not merely taught to do research but were *professional*: i.e. people who expected to make a living from it other than as teachers. This was effectively the birth of true applied science, the moment when laboratory work fed directly into a factory and generated an industry.

In Britain there were all sorts of calls for the state to support industrial research. True, Cambridge University had created its Natural Sciences Tripos in 1848, followed by Oxford's Honours School in Natural Sciences in 1852. But such courses largely taught academic rather than applied science, and to predominantly middle- or upper-class students. They were scarcely geared to any idea of the students having to earn a living once they had graduated, although it was appreciated that a good few would stay in academia.

In 1900 Lord Salisbury's Conservative government created the National Physical Laboratory (NPL) at Bushy Park in Teddington, just outside London. This was initially funded by the Treasury and the private sector but controlled by the Royal Society.[91] It remains to this day a highly prestigious research establishment but is not – and was never intended to be – a college of advanced technology, whether for full-time students or evening class attendees. As the science historian Donald Cardwell pointed out half a century ago:

> The ruling philosophy in England throughout the nineteenth century appears to have been that an individual who wanted higher education must be prepared to pay for it, even in colleges that were maintained in part by the State. ... It is not surprising, therefore, that the lower middle classes could not afford to send their children to London or provincial university colleges. ... The

scales were heavily weighted against talent from the lower classes; from, that is, the great bulk of the population.[92]

Even at the end of the nineteenth century, when secondary schools and universities had expanded and various kinds of social welfare at last made it possible for numbers of young men and women to get a higher education in technology, typically via evening classes, the opportunities for them to make a living from it other than by teaching were still limited. According to the Board of Education's Report for 1908–9:

> The slow growth of these technical institutions is in the main to be ascribed to the small demand in this country for the services of young men well trained in the theoretical side of industrial operations and in the sciences underlying them. There still exists among the generality of employers a strong preference for the man trained from an early age in the works, and a prejudice against the so-called 'college-trained' man.[93]

This was particularly true for older, craft-based industries like shipbuilding that were suspicious of 'book learning', and truer still for highly physical industries like mining where almost everything depended on traditional ways of working combined with deeply ingrained codes of personal toughness.

At a more intellectual level a counterpart to this attitude was identified by the Committee on the Neglect of Science in 1916. This clearly articulated the 'Two Cultures' problem more than forty years before C. P. Snow made it famous. At a meeting that took place in the depths of the First (and overwhelmingly technological) World War, all the attendees – including a number of classicists – agreed it was high time to break classical education's stranglehold on the Higher Civil Service examinations. A year later H. G. Wells attended a meeting of the British Science Guild and demanded an end to the 'Greek shibboleth' that set up a barrier between science and philosophy and history. 'Until you do that,' he said, 'your man of science will still be an unphilosophical specialist... and your literary and political men will be unscientific, unprogressive and unenterprising, full of conceit about their "broader outlook", and secretly scornful of science.'[94] Nevertheless, as late as 1920 Oxbridge colleges were still demanding a qualification in Greek from their future engineers and scientists.

But never mind mere science. There are times when anybody might be excused for wondering whether the British are innately opposed to *all* education. This, for example, was the situation the Board of Education found in 1917 while researching the prospects for Britain's post-war recovery: 'Public education after the Elementary School leaving age is a part-time affair. And there is very little of it. In 1911–12 there were about 2,700,000 juveniles between 14 and 18, and of these about 2,200,000 or 81.5 per cent were enrolled in neither day schools nor in evening schools...'[95] Thirty years went by until after the Second World War, when the Butler Act of 1944 introduced a 'Tripartite System' of state education that provided for grammar schools, secondary technical and secondary modern schools. Yet not much changed. Ninety-nine per cent of working-class children were now leaving school at fifteen but still devoid of any kind of qualification, scholastic or vocational. They were no more than 'ignorant coolies for a world of rapid technological change'.[96] An ex-grammar school boy later described how it had been:

As a beneficiary of the Butler Act, which gave me the chance of a grammar school education, it pains me to admit … that the 70 per cent of children who attended a secondary modern after the war got little or nothing out of it in skills or qualifications. The failure of governments to think constructively about the needs of the secondary modern pupils, or to devise for them any form of continuing education after the age of 15 was a scandal. For the great majority of working-class children the Butler Act might just as well never have happened. 'Secondary education for all' was the cry; but the educationalists who raised it were masters of abstract windbaggery – a vague secular religion of moral and spiritual uplift. What it came down to in the end was another year at school, with boys learning to bake a cake and girls to mend a fuse: all very well-meaning, but hardly the stuff of a great educational advance.[97]

Fast-forward another twenty years to the 1960s and we come to this:

With regard to higher technical education, it was not until 1960 that Britain was to create her first colleges of advanced technology, some 120 years after Germany; and not until after 1963 that these were to become full technical universities, some 70 years after their German equivalents. It was not to be until the mid-1960s, in the wake of the Robbins Report on higher education, that Britain embarked on the large-scale creation of new universities, and even then the liberal-arts tradition proved so strong that it came to dominate them too. In 1969, for instance, more than 1500 places, mostly in science and engineering, were to remain unfilled. And not until 1965 were the first two British business schools to be set up – sixty-six years later than the Harvard Business School.[98]

Half a century after that, and as evidence of how little changes in Britain, figures released by the Cabinet Office showed that in 2016 poor white (i.e. working-class) pupils performed worst at school of any ethnic group of Britons and had the lowest university entry rate.[99] Tony Blair's fulsome slogan of 'Education, education, education' had had as much tangible legacy as any other politician's catchy mantra. Mark Tavener's early noughties' radio serial *Absolute Power* stripped it bare as a question in a mock school maths exam: 'Divide "Education, education, education" by a lack of investment and express your answer as a fraction of an election promise.'[100] In any case, the reality is that today's state school teachers often have to act more as social workers than as educators. Finally, here is Carolyn Griffiths delivering her Presidential Address to the Institution of Mechanical Engineers in 2017:

> Already 64 per cent of UK engineering employers say a shortage of engineers in the UK is a threat to their business. … It is doubtful that the Government will ever make the radical changes to our curriculum to make it STEM [Science, Technology, Engineering and Mathematics]-focused. This would be unpopular with large parts of the education system, costly, highly disruptive and would probably be met with resistance from almost all other disciplines. Here there seems little prospect of change.

This pessimism was echoed by the Royal Academy of Engineering in its January 2017 response to a recent House of Commons Committee inquiry into how to close the STEM skills gap. It recognised that 'the chronic failure to encourage enough young people to become engineers and skilled technicians is a serious threat to the UK's engineering competitiveness'.

To be fair, this is a many-faceted problem. Difficulties for potential engineers trying to decide on a career today include a very uneven jobs market in which competition for joining big companies such as Airbus is fierce, while highly specialised disciplines (the nuclear industry, for example) or small rurally situated companies often attract no applicants at all for an advertised job. This is where companies may have no alternative but to recruit from abroad. Moreover, many students have little idea what engineering can offer as a career. One reason is that, in general, engineering firms fail to sell themselves well. This is in sharp contrast to companies offering careers in financial and professional services to numerate graduates.

'The major engineering employers only go to the top 10–15 universities, while all the banks and accountancy firms are very visible on all campuses.'[101] In addition, many companies that badly need genuine engineers complain of a lack of quality in today's graduate applicants. As one correspondent wrote in *The Engineer*:

> Many degrees just do not deserve the title. Even a good MEng in terms of technical depth is not as strong as the level of achievement we used to get at the end of the second year in a BSc. … It's not the graduates' fault – the failure of our education system and the Institutes is the problem.[102]

A friend of mine endorses this sentiment. He co-founded a very successful company making hi-tech sensing equipment for various offshore uses and recently had difficulty recruiting a suitable graduate for a very well-paid job. He ended up having to solicit applicants from Pakistan to find someone with the right educational background in analogue – as opposed to digital – electronics. He spoke disparagingly of the situation in the UK where 'too many universities are doing bollocks degrees. When everybody in the country's got a degree in media studies then nobody's qualified to do anything useful.'

In the same issue of *The Engineer* a letter from an S. Martin suggested that the problem lay less with the engineering industry than with society and a basic ignorance of old-fashioned skills until recently taken for granted:

When I was young we had toys such as Lego and Meccano that encouraged logical thought and practical assembly. Now it's all computers, which resolve problems on a screen hypothetically. This is a major problem. Hypothesis is fine up to a point, but come the practicalities and hypothesis doesn't work. Engineering is all about making the hypothesis a practicality and a reality.[103]

As a boy who spent much of his time making model aircraft and explosions, trying to fix a long series of defunct second-hand radios and taking down and cleaning the carburettor and jets of our Atco motor mower, I find this an entirely sympathetic argument in favour of a hands-on approach right from childhood, and never mind the minor injuries and occasional lack of eyebrows. It is irreplaceable groundwork on which later to graft theoretical learning that can then be more vividly and intuitively internalised.

Finally, as a further disincentive to consider engineering as a career, while a few graduates can expect a starting salary of £30,000, ordinary apprentices are often paid the official minimum of £3.50 an hour, which for an eight-hour day and a five-day week for forty-eight weeks might amount to a princely annual salary for someone aged 22 of £6,720, a sum on which no young urban Briton can possibly survive today. Such is the official rate; and it perfectly expresses the degree of importance the country attaches to educating its future engineers.

Thus it is that the two centuries-old complaint is still raised, year in and year out. Quite apart from the ongoing reluctance of successive governments to make large-scale investment to change this state of affairs, there is still the matter of public attitudes towards science and technology as a career option, which in a democracy must always to some extent underlie governmental policy. At the start of *I'm All Right Jack* (1959), the Boulting Brothers' oddly affectionate film satirising industry and the unions, Miles Malleson reacts to his newly graduated son (played by Ian Carmichael) expressing a desire to go into industry by saying, 'I still don't understand why anybody brought up as a gentleman should *choose* to go into industry.' Even sixty years ago this would have sounded snobbish although quite familiar enough to earn a laugh, whereas today few would risk expressing such a sentiment as though they believed it. It is worth briefly examining the history of the way we have trained our technicians and engineers because it partly explains a faint but lingering disdain which many people seem to feel – often quite unconsciously – about the entire enterprise.

Engineering's academic history in Britain has not much helped its cause. As we have seen, some of those little mechanics' institutes of the early nineteenth century were eventually translated into polytechnics, which in the following century began to proliferate after the Second World War. Since they initially focused on technical subjects more at a practical than an intellectual level they were generally viewed as inferior to universities. Polytechnics were converted into universities in 1992 with what looked like an unseemly haste that led to a certain amount of mockery. At the same time several existing university institutes of science and technology (such as UMIST in Manchester and UWIST in Wales) were absorbed into their respective universities and lost their identities. None of this did much to improve the public image of engineering and technology, where a faint miasma of 'second best' (but not necessarily second-rate) hung about them.

We can thank Britain's peculiar class structure for this. The status of engineer still has not made the transition from a trade to a profession, unlike the surgeon-barber who has long since been elevated to surgeon proper (while still being addressed as Mister). The legal clerk has likewise been transformed into a solicitor; the book-keeper into an accountant. Many European countries have long allowed and even encouraged the rise of diverse trades to the status of professions, and with it their social standing. The unimpeachable professional status of engineers in technologically advanced societies like Germany is long established; and in Italy the courtesy title of 'ingegnere' is in daily use (usefully so when addressing an educated person whose exact qualification one doesn't know).

In Britain, by contrast, the term 'engineer' is vague and, far from having acquired the dignity of professionalism, is still often associated with oil-stained overalls in grubby backstreet workshops and even with car repairs. Many people have no idea of the complex grounding in theoretical science needed before one can hope to become a 'chartered' engineer, nor how long it can take to acquire this status. Neither do most people realise how extremely diverse engineering is with its sundry divisions such as Mechanical, Electrical, Electronic, Agricultural, Civil, Structural, Telecommunications, Chemical, Nuclear, and so on; nor that there are many subdivisions and mergings of these into Aerospace, Automotive, Marine, Medical and other specialised forms of engineering.

A careers adviser with thirty years' experience in the field points out how very few examples there are in Britain of politicians and public figures with technological connections or qualifications. Gone are the 1960s when the Industrial Training Boards were established and for a brief period Harold Wilson openly identified with the 'white heat' of technology. There was governmental backing for Concorde, the Hawker Harrier, telecommunications and some manufacturing – mostly connected with the defence industry. But the following decade ended in the Winter of Discontent with increasing industrial strife and a slowdown in manufacturing, while the 1980s brought the demise of heavy engineering and mineral extraction such as coal mining, the transfer to the Far East of a good deal of manufacturing and the steady rise of financial and other services in London and the south-east. That decade also saw the dismantling of the Industrial Training Boards in response to pressure from what remained of industry, which collectively was reluctant to pay for training but apparently didn't mind cutting its own throat. What was more, the trade unions also failed to make a case for high-quality engineering jobs, preferring to focus their energies on maintaining the differentials between members who had been traditionally trained through apprenticeships and those who had acquired the same level of skill by other means.

The same careers adviser admits that trying to overcome engineering's negative connotations in the public's mind has not been made any easier by a chronic lack of investment. 'I have visited companies where equipment made before the First World War was still in daily use. It was readily admitted that the level of accuracy that could be achieved did not meet the contract requirements.'[104] In other words Britain is open for business provided customers don't mind hundred-year-old standards of manufacture. The same adviser added location as often affecting attitudes to engineering. Negative memories are not easily forgotten in hard-hit areas:

All my careers guidance experience has been based in the Midlands and much of this in Rugby. This town was once strongly focused on a variety of engineering activities and was home to several branches of GEC [General Electric Company] who employed thousands. British Rail also had significant repair and maintenance workshops there and many small companies were specialist suppliers to the motor manufacturing and machine tool firms in nearby Coventry. BR moved their facilities back to Derby and bit by bit GEC shut down their facilities to the point that within ten years they went from taking on over 150 craft and technician apprentices per year to ten, and now none. The demise of the car makers in Coventry meant the closure of many parts suppliers and the rapid decline led to many redundancies and the loss of highly skilled jobs. This collapse still echoes because the students' parents have deep memories of the unreliability of employment in engineering. ... As for universities, I have also visited plenty to view their engineering courses and when I asked one tutor about entry requirements he told me he used the 'mirror test'. This involved holding a mirror to the mouth of the applicant and if condensation formed they were accepted. This was obviously meant as a joke, but it surely illustrates a sadly unsatisfactory state of affairs.[105]

Coventry had long been prosperous as 'Motor City' and was latterly home to BL's Standard-Triumph, Jaguar, and Hillman-Chrysler (later Talbot and Peugeot), not to mention Alvis. But by the early 1980s upwards of 20 per cent of the workforce was unemployed. The city's recent self-reinvention as an automotive R & D hub, while obviously good news for engineers, serves to hide the profession's unpredictability in terms of both jobs and geography. Anybody who can remember Sheffield in its heyday as 'Steel City' would be even more wary. The opening sequence of the 1997 film *The Full Monty* is a 1972 documentary about booming industrial production in Sheffield that promptly contrasts with six unemployed steel workers resorting to strip-tease in order to earn a living. The comedy only partially obscures acute social tragedy. Today Sheffield is Britain's low-pay capital, with average hourly rates 10 per cent lower than those of the rest of the country. 'It never recovered from the decimation of industry under Thatcherism in 1984 [when] unemployment in the city surged to over fifteen per cent, and industrial suburbs with flickering furnaces were reduced to wastelands of weeds and fences.'[106]

Such imagery has long taken root in popular culture. In June 1981 the pop group The Specials recorded 'Ghost Town', which stayed at no. 1 for three weeks and was elected Single of the Year. In March 2002 Jerry Dammers, the group's keyboardist, was interviewed by the *Guardian* and vividly recalled the period. 'You travelled from town to town and what was happening was terrible. In Liverpool all the shops were shuttered up, everything was closing down... You could see that frustration and anger in the audience. In Glasgow there were these little old ladies on the streets selling all their household goods, their cups and saucers. It was clear that something was very, very wrong.'[107]

If one looks back over nearly three centuries of Britain as the world's first industrial nation, one single feature stands out. It explains nearly every aspect of Britain's lurching and sporadic economic progress, right down to today's farcical chaos surrounding the crucial Brexit negotiations. That is, the utter want of any serious, thoroughgoing *plan*. No social plan; no economic plan; no industrial plan; no overall vision; no nothing. All is casual, amateurish, as though there will always be a safe distance between those who govern and the outcome of their policies. Only twice in the past century has serious planning been sustained for as much as a few consecutive years, and both occasions were made mandatory by world wars. Outside wartime, British political strategy has mainly relied on muddling through to the end of the week. Far from planning, these days a government's entire energy is swallowed up in trying to remain in office by means of constant damage control and keeping the lid on by robbing Peter to pay Paul. That and bluster. Small wonder that students tend not to be easily seduced by the prospect of a career in engineering when all history has shown that it is a misunderstood and undervalued profession, socially speaking, as well as prey to abrupt changes of the political wind that within a decade or so can render destitute whole towns and cities, even entire regions. Admittedly, nothing is guaranteed in this world; but without some kind of earnest that one's hard-won qualification will be recognised by continuity of employment rather than being forever at the mercy of the sudden whims, caprices and indifferences of whichever government, there is understandably little incentive to commit to the profession. So much for 'the knowledge-based economy'. We sometimes feel like a culture that has lost the will to live.

ELLING ENGLAND BY THE POUND

10.
Latterly

*'The world is disgracefully
managed, one hardly knows
to whom to complain.'*

—RONALD FIRBANK, *Vainglory*

Alluding to the 1908 tourism poster 'Skegness is so bracing', Gary Barker's November 2013 cartoon shows prime minister David Cameron and his City cronies exultant after selling off tranches of Britain's nuclear industry to China and France.

What, then, can be concluded about the manner in which so many of Britain's major industries slid – or were allowed to slide – into oblivion in the latter half of the last century? All those myriad British products from watches to transatlantic liners, from Dinky Toys to supersonic fighters: how could our ability and will to make and keep them simply fade away? World-famous names like Cammell Laird, Dunhill and Purdey were forcibly cut from their pasts to float in the commercial mid-air like the Cheshire Cat's grin for shape-shifting consortia to snap up as 'brands' to swell their investment portfolios and give an aura of dignified quality to their ventures. Whatever happened? From a septuagenarian's perspective the usual explanations (changes in world trade, bad management, obstreperous unions, slumps and so forth), while often convincing enough as far as they go, never quite satisfy.

For one thing, too much attention is paid to the *coups de grâce* Margaret Thatcher administered. She made no secret of what was clearly a visceral dislike of heavy industry with its connotations of grime and strikes and a bolshie working class that lacked petit-bourgeois rectitude and patriotism. Yet the truth is that the writing had been on the wall for most British manufacturing industries long before her accession in 1979. None of Britain's successive post-war governments, union leaders and managements ever succeeded in drawing up – let alone implementing – a coherent and long-term national plan, not just for survival but for prospering. No remedy for setbacks, whether temporary or terminal, was ever found beyond the injection of huge doses of public money to postpone collapse. Given this, Thatcher's conviction that the day was over for Britain's great nationalised industries was reasonable, as was her certainty that their place could be taken by new economic sectors such as banking and insurance: a shift towards the service industries that the European single market would make that much easier. The mistake for which she will never be forgiven was the brutal manner in which the shift was carried out. The erstwhile 'northern powerhouse' was dumped in favour of a new south-eastern powerhouse centred on the City of London without the slightest sympathy or provision for dealing with the social consequences. In keeping with British governmental tradition, no proper plans were ever made to alleviate the miserable social consequences of the greatest economic upheaval since the Second World War.

This lack of planning has a history going back to the very Industrial Revolution that Britain had the great misfortune to inaugurate. The revolution itself sprang up in scrappy fashion and until around 1870 was pushed ahead by engineering geniuses in stovepipe hats and lumpy trousers plus hordes of nameless navvies. At this point the country began paying the price most innovators wind up paying: that of being overtaken by others able to skip comparatively nimbly over the stepping stones the pioneer has so painfully laid. As recounted in Chapter 2, purely technical innovation was never a British monopoly and a good deal of cross-fertilisation of ideas and inventions quickly took place among the industrialising nations. In due course the trade figures tell the story, although the British Empire's enormous 'tame' market skewed Britain's export record to give a more favourable impression than perhaps was merited. By the mid-1880s the UK was accounting for 43 per cent of all the world's manufactured exports, while Germany produced 16 and the USA 6 per cent. By 1913, the UK's share had fallen to 32 per cent while Germany's had increased to 20 and the USA's to 14 per cent.[108] Britain proved slow to keep up with technological improvements, and where we ourselves had invented a new technology we seldom had the ability to make it pay commercially. The cotton industry's failure to profit from young William Henry Perkin's chance discovery of aniline dye was but one example. We were also bad at renewing factory equipment to keep up with foreign competitors who offered new standards of efficiency and precision. This was a protracted failing. In both world wars a good deal of our production of aircraft parts and engines could not have been achieved without the thousands of German and American machine tools that British companies had imported in peacetime for lack of suitable home-grown versions.

Seriously compounding this downward trend were a low-skilled, poorly housed and often half-starved labour force and equally low levels of investment. In the ongoing absence of any overall national plan, as late as the 1920s and 1930s less than a quarter of all Britons had any secondary or tertiary education, which made it impossible to build a skilled labour force even if that had been the manifest goal of successive governments – which it clearly never was. During the Second World War British industry flourished because it had the undivided backing of the Coalition government and the War Cabinet and was given absolute priority. At the time all that mattered was the nation's survival, even though, as we have seen, it was never enough to keep strikes and stoppages from holding up production, particularly in the shipyards. This fact alone ought to alert any observer to an underlying division within British society that dated back to at least the beginnings of the Industrial Revolution and which no amount of threats, exhortation or propaganda could cover up. That our industrial wealth and production depended to such an extent on an ill-educated underclass was an open sore that, unaddressed, would play its own inexorable part in the country's industrial downfall in the decades following 1945.

Given all these factors plus some bad luck, the demise of Britain's major industries was surely inevitable, especially once foreign competition had leaped ahead. It is only too easy now to see how Clement Attlee's post-war Labour government failed to take the one step that might possibly have averted disaster by coming up with a comprehensive long-term plan for British industry, and hence for the whole economy. But again, history shows that we are neither good at nor really interested in that sort of thing, least of all in peacetime. Maybe it smacks too much of command economies and collectivisation, of Nazi Germany and the Soviet Union? In any case excuses can be made for Attlee, given the workload facing his government. Much of it was admittedly self-imposed, like the introduction of the massively expensive welfare state; but a good deal of the rest was necessitated by the recent war and included the urgent reconstruction of towns and cities, housing and infrastructure. All these tasks were further hampered and exacerbated by an acute shortage of money.

What Margaret Thatcher was to import from America – but with not the slightest understanding of its implications and future consequences – was the idea of running a country as if it were a company, with the prime minister and Cabinet playing the roles of chairman and board of directors while sixty-five million citizens were turned into 'stakeholders'. She was besotted by the fashionable economic theories of American neoliberal economists like Friedrich Hayek and Milton Friedman that extolled the private sector and berated government spending. However, as previous chapters have shown, the British with their innate laissez-faire attitude have never really shown much flair for management of any sort. Likewise, boards of directors drawn chiefly from the upper echelons of society with more interest in the City than in the rest of the country beyond the Home Counties have often proved incompetent. The tragic outcome of this 'Britain plc' business model is today revealed in all its enforced austerity and ever-widening disparities of wealth. That this neoliberal nonsense ever managed to take hold suggests that our long drawn-out industrial failure probably had as much to do with Britain's pre-existing social attitudes and governmental system as it did with external factors like oil embargoes, global economic downturns and the rest. Somewhere in this mix, and at an inchoate motivational level, there is the national character to take into account. If this is correct, then the polarity between the 'cultural' and 'scientific' explanations outlined in Chapter 2 must be false, and a true explanation would have to include both.

One of the most obvious failures of the 'Britain plc' business model with its wholesale privatisations has been that 80 per cent of Britain's economy is now composed of service 'industries', not one of which could manufacture so much as the proverbial bag of nails. It is hard to pretend that this idea of putting four-fifths of a nation's economic eggs into one basket inspires the remotest confidence. Common sense suggests that the safest defence against unforeseeable events is a well-mixed economy; and that one chiefly composed of bankers and nail parlours does not qualify. It is precisely this dumping of common sense in favour of an unproven economic theory dreamed up by a couple of disaffected foreign academics that has left the nation's fortunes so dangerously vulnerable. This is interesting for two main reasons. First, because it gives the lie to the idea – much touted by the natives themselves – that we British are innately wary of any ideology, especially if it is foreign and fanatically endorsed. (After all, we have been swallowing the notion of 'Britain plc' for nigh on forty years.) And second, our generally slavish aping of the United States hides how often we have misinterpreted the model. Hayek and Friedman might well have extolled the private sector at the expense of government spending, but unlike Britain plc the United States has shown itself to be highly flexible when it judges that the nation's interests are at stake. More than that, the US government has shown itself to be the world's biggest venture capitalist.

As the economist Mariana Mazzucato has shown, far from only ever stepping in reluctantly to save failing industries (the most that doctrinal neoliberalism might allow), the US government has actually generated entirely new markets by means of canny long-term investment.[109] For instance: although Silicon Valley is everywhere hailed as the ultimate symbol of multi-billion-dollar private enterprises that germinated in garage start-ups, the ground in which they took root was already heavily manured. Silicon Valley's present vast economic power owes everything to crucial government support at an early stage. Mazzucato details how practically every one of the new technologies that lie behind the success of the iPod, iPad and iPhone – the internet, GPS, lithium-ion battery, hard drive, touchscreen, voice recognition and even SIRI – has it roots in federally funded projects. By contrast, Britain plc is loath to back almost anything in the private sector without the guarantee of short-term shareholder dividends. The dead hand of ideology and the Treasury will not permit it. It therefore comes as no surprise to learn that the rechargeable lithium battery was invented by an English chemist, M. Stanley Whittingham, when he was working for Exxon in the 1970s, nor that today he is a materials science professor at New York State's Binghamton University rather than at his alma mater, Oxford.

It is perfectly true that the US government was never going to turn the research it funded into an iPhone: that is the role of entrepreneurs like the late Steve Jobs, gifted with the ability to transmute innovation into cash. But the groundwork was laid by American taxpayer-funded research.

In any case, if the proof of a pudding is in its eating we ought by now to be able to give a gourmet's verdict on Britain's uniquely flavoured economy. Since this has been running at a deficit for years (the national debt is now £1.6 trillion or so), it is scarcely a glowing advertisement for neoliberalism, Britain plc or the British way of doing things. If after 1945 we couldn't even run a comparatively straightforward and self-contained motorcycle industry with lasting success, by what hubris do we imagine we can run an entire country as a company? To judge from its own ledgers Britain's version of capitalism since the 2008 global banking crisis has scarcely been a triumph for monetarism. The country's inability to recover, let alone to prosper, while other European countries have managed both reveals our economic model as a failure, as well as no way to govern human lives. *Si monumentum requiris, circumspice.*

That this is not mere rhetoric is shown by the profound gulf that has progressively opened up between the 'Them' of the board and the 'Us' of the 'stakeholders', a majority of whom have long given up all hope of influencing the way their country is run. If Britain's record over the last half-century has all the hallmarks of a failed economy, it also now presents symptoms of a failing society. Back in 1965, the year after I left university,

Brian Abel-Smith and Peter Townsend wrote in *The Poor and the Poorest* that 7.5 million Britons were living below subsistence level (using the National Assistance Board's definition): some 13.4 per cent of the population. All but half a century later, the 2014 Poverty and Social Exclusion (PSE) report stated, 'Today, 33 per cent of the UK population suffers from multiple deprivation by the standards set by the public. It was 14 per cent in 1983.' According to OECD figures the UK is now the least economically egalitarian country in Europe, with public spending lower in Britain than in almost every other Western European country. Our growth is virtually nil.

> Our under-30s are near the bottom for technical qualifications, with low literacy and numeracy, while our research and development falls below the OECD average. Our low corporation tax encourages companies neither to invest – they sit on shedloads of capital – nor to upskill. Eurostat shows UK companies invest half as much as the EU average in training. Apprenticeships fell by over 60 per cent last year, and investment in skills by 9 per cent in the decade. Failure in early years education is just one more glaring error stressed by the OECD, while 54 per cent of schools offer no computer science GCSEs.[110]

All very tragic, but hardly a surprise. Right from the start of the neoliberal experiment in around 1980 we could see how things would probably go. On the one hand the City's Yuppies were soon modelling for 'Alex' cartoons, roaring around in Porsches and lighting their cigars with five-pound notes, while on the other regional industries were going out of business at an alarming rate. Yet government money was more likely to be spent on propaganda claiming that Britain was open for business than it was on trying to save companies. A good example of this was the Welsh Tourist Board's late 1981 television campaign 'Made in Wales', promoting the idea that, far from being a scene of growing devastation and unemployment, the Valleys were alive with the sound of factory hooters and joyous rugby songs. The ad listed various industries in Wales that employed thousands of workers, with the names of the companies running along the bottom of the screen as a Welsh choir sang them to the tune of Cwm Rhondda.

This was so outrageous it begged to be lampooned, and the TV satirical programme *Not the Nine O'Clock News* obliged with a savage version that exactly copied the Tourist Board's format. The only differences were that it listed sixteen companies that had failed and the voice-over at the end was by Griff Rhys Jones rather than Philip Madoc. You need to hear the tune in your head to take the necessary liberties with the scansion:

Dunlop, Jaeger, Firestone, Triang
Ethylene Products, Potter and Sons;
Inglefield Power Engineering,
Richards and Wellington Industries Group.
E.C. Cases, Tubal Cain Foundry,
T.I. Helliwell, Curran Steels;

Louis Edwards, D. A. L. Builders Merchants,
Leiner Limited and Duport Steel.

Failed in Wales, failed in Wales,
Please help us to work again, work again...

V/O: We've called in dozens of receivers, closed hundreds of
factories, and there are thousands more teetering on the brink in
Wales ...[111]

In order to sustain the illusion of Britain plc keeping the country open for business, successive governments have often needed to use means that are, frankly, questionable. These include the short-termism imposed by trying to keep the books balanced and looking good while buying off the stakeholders with dividends; generating cash by selling off public property that was not theirs to sell (such as houses paid for by generations of council ratepayers); and doing much of this under cover of subterfuge. British governments have always been able to rely on the more influential part of the electorate having little curiosity about the social conditions in which so much of the nation's wealth is generated. Beyond that, though, official secrecy is evidently a vital part of our version of democracy, as was obvious when it came to choosing the best design of nuclear reactor to supply electricity to the national grid. The Freedom of Information Act 2000 – a measure grudgingly passed although long overdue for a country that has always congratulated itself loudly on its freedom of speech and the public accountability of its workings – is itself under constant threat from the government of the day. According to the 2018 World Press Freedom Index, and thanks partly to a recent series of press-muzzling laws, the UK is now one of the worst countries in Europe in terms of press freedom. Overall it has sunk to 40th out of 180: a loss of eighteen places since the Index was started in 2002. It is as though at an AGM the board of directors was anxious lest shareholders examine too closely what they are up to. 'Transparency' can thus be indistinguishable from a carefully constructed opacity. The parallels with the corporate world are obvious. The Reuters reporter Tom Bergin was formerly an oil broker who knew the oil industry from within. Here he might be describing the working ethos of Britain plc as much as that of oil companies:

> A general lack of transparency in the corporate world makes it hard ever to know what is going on inside a company. All information is controlled by the management, whose primary goal is to manage perceptions of their own performance. Obviously their primary duty is to protect shareholders' interests, but anyone who thinks this duty will ever trump an executive's desire to manage his or her reputation is naïve. Indeed, information that might be highly beneficial to shareholders yet damaging to management is often withheld from investors on the grounds that releasing it would hurt shareholders. The term 'commercially sensitive' can be stretched to audacious extremes.[112]

This doubles as a perfect description of the way Britain is governed.

If all the foregoing has something to say about the British national character, not least a peculiar tolerance for social injustice that we would roundly condemn in another country, it is not hard to see the bearing it might have on the way so many of our industries proved beyond resurrection. Almost half a century ago a familiar public figure gave the Rectorial Address at Glasgow University. He spoke passionately of a growing social alienation in Britain in terms that were to become commonplace among journalists writing about Them and Us and the large section of those Brexit 'Leave' voters who had suddenly surfaced as the ignored Other Nation. Small wonder that it should have played a central role in our industrial decline:

> What I believe to be true is that today [alienation] is more widespread, more pervasive than ever before. ... It is the cry of men who feel themselves the victims of blind economic forces beyond their control. It is the frustration of ordinary people excluded from the processes of decision-making. The feeling of despair and hopelessness that pervades people who feel with justification that they have no real say in shaping or determining their own destinies.

Of all people, this speaker in 1972 was Jimmy Reid: a man the nation's mainstream press had denounced as a 'Communist firebrand' and who led not a strike but a 'work-in' at the Govan shipyards to protest against their incipient closure thanks mainly to decades of mismanagement. The rest of his address was in a moral, humanist tone, quoting Jesus Christ and Robert Burns; but the anger that underlay it was unmistakable.

> Profit is the sole criterion used by the establishment to evaluate economic activity.... The whole process is towards the centralisation and concentration of power in fewer and fewer hands. Giant monopoly companies and consortia dominate almost every branch of our economy. ... From the Olympian heights of an executive suite, in an atmosphere where your success is judged by the extent to which you can maximise profits, the overwhelming tendency must be to see people as units of production, as indices in your accountants' books. To appreciate fully the inhumanity of this situation, you have to see the hurt and despair in the eyes of a man suddenly told he is redundant without provision made for suitable alternative employment... Someone, somewhere has decided he is unwanted, unneeded, and is to be thrown on the industrial scrap heap.

The trends that Reid noted all those years ago have since become entrenched and blatant; are even promoted as the natural order of things. In today's Britain plc, the land of the gig economy and the zero-hours contract, millions daily face the threat of redundancy or below-minimum-wage income, usually while already in debt. The country has wandered into a chill shadow that makes Beveridge's meliorist vision in the depths of war look positively Edenic. The general insecurity is further fed by almost daily predictions that within a decade or two automation and robots will anyway make practically everybody redundant.

We are left with a sense of a country either stalled or heading relentlessly backward after a brief post-war glimpse of civic fairness. This feels true at both a general and a specific level. The British political writer Owen Hatherley recently addressed with passion the fate of the Beveridgian plans for Britain's social recovery that evolved during the latter part of the Second World War, summing up: 'In Britain today we are living through exactly the kind of housing crisis for which council housing was invented in the first place, at exactly the same time as we're alternately fetishising and privatising its remnants.'[113]

It goes still deeper. Behind the retrogression lies something that has changed little in over a century: a pervasive infantile element in Britain's national psyche that means some social attitudes have barely moved. In his 1939 essay 'Boys' Weeklies', George Orwell remarked how this ethos was a mixture of Dickens and Kipling, 'sodden in the worst illusions of 1910'. Orwell pointed out that this was not accidental. It simply promoted the ruling class ethic of the magazines' proprietors like Lord Camrose, whose Amalgamated Press also owned the *Daily Telegraph* and the *Financial Times*. What was being pumped into Britain's youth was 'the conviction... that there is nothing wrong with laissez-faire capitalism, that foreigners are unimportant comics and that the British Empire is a sort of charity concern which will last forever. Considering who owns these papers, it is difficult to believe that this is unintentional.' Indeed. Fast-forward nearly eighty years to the 2016 Referendum and an almost identical message was being trumpeted by such papers as the *Daily Mail* (prop. Jonathan Harmsworth, the 4th Viscount Rothermere, with non-domicile tax status and an estimated fortune of £1 billion); the *Daily Express* (prop. Richard Desmond, net personal worth £2.25 billion); and with hardly less restraint by the *Daily Telegraph* (props. the tax exile Barclay twins, Sir Frederick and Sir David, with an estimated joint net worth of £6.5 billion); and *The Times* and the *Sun* (prop. Rupert Murdoch, global tycoon with a personal fortune of £12 billion). This is scarcely a roll call of men-of-the-people, still less of radicals. The power these moguls jointly exercise over British public sentiment would have been instantly recognisable to George Orwell. Under their tutelage foreigners are still a collective joke ('Up Yours, Delors'); Britons are naturally superior (We Won the War – not to mention the 1966 World Cup); and in some ghostly and wholly fictitious manner Britannia continues to rule some prudently unspecified waves. As with all determined self-delusions, a deep pathos adheres to this gangrenous form of patriotism.

Ironically, far from moderating Britons' insularity, the spreading of the Empire in the nineteenth century may well have encouraged a national disdain for foreigners. We now rightly lament the damage the Empire did to dozens of societies around the world; but we have spent far too little time assessing the damage it did to us, too. The survival of such xenophobic snobbishness into the twenty-first century is worse than merely uncivil. Britons' reluctance to learn foreign languages, and increasingly that of many British schools to teach them, undoubtedly carries economic penalties. It often seems as though many Britons' affectation of a lordly disparagement of the Continentals they are expected to trade with – not to mention towards their own working class – has changed remarkably little in the last half century. Back in the early sixties both attitudes were skewered by Michael Frayn in his weekly newspaper column. It is satire; but only just:

Christopher Smoothe, the Minister of Chance and Speculation, is overcome by an unforeseen attack of truthfulness when opening the British Bingo Exhibition in Brussels:

'The intention of this exhibition, I am told by my advisers, is to show bingo as part of the so-called British way of life. What the British way of life consists of, apart from unofficial strikes and industrial squalor, I am not qualified to say, but let me point out at once that neither I nor anyone else of the social class to which I happen to belong would be seen dead in a bingo hall.

'The exhibition is also being represented, in some nebulous fashion which I have not fully comprehended, as a contribution to the concept of the Common Market. If this means that foreigners are expected to buy the bingo equipment displayed here, let them be warned that it is of British manufacture, and is therefore likely to fall very swiftly to bits.

'I suppose it is expected that on an occasion of this nature I should make some comment on Britain's entry into the Common Market. I must say first that neither I nor my colleagues have any clear idea of what the economic consequences of going in will be, and that frankly none of us greatly cares. I myself find the idea of any closer association with one nation which we have just denazified and another which urgently needs to be degaulled unappealing to say the least, but my colleagues and I did agree to bide by the spin of the coin on this, and I shall reluctantly say no more.'[114]

One of the stranger ironies of Britain plc's last forty years is how much of the country's patrimony has been sold off quite precisely by governments that describe themselves as conservative. It was ex-prime minister Harold Macmillan, newly ennobled as Lord Stockton, who famously addressed the Tory Reform Group on 8 November 1985, full of foreboding after witnessing six years of Margaret Thatcher's brand of Conservatism. 'The sale of assets,' he noted glumly, 'is common with individuals and states when they run into financial difficulties. First, all the Georgian silver goes, and then all that nice furniture that used to be in the saloon. Then the Canalettos go.' This is usually referred to as Macmillan's 'selling off the family silver' speech. Unlike Anthony Eden he was actually middle class rather than landed gentry, but as a true Tory he shared an aristocrat's horror of selling ancestral lands and heirlooms of which he considered himself the custodian for future generations of the family, never their owner. The livelier half of his misgiving was that of an ex-statesman who recognised the cardinal error in confusing the money thus raised with income. It would find its way into the nation's current balance sheet looking like profit to offset against the lengthening column of figures in red, whereas it was nothing of the kind: it was simply a deficit in assets. The nice furniture had, in effect, been chopped up for firewood to heat the house.

However, there is a less easily quantifiable aspect of national loss. We have already alluded to many famous British industrial names that have vanished into oblivion or foreign ownership. The 'giant monopoly companies and consortia' that Jimmy Reid mentioned in his Rectorial Address are today almost always foreign-owned. What is never taken into account by governments is the sapping effect on national morale these takeovers and sellings off can have. No matter that a few thousand stakeholders benefit from making a nice bit of cash; when favourite brands either disappear or vanish into foreign ownership it simply adds to the public's unexpressed but glum feeling that the once-familiar is being steadily and ruthlessly dismantled and that their lives and even the country are in some way diminished. It is, of course, in the order of things that the familiar can disappear without warning; but confidence that something of equal value and enjoyment will replace it can make the loss more bearable. A lack of this confidence leads to a chipping away of morale that bit by bit affects how the country views itself and its governance. To show that it is not only Tories who lament this, in 1973 an issue of the *New Statesman* led with an appreciation of John Betjeman's popular stand against urban redevelopments:

> [A] Poet Laureate has expressed the nation's feelings. This week Sir John Betjeman observed that destroying the surroundings in which people live – and which they like, and are accustomed to – amounts to straightforward robbery. It is stealing the people's property, said Sir John, exactly the same as being burgled. In some ways, maybe worse. You can buy substitutes for the contents of a house. A familiar narrow street, with its obscure chapel, tree and corner shop, is irreplaceable.[115]

In our day Iain Sinclair's memoir *Ghost Milk* (2011) was a passionate denunciation of a classic Britain plc move: the brutal way in which the forcible land clearances for the 2012 Summer Olympics dispossessed many of London's poorest citizens of their homes in the name of redeveloping an allegedly derelict area at prodigious profit to the developers.

If this is true for people's surroundings, it can be equally so for commonplace products, especially those whose origins were coeval with the dawn of the Industrial Revolution and England's prosperity. The sale of Cadbury (founded in 1824 and formerly Cadbury's) to the American giant Kraft Foods was a case in point. Nothing could have been more English than this favourite chocolate maker, for generations associated with Christmas and Easter as well as with daily pleasures and treats. Consequently, nothing could have been more bitterly resented by much of the British public when Cadbury was sold to an American food giant in 2010 – unless it was learning the following year that it had been further hived off to a Kraft subsidiary, Mondelez International, to join two other British Quaker-founded confectioners, Fry's (founded in 1761) and Terry's of York (founded in 1767). No matter how illogically, people felt that Cadbury's, in particular, had the status of a British institution and in some mystical fashion hadn't really been the property of its shareholders to sell. But because in Britain plc the marketplace trumps all, a gloomy resignation settles on people as they hear of the demise or foreign acquisition of a favourite brand, especially if it is one they associate with their own childhoods. It seems not right that something belonging to everybody can be sold off abroad to make a few shareholders richer. It felt like the final straw when the public learned that the very machinery to make some of Cadbury's favourite lines had been unbolted from the factory floor in Bourneville over one weekend and shipped to Poland where it soon resumed production for a foreign workforce.

Very occasionally when a foreign takeover bid unexpectedly fails – as in the case of the UK-based pharmaceutical company AstraZeneca rebuffing a bid by the US company Pfizer in 2014 – it can arouse a cheerful response in people who otherwise have no vested interest in the matter. At last someone is fighting back. But such are minor enough triumphs to offset against the news that Thames Water is part of an Australian group with substantial shareholdings by Abu Dhabi and China. Old Father

Thames? The lifeblood of southern England? The immortal setting of *The Wind in the Willows*? That same river. Only thirty
years ago the idea that we would have allowed a major energy
company supplying millions of British households with their
electricity to be wholly owned by a foreign government would
have been considered unthinkably stupid. That EDF is owned
by the *French* government would have provoked uproar in
parliament. Today it seems to be accepted with leaden resignation, as it is that British Airways is now a subsidiary of IAG, a
company based in Spain.

This remorseless whittling away of minor but cumulatively
profound sources of national pride takes its toll. No more
Vickers-Armstrong? No more English Electric? ICI? Britain's
post-war decline has involved too many sectors for it not to
have contributed to a chronic if subclinical national demoralisation that today is evidenced by its citizens' cynical mistrust
of government, their formerly bovine but now fast lessening
passivity over austerity, their lack of real hope that the future
will be much better, whatever the outcome of the crassly incompetent Brexit negotiations. Aside from entire industries, we
have simply lost too many names that millions of households
once thought of as unequivocally British and that in some way
represented or at least bolstered our collective selves. Rolls-
Royce cars, Land Rover, de Havilland, EMI, Vickers, Plessey,
Bentley, Decca, Jaguar, Harrods, Avro, GEC, GKN... All have
been knocked down in the great car boot sale or else have
vanished altogether, now to be found only as advertisements in

yellowing archives. And not only this; so much of the country's reputation has equally been frittered away. When I was young the City of London was internationally esteemed (or so we were told) as a citadel of irreproachable probity where a banker's word was his bond and honesty was taken for granted. In 2016 Roberto Saviano, an investigative journalist and author who has spent more than a decade exposing the inner workings of the Italian Mafia, told a Hay-on-Wye audience that Britain is now the most corrupt country in the world.

> It's not the bureaucracy, it's not the police, it's not the politics. What is corrupt is the financial capital. Ninety per cent of the owners of capital in London have their headquarters offshore. Jersey and the Caymans are the access gates to criminal capital in Europe, and the UK is the country that allows it.[116]

Once again, this is the direct result of ideologically driven lunacy. In 2011 the business secretary, Vince Cable, changed the requirement for registering a company with Companies House. From then on, and for a mere £18 fee, anyone in the world could register their company online and in any name they chose, no matter how fictitious. Ever since, such supposedly bona fide British corporate vehicles have facilitated fraud on a global scale. In 2017 a National Crime Agency report claimed that the UK is now losing £193 billion *annually* from fraud, with maybe a further £100 bn being laundered via our relaxed financial system – sums that could transform the NHS, education and other social services.[117] Of course we are not the only country to suffer bouts of humbling exposure. National reputations come and go. But it is particularly galling that most other countries manage not to sell off their nations' figurative crown jewels, loot their own assets and blithely sacrifice their good names. Rather, the cannier of them protect and support their industries, which we British almost never do except in the case of those with defence and pharmaceutical connections: almost the only sectors ever to see government investment. The motoring correspondent James Ruppert noted this when summing up the fate of the British car industry:

> Whereas foreign governments have been cleverly protective of their car industries, the British simply interfered and relocated parts of it to inappropriate areas of the country. It is no accident that Volkswagen, the company that the British Army once ran, was immune from takeover, however many shares any other company bought. Just as it is unthinkable that Mercedes or BMW would fall into foreign-owned hands. They have been guided, protected and subsidised by the regional governments where the factories are based.[118]

I think back to the old V-bomber pilot I visited in his freezing, newspaper-crammed house in Sussex all those years ago. His trick for avoiding the threat of the future was to live in the past, surrounded by the reassuring trade names of his boyhood, writing off to companies whose printed addresses held out the promise that they were still there, as busy as ever in a parallel universe. His particular England was imperishable. In its way, my own is, too. Those Tri-ang toys and Banner pyjamas are still there, just as is the threepenny bar of Fry's Five Boys chocolate I might pick up on my way to school and later, when I was a student, the tin of Crosse & Blackwell's Mulligatawny soup (so much better than Heinz's). The difference is that the old wing commander had taken up residence in his private version of England, whereas mine is less nostalgia than an ordinary recollection of the once commonplace that, when the light is turned up in an inner memory room, produces a sort of Pepper's Ghost illusion whereby I feel I could reach out in the real world and touch something that isn't there.

Such ghosts remind me of my paternal grandmother: one of the first women science students at Leeds University, a tough lady who in the early years of the twentieth century went to China as a missionary midwife. Fifty years later she was devastated when her beloved eldest son – my father – died at the age of forty-six. It so shook her faith that not even her own Congregational Church in Eltham could give her solace. In the depths of misery and more than a little shamefaced she took herself off to the Society for Psychical Research in London and paid for a séance during which, she assured me, the medium had been in direct contact with my father. There was no question, she said, that it was John: the medium described him far too accurately for any doubt. She had told my grandmother that my father was happy in the other world, helping *his* father with his medical work. My grandfather had been a missionary doctor in China where he met my grandmother and where my father was born in 1915. By the time he died my father was a consultant neurologist at London's National Hospital, Queen Square, researching Parkinsonism. It was inconceivable that his highly specialised medical skills could ever have usefully over-lapped with those of his own father, who had been more of a bush doctor doing his best to patch up the Chinese victims of periodic bandit attacks in the hills of Jiangxi Province during and after the First World War.

At some level my grandmother – a Yorkshire woman who was ordinarily nobody's fool – must have known this even though she was probably ignorant of the medium's professional skill at cold reading. With her normal rationality she would have asked herself why on earth doctors were still needed in the supposedly blissful afterlife. But however she had managed temporarily to repress her intelligence, the emotional relief she derived from her visit was clearly profound. Both her husband and her son were confirmed as happy and productive in a next world whose existence she had never doubted. For months afterwards when I thought of this I was needlessly haunted by a feeling of pity just as, when I was a child, my eyes would reliably fill with tears whenever I read the last sentence of *The House at Pooh Corner*: 'In that enchanted place on the top of the forest, a little boy and his Bear will always be playing.'

A lapse into sentimentality is easy to forgive in a child who has had a terrifying glimpse of the present's essential flimsiness. Our imagined worlds of the everlasting transcend the sundry erosions of daily life, stable and infinitely touching, deeply rooted in a fictitious permanence.

However, if it is not entirely infantile to regret the passing of household brands, it is fully adult to lament the selling off of enchanted but real places. As a Londoner by birth I had no idea until a short time ago how much of my native city was no longer a truly public space. I knew about and deplored the sale of individual properties, often to overseas speculators, with thousands of apartments and houses standing empty despite London's housing crisis. But I had not realised that open air places one had taken for granted as belonging to Londoners could be privately owned, often by foreigners who have the right to prevent access to citizens even while calling them 'public spaces'. One such is Paternoster Square, in the shadow of St Paul's, currently owned by the Mitsubishi Estate Company. Bishops Square and much of Spitalfields is owned by J. P. Morgan asset management. King's Cross's Granary Square is likewise privately owned. Much of the South Bank belongs to Kuwait. It is a syndrome repeated in towns and cities all over Britain. No doubt this is another skewed manifestation of globalisation, but I am prepared to bet it is one-sided. I doubt if any UK pension fund owns much of downtown Riyadh or Tiananmen Square even though Saudi and Chinese concerns have bought acres of my native city.

It is not only old Tories like Harold Macmillan who would have been shocked to the core by this. So would my own socialist-leaning parents and everybody else of their generation. The spectacle of the fire sale of the nation's assets was already far enough advanced by the mid-1980s to cause alarm to Britons who, like Macmillan, had fought for their country, just as my father had. Yet again the irony is extraordinary. On the one hand there was Mrs Thatcher, the Wesleyan Methodist petite bourgeoise from Grantham extolling the virtues of prudence and thrift; and on the other the spectacle of her Britain plc as the *Antiques Roadshow*, a huckster's free-for-all scouring the nation's attics for bargains to sell off. And once more there is a deep pathos: this time of a Britain that can never come again because so much that was original and characteristic has gone under the hammer for cash which has long since disappeared into the black hole of the national debt. What is left is widespread foreign ownership, with overseas landlords employing security guards to tell Britons where they may and may not go in their own cities. These days permission can even be required to stand in a 'public space' and take a photograph, while gatherings of more than ten people can be banned, with British police and security companies acting as the whip hands of foreign landlords.

So we have come to this. My country has been sold off to defray charges, and to nobody's profit save that of a lot of bankers and property developers. Even Winnie the Pooh has long been kidnapped by Disney. Britannia does not rule the waves and Britons are ever more slaves who have inertly connived at their own surveilled serfdom. Looking around for enemies of their Britain, apoplectic Brexiters inveigh against the easy target of Brussels; but they conveniently choose to ignore Arabia and the Gulf States and Beijing and Kuala Lumpur, not to mention Dallas and Toronto and the unaccountable complexities of transnational hedge and pension funds. Above all, they choose to forget that it was British politicians and City financiers who alone made it all possible.

Meanwhile, the Britain they fondly believe they are defending is long gone. Its ghosts gibber from cenotaphs, from worn recordings of *Hancock's Half Hour*, *The Goons*, *Round the Horne*, *Dad's Army* and other touchstones of poorer but undeniably kinder times. The price of a lot more wealth, unevenly distributed and now severely rationed for most, is a disunited and altogether nastier kingdom, much of which no longer belongs to its people. You know your country has vanished when you find yourself almost daily thinking – and often saying aloud – 'Thank God my parents never lived to see this'.

Was it inevitable? Maybe. Similar effects of glaring disparities in wealth are plain to see in countries around the world, although until 1979 reversing our own inequalities used to be an aim to which all our political parties claimed to aspire. Certainly people then would have been deeply shocked had they known they would live to see a day when tens of thousands of Britons would be homeless or sleeping rough in the depths of winter, dependent on shelters and food banks. *Food banks?* A return to the poorhouse and Victorian charities' soup kitchens? Sometimes it seems as though the calamity that has overtaken Britain has to do with a comparatively recent indifference to a social purpose that might have transformed the economic model. The country has long craved a direction, no doubt; but it is impossible to overlook that the last time its factories hummed and there was a determination to bring about a better and more egalitarian Britain was during and immediately after the Second World War. Without a desperate but unifying purpose we seem unable to progress.

Our moral stagnation is made infinitely worse by that of Westminster. That Britain plc is still not open for business is a charge which, as of writing, is easy enough to explain. The country has long valued stability (aka the status quo) above nearly all else. Prime Minister Theresa May's disastrous 2017 Election slogan of 'strong and stable' government was especially derided when for the past year Britain had had a government with all the strength and coherence of a bale of rice paper left out in the rain. Small wonder that people lack enough confidence in Westminster's soggy parade of political jobsworths to start business ventures when they cannot rely on government support and, like the government itself, have no remote idea of what the current squabble with Brussels portends for the future of British business. An image comes to mind of the whole solemn realm – the men and women of both Houses of

Parliament – leaning over the parapet of Westminster Bridge desperately playing Poohsticks as the tide below them ebbs and flows. The system is irreducibly amateurish.

And yet there are many principled MPs who campaigned and were elected to change things for the better but who are perpetually frustrated and thwarted by party discipline and stupidity – even as Parliament as a whole is increasingly hamstrung by an increasingly ragged civil service. Since the days depicted in *Yes, Prime Minister* this once reliable, if elitist, instrument of governance has been decimated and reformed to the point of demoralisation. As the CEO of one of the UK's two largest private companies by turnover recently remarked: 'Whitehall is full of absolute idiots. It's become a self-fulfilling black hole of hope. This idea that you can get civil servants who are paid a fraction of the money that you could earn in industry, somehow making better judgements than industry – it's nonsense.'[119]

It's so sad. Had we been halfway competent at running our industries profitably there would have been no need for Thatcher and her ideologically obsessed cohort; none for a stagnant economy and protracted austerity; and none even for Brexit, which could never have occurred in good times but which stands for Britons' collective fury at getting steadily poorer, egged on by non-dom press barons into looking for an external enemy to blame.

Yet it is an internal enemy in the shape of national character that provides the fuller explanation. I began this book by depicting Britain's attitudes to industry and even commerce as having appeared equivocal from the very start of the Industrial Revolution: a theory both supported and rejected by conflicting historians. I now think it is simpler to forget about theory and merely look at the evidence of the last sixty years. Endlessly repeated calls for more engineers have fallen on deaf ears. Provision was made for technical education, but it turned out that not enough potential students wanted to take it up. Despite at least a century of official lament that the majority of Britons are undereducated, stubbornly undereducated they mostly remain compared with many Europeans. A thousand ringing proclamations about Britain being open for business have accompanied wholesale industrial withering and productivity that has been flat-lining for the past decade. Back in the mid-1960s prime ministers as unlikely as Harold Wilson were actually reduced to telling the country to pull its collective socks up. This set Michael Frayn off once more:

> What I can't understand is why these endless appeals to the nation are necessary. Isn't its self-regulating natural efficiency the point of a free economy? Isn't the God-given desire to maximise profits the whole basis and justification of capitalism? Why do the nation's leaders have to keep getting down on their knees and begging businessmen to install more efficient plant and sell more goods? Why do industrialists have to be coaxed and wheedled to make some more lovely nourishing profits by appeals to their patriotism?[120]

Excellent questions. The conclusion surely has to be that, fundamentally, Britain isn't really very interested in business at all, or in industry, otherwise it would long since have done something radical to improve both. Our culture is evidently all wrong for it. Our genius is for gifted boffins and amateurs inventing things. Our talent is for preserving the status quo if possible or for fond remembrance of sunnier times if not. What looks like chronic indecision may after all be Humpty Dumpty on top of his metaphorical wall preferring the lofty view it affords over an inner private empire to the risk of committing himself and coming down fatally on one or other side. In any case, should he actually make a choice and fail, the King's horses and King's men who might once have come to his rescue will have been ruthlessly decimated by Ministry of Defence cutbacks and couldn't possibly get clearance to mount a rescue sortie for a lone fence-sitter who overbalanced. Maybe this is how our deep individualism sometimes takes us. At other times we prefer to hunch in front of a popping gas fire, writing letters to long-defunct companies, than do something to bring about a better future for all. Our forebears may have brought the world industrialism, but we have little desire to practise it ourselves. We have moved on to somewhere different, although quite where cannot easily be pinned down. Bored by the exhortations of leaders for whom we have lost all respect, we have wandered forth from Britain plc's AGM in quest of a Britain that is not open for business but for pleasure, a land somewhere quite else – between Ambridge and Facebook, maybe: a place full of rural longings and savage gossip, and where losing is a form of national superiority.

Perversely enough, I find an odd source of pride in the idea that Britain, contrary to its official protestations, is just not very interested in business at a national, as opposed to local, level. We will muddle along as always, grousing. The curious national mix of dogged individualism and occasional creative genius that can throw up entrepreneurs as well as engineers and artists was evidently never destined to jell into industrial efficiency and wealth for all. Apart from anything else, it is too liable to burst into laughter in the middle of a serious meeting at the thought that there really *is* a Rupert Murdoch Chair of Language and Communication at Oxford. Or it might run a wonderful bookshop or a famous whelk stall but would have not the slightest qualm about pinning a notice to the door saying 'Probably closed for the rest of the month' and going off to Hungary for a hair transplant. Its disrespectful sense of bleak amusement reminds me of an episode in my neophyte journalist days when I accompanied a pickled old *Oxford Mail* foot-in-the-door reporter to a church somewhere out Cowley way that had suffered a break-in. It was superficially Christmas Eve; in reality it was the day I belatedly learned to dump optimism with a disburdening that has lightened my life ever since. We passed the Pressed Steel Fisher factory in whose padlocked forecourt a car transporter stood, apparently abandoned and laden with red-rusted Rolls-Royce bodies. We found the church plastered with banners proclaiming the birth of Jesus as the Good

News. My escort gave it a withering glance through the windscreen. 'Ah, shit,' he said under his breath, braking to a halt. 'One of those.'

We were met on the church's steps by a jaunty evangelical. 'Have you heard the Good News?' he greeted us – rather oddly, I thought, given the break-in. The *Oxford Mail*, having speechlessly exhaled whisky fumes towards him for a moment, growled: 'I'm a reporter, for fuck's sake. I'm not interested in *good* news.' Then gave a great phlegmy guffaw.

A single pump serving the surrounding houses in a London slum in the 1930s. The lime-washed doorsteps and windowsills were a valiant attempt at respectability amid squalor.

Sometime in the late 1980s my mother, who would herself have been over eighty, burst into tears on Victoria station. Quite how shocking and out of character this was can be judged by the fact that retired doctors of her generation and upbringing who had survived two world wars were not given to weeping, and definitely not in public. That she had trained at University College Hospital in the early 1930s was anyway the mark of a certain toughness and independence of character. It was not a time when well-bred girls who had been presented at Court (reluctantly, in my mother's case) elected to study for the medical profession.

She was frequently shocked by the state of the outpatients she treated, remembering in particular a man who had dragged himself to the hospital early one morning to have an immense boil on his neck lanced and who pleaded with the doctors to hurry, otherwise he would be late for work and find his job given to one of the other casual labourers who queued for work at dawn each day. This was only four years since the discovery of penicillin, which would not be used therapeutically until 1942 – another decade. The man survived without antibiotics, but only after being hospitalised as a charity case. How his family fed themselves while he was off work is anybody's guess.

My mother's moment of true revelation came when doing her midwifery course. She was sent over the road from UCH into the Somers Town slums around Euston, St Pancras and King's Cross stations and I have never forgotten her accounts of the conditions she found there. Nothing in her upbringing had prepared her for such squalor. She described visiting houses whose top floors were unreachable as well as uninhabitable because most of the floorboards as well as the staircase had been burned for fuel. She delivered babies onto the day's newspapers, having been told at the hospital that fresh newsprint was the most nearly sterile thing that was easily available. If there was a remaining chest of drawers in the dark and smelly house the baby would be put into a drawer as the nearest thing to a cradle. In the midst of such dirt it seemed impossible that infants could survive, but they often did. 'Babies are tough little creatures,' my mother would observe. It was a hope to which a middle-class student might cling as she picked her way down noisome alleys strung across with washing and with a single putrid jakes serving several households.

There are few Britons alive today to remember how different London was in those inter-war years. My mother's family lived in a flat in Eaton Terrace, just around the corner from Sloane Square, which now sounds positively grand rather than merely respectable, as it was then. In order to travel to and from UCH she would use the underground at Sloane Square, but her walk took her past the pub on the corner of Cliveden Place. She was no faint-heart but she did confess to having been scared to pass the gang of drunks and loungers that at all hours thronged the pavement outside it. Women would often get off the Tube and, total strangers to each other, band together for mutual protection in order to run the gauntlet past these jeering and menacing ruffians. *Sloane Square?* But yes. The rapid gentrification of so much of London is a comparatively recent phenomenon. Even in 1964 when, fresh from university, a friend and I took a couple of grotty rooms above a cleaner's towards the top of Marylebone High Street there was no question that despite Daunt's bookshop we were at the rough end of an unglamorous road, with dismal tenements around Paddington Street where drunks and occasional muggers lurked. From the Kardomah Café southwards a certain gentility reigned, but it was not remotely like today's multinational souk where foie gras and artisanal gin may be had at the wave of a credit card at any hour of day or night.

In due course my mother, once qualified, taught anaesthetics to my father at UCH and no doubt in turn he also did his midder practice in the same slums. The conditions there might have come as less of a shock to him since, having been born in rural China, he had probably seen things that were quite as bad. Even so, when they married in 1940 my parents were clearly in agreement that the living conditions of so many native Britons in the capital city of the world's largest empire were shameful and intolerable. Once the war was over and my father returned from France and had been demobbed, both he and my mother became founder members and staunch lifelong supporters of the new National Health Service. To many older consultants this was anathema. They could only see the NHS as a threat to private medicine and to their godlike right to command large fees for their services, irrespective of their patients' ability to pay. They saw it as the state having the audacity to tell them how to practise their profession. It was decades before I realised that while we were living in Sidcup both my parents had voted Labour. At that time the Conservative MP for the constituency was the tirelessly campaigning Pat Hornsby-Smith, and when as children my sister and I would ask our mother whether she had voted for her she always laughingly replied, 'Never you mind.' She later explained that she was worried lest our casually mentioning it at school might lead to us being victimised. However, this probably said more about her own experience of having been enfranchised by the 1928 Act and expected by her Tory-voting family to vote Conservative than it did about social attitudes in post-war Sidcup.

In any case both my parents worked long and hard years in the NHS, with occasional private work thrown in. I was somewhat aggrieved to learn that although my father and a fellow neurologist jointly rented a small consulting suite in Wimpole Street he, with inherited Low Church principles, had charged the Aga Khan exactly what he would have charged any other private patient and not a penny more. (This emerged only after my father's early death when his colleague remarked on it at the funeral.) Neither of my parents ever lost their belief that continuing social improvement was Britain's duty and most urgent priority, and they took pride in the immense strides that medicine was making with the steady eradication of childhood epidemic diseases like whooping cough, scarlet fever and diphtheria as well as more stubborn conditions such as tuberculosis and polio. Meanwhile, the slum areas that the

Luftwaffe hadn't already cleared were bulldozed and decent housing built. For three decades conditions for the vast majority of Britons generally improved; outside lavatories retreated indoors and jokes about baths filled with coal lost their point.

Then came the fateful day when my mother, crossing the concourse at Victoria station, came face to face with three clearly destitute girls sitting on a flattened carton and begging: a cardboard island of castaways amid a surging ocean of commuters' legs. They were, she saw, youngish teenagers of much the same age as her own granddaughters. In one of those epiphanic moments these thin children suddenly seemed to her to personify what was happening to Britain in the eighties. Whether or not the girls' circumstances were really as they appeared, the sight reduced her to helpless tears of rage. 'It's all going backward,' she said when she could speak. 'After all our gains. Those bloody politicians, that *bloody* woman – they ought to hang their heads in shame.'

My mother died in 2001 aged nearly ninety-three; and I am thankful that neither she nor my father could have seen the steady recolonisation of London's doorways by today's growing legion of homeless rough sleepers, the increasingly malnourished children who come to school unfed and inattentive for hunger, the food banks on which many families now depend, the disgusting premises ineffectually condemned by councils and run by a new generation of rapacious slum landlords: Perec Rachmans reborn. Truly, human nature does not change; but our ideological refusal to curb it for the common good is enough reason finally to dissever the epithet 'Great' from the name of Britain.

Notes

Chapter 1: Formerly

1   John Crace, *Guardian* (1 April 2017).

Chapter 2: The Problem

2   P. G. Wodehouse, 'The Purity of the Turf', in *The Inimitable Jeeves* (London, 1923).
3   Jonathan Gathorne-Hardy, *The Old School Tie* (Viking, 1978), pp. 62–3.
4   J. J. Findlay (ed.), *Arnold of Rugby: His School Life and Contributions to Education* (Cambridge University Press, 1897), p. xvii.
5   T. W. Bamford, *The Rise of the Public Schools* (Nelson, 1967), p. 88.
6   C. P. Snow, *The Two Cultures* (Cambridge University Press, 1959, 2001).
7   Quoted in Martin J. Wiener, *English Culture and the Decline of the Industrial Spirit 1850–1980* (Penguin, 1985), p. 131.
8   Christopher Benjamin, *Strutting on Thin Air* (published by the author, 2009), p. 301. The ISBN of this valuable source is 978-0-9561579-0-4.
9   C. Peattie and R. Taylor, *Alex IV* (Penguin, 1991).
10 Peter Drucker, *Post-Capitalist Society* (Butterworth-Heinemann, 1993).
11 Peter L. Payne, in Bruce Collins et al. (eds), *British Culture and Economic Decline* (Weidenfeld & Nicolson, 1990), p. 33.
12 David Edgerton, *Science, Technology and the British Industrial 'Decline' 1870–1970* (Cambridge University Press, 1996), pp. 29–30.
13 Ibid., p. 46.
14 Correlli Barnett, *The Verdict of Peace* (Macmillan, 2001), p. 307.
15 Michael Shanks, *The Stagnant Society* (Penguin, 1961), p. 207.

Chapter 3: Trains and Planes

16 See 'Signal Failures' column, *Private Eye*, no. 1441 (7 April–30 April 2017), p. 14.

17 'Signal Failures', *Private Eye*, no. 1449, p. 17.

18 P. D. Henderson, 'Two British Errors: their probable size and some possible lessons', in *Oxford Economic Papers*, vol. 29 no. 2 (July 1977). The other error was the Atomic Energy Authority's Advanced Gas-cooled Reactor, the blighted AGR. The third 'worst decision', in his view, was 'Concordski', the Russian Tupolev Tu-144.

19 *Uxbridge Informer*, 25 March 1994.

20 Hansard, 20 November 2001.

21 'Heathrow News, Produced for Local Residents by BAA Heathrow', May 1997.

22 BBC News (online), 14 April 2017.

23 Andrew Adonis, speech to the Institution of Civil Engineers, 26 June 2017.

24 BBC News (online), 7 July 2017.

25 John Grindrod, *Outskirts* (Sceptre, 2017), pp. 310–11.

26 See *Guardian*, 8 February 2016.

27 Quoted by Simon Calder in 'Aviation Bursting at Seams', *Independent*, 31 July 2017.

Chapter 4: Cars

28 *The Times*, 6 February 2018, p. 18.

29 Buchanan Report (Penguin, 1964), Introduction.

30 Ibid., para. 68.

31 Ibid., para. 30.

32 See Swati Dhingra and Nikhil Datta, 'How Not to Do Trade Deals', *London Review of Books*, 21 September 2017, p. 31.

33 Huw Beynon, *Working for Ford* (Pelican, 1984), p. 146.

34 Ibid., p. 86.

35 Ibid.

36 See www.youtube.com/watch?v=LL30Y1Mzq-A. It is claimed this was not a *Motorworld* episode but a 1997 special called 'Apocalypse Clarkson'. Whichever, the quotation is authentic and was made to camera.

37 Ibid.

38 *Daily Telegraph*, 17 July 2008.

39 Ibid.

40 See no. 4 (22 June 2000) of the BBC series *Clarkson's Car Years*. This episode was titled 'Who Killed the British Car Industry?' www.youtube.com/watch?v=TGJty_Rdp1U.

41 Ibid.

42 Ibid.

43 Chris Benjamin, *Strutting on Thin Air* (published by the author, 2009), p. 131.
44 Michael Edwardes, *Back from the Brink* (Pan, 1984), p. 41.
45 Ibid., p. 125.
46 Ibid., p. 297.
47 James Ruppert, *The British Car Industry: Our Part in its Downfall* (Foresight, 2013), p. 4.

Chapter 5: Shipbuilding

48 Correlli Barnett, *The Lost Victory* (Pan, 1996), p. 38.
49 Correlli Barnett, *The Verdict of Peace* (Macmillan, 2001), p. 209.
50 Quoted in Correlli Barnett, *The Audit of War* (Papermac, 1987), p. 121.
51 Anthony Slaven, *British Shipbuilding 1500–2010* (Crucible, 2013), p. 109.
52 Barnett, *The Verdict of Peace*, pp. 220–22.
53 Christopher Benjamin, *Strutting on Thin Air* (published by the author, 2009), p. 540.
54 Slaven, *British Shipbuilding 1500–2010*, p. 143.
55 Interviewed by Dan Milmo in *Guardian*, 6 November 2013.
56 Benjamin, *Strutting on Thin Air*, p. 541.
57 Ibid., pp. 305–6.

Chapter 6: Defence

58 Quoted in Quentin Letts's obituary of Jay, *Daily Mail*, 25 August 2016.
59 See Hansard, 30 July 1964.
60 Quoted in de Ferranti's *Daily Telegraph* obituary, 26 October 2015.
61 See 'Squarebasher', *Private Eye*, no. 1424, 5–18 August 2016, p. 9. 'Squarebasher' was the byline of the late and much missed Paul Vickers.
62 A. R. W. Purton, letter in RUSI *Journal*, October 2000. I am much indebted to the same author's invaluable MoD booklet *Legal Awareness in UK Defence Procurement* [1991].
63 See article by Tony Skinner, 'Farnborough 2016: Industry continues to fleece UK MoD', in Shephard Media's *Defence Notes*, 15 July 2016.
64 *Private Eye*, no. 1426 (2–15 September 2016), p. 20.
65 Chris Roberts, email to the author, 25 February 2016.
66 John Farley, email to the author, 22 February 2016.
67 See Admiral Sir Raymond Lygo, *Collision Course* (The Book Guild, 2002), pp. 433–4.
68 In 2017 *Defense News* listed ten UK companies in its Top 100. Of these,

BAE Systems is ranked as the world's third largest defence company, with 91 per cent of its revenue deriving from defence. Rolls-Royce remains the world's third largest aero-engine manufacturer, with 25 per cent of its revenue coming from defence.

69 See 'Government on Trial' (Channel 4 Midnight Special, x/y/1996)

70 Hansard, 25 January–4 February 1966.

71 Source: MercoPress, July 2017.

72 *Aerospace*, September 2017, p. 28.

Chapter 7: Motorbikes

73 Mabel Lockwood-Tatham, 'The Modern Girl and the Motor Cycle: A Defence of the Motor Cycling Sporting Girl', *The Motor Cycle*, 5 October 1927, pp. 472-3.

74 The phrase is that of Steve Wilson, in his introduction to Bert Hopwood's autobiographical *Whatever Happened to the British Motorcycle Industry* (Haynes, 1999).

75 Hopwood, *Whatever Happened to the British Motorcycle Industry*, p. 81.

76 Ibid., p. 101.

77 Ibid., p. 303.

78 Chris Benjamin, *Strutting on Thin Air* (published by the author, 2009), p. 149.

79 Peter Mathias, in Harold F. Williamson (ed.), *Evolution of International Management Structures* (Newark, Del., 1975), pp. 41-3.

80 Hopwood, *Whatever Happened to the British Motorcycle Industry*, p. 128.

81 Ibid., p. 143.

82 Mat Oxley, *Stealing Speed* (Mat Oxley, 2014).

83 Hopwood, *Whatever Happened to the British Motorcycle Industry*, p. 140.

84 Benjamin, *Strutting on Thin Air*, p. 131.

Chapter 8: Nukes & Fish

85 For a fascinating account of this extraordinary transaction, told from the American side, see Jennet Conant, *Tuxedo Park* (Simon & Schuster, 2002). It was largely the enthusiasm and private enterprise of the millionaire scientist Alfred Lee Loomis that ensured the magnetron was first examined on the other side of the Atlantic by precisely those few scientists who could immediately understand and exploit it.

86 David Henderson, in *Nuclear Engineering International*, 21 June 2013: 'The More Things Change'.

87   Christopher Booker, 'How Heath Betrayed Our Fishermen', *Sunday Tele-graph*, 14 January 2001.
88   See Polly Toynbee in *Guardian*, 23 April 2018.

Chapter 9: Engineering

89   Correlli Barnett, *The Verdict of Peace* (Macmillan, 2001), pp. 311–12.
90   Jonathan Lynn and Antony Jay, 'The Greasy Pole', in *The Complete Yes Minister* (BBC Books, 2003), p. 254.
91   David Edgerton, *Science, Technology and the British Industrial 'Decline'* 1870–1970 (Cambridge University Press, 1996), p. 42.
92   D. S. L. Cardwell, *The Organisation of Science in England* (Heinemann, 1972), pp. 219–20.
93   Report of the Board of Education for the year 1908–9, p. 90.
94   H. G. Wells, Eleventh Annual Report of the British Science Guild (June 1917).
95   Referenced in Correlli Barnett, *The Audit of War* (Macmillan, 1987), pp. 208–9.
96   Barnett, *The Verdict of Peace*, p. 446.
97   Paul Addison, 'Warfare and Welfare', *London Review of Books*, 24 July 1986.
98   M. Sanderson, *The Universities and British Industry, 1850–1970* (Routledge, 1972), p. 377.
99   Reported by James Tapsfield, Mailonline, 11 October 2017.
100   Spoken by John Bird in the character of the spin-doctor Martin McCabe.
101   Stephen Harris, 'Why are engineering firms struggling to recruit gradu-ates?', *The Engineer*, 1 April 2014.
102   Ibid.
103   Ibid.
104   Alan Johnson, email exchanges with the author, October 2017.
105   Ibid.
106   Owen Jones, 'Brexitland', *Guardian*, 13 April 2017.
107   Interview by Alexis Petridis, *Guardian*, 8 March 2002.

Chapter 10: Latterly

108   R. C. O. Matthews, C. H. Feinstein and J. C. Odling-Smee, *British Eco-nomic Growth, 1856–1973* (Oxford University Press, 1982), p. 435.
109   See Mariana Mazzucato, *The Entrepreneurial State* (PublicAffairs, 2014).
110   Polly Toynbee, *Guardian*, 21 November 2017.

111 *NTNOCN*, Series 4, Episode 5: 1 March 1982.

112 Tom Bergin, *Spills and Spin: The Inside Story of BP* (Random House, 2012), p. 130.

113 loc. 2381/Owen Hatherley, *The Ministry of Nostalgia* (Verso, 2016).

114 Frayn, Michael: *The Book of Fub*, 'Christopher Smoothe Opens His Heart' (Fontana, 1965), p. 189 [It was a piece for his column in the *Guardian*. The collection was first published in 1963.]

115 *New Statesman*, 23 February 1973.

116 *Independent*, 29 May 2016.

117 See 'Britain, headquarters of fraud' (*Guardian*, 22 April 2018), based on Oliver Bullough: *Moneyland* (Profile, 2018).

118 James Ruppert, *The British Car Industry: Our Part in its Downfall* (Foresight, 2013), p. 241.

119 Andrew Owens, quoted by Aeron Davis in *Guardian*, 27 February 2018.

120 Michael Frayn, from his column in the *Observer*, as collected in *At Bay in Gear Street* (Fontana, 1967), p. 77.

Acknowledgements

Grateful thanks to:

AVM Nigel Baldwin, for sundry kindnesses including permission to re-use part of Chapter 6 that originally appeared in the RAF Historical Society's 2017 publication, *Cold War Air Systems Procurement*; **Neil Belton,** for decades of friend- and editorship; **Georgina Blackwell,** for patience and help with this book's production; **Anthony Cheetham,** for welcoming me as one of his authors and in particular for insisting that I write this book; **Richard Collins,** for first-rate copyediting; **John Grindrod,** for permission to quote from his latest book on architecture; **Andrew Hewson,** for having been both friend and agent for half a century; **Quentin Huggett** and **Sally Marine,** oceanographers and directors of Geotek Ltd, for years of friendship and most recently for hospitality and an introduction to Alan Johnson; **Alan Johnson,** polymath and former careers adviser, for vital information in Chapter 9; **Lindsay Peacock,** for hospitality and particularly for his professional knowledge of obscure aircraft and aviation matters generally; **Tony Purton,** for all his help with my original article for Chapter 6 and for his own publications; but above all for recommending Chris Benjamin's *Strutting on Thin Air*. I have regrettably failed to track down this author, but his book is a treasure trove of information, reminiscence and invigorating invective by a man who was a senior civil servant in the Thatcher years. It is marred only by being privately published and lacking an index, but as source material about shifting governmental attitudes to industry it is invaluable. I would also like to thank **Simon Sanders**, for information about British industry back in the days of Plessey; **André Teissier-duCros**, for his thoughts on the French post-war aircraft industry and more, and **Ed Wilson**, for being an inspirational and assiduous agent.

Image credits

pp. 266–7 The engine workshop at RAF Halton. Courtesy of RAF Halton.

pp. 296–7 'Selling England by the Pound'. © Gary Barker.

p. 335 London slum, 1930s. Topfoto.co.uk.

Index